The End of Realignment?

The End of Realignment?

Interpreting American Electoral Eras

Edited by

Byron E. Shafer

THE UNIVERSITY OF WISCONSIN PRESS

JAN 1 9 1992

The University of Wisconsin Press
114 North Murray Street
Madison, Wisconsin 53715

3 Henrietta Street
London WC2E 8LU, England

5 4 3 2 1

Printed in the United States of America

Library of Congress Cataloging-in-Publication Data
The end of realignment?: interpreting American electoral eras / edited
  by Byron E. Shafer.
    200 pp.   cm.
    Includes bibliographical references and index.
    ISBN 0-299-12970-5   ISBN 0-299-12974-8
    1. Party affiliation—United States. 2. Party affiliation—United States—History.
3. Elections—United States. 4. Elections—United States—History. I. Shafer, Byron E.
JK2261.E475   1991
324.973—dc20   91-7505
                    CIP

Contents

Contributors   vii

Preface   ix

1. Beyond Realignment and Realignment Theory: American
   Political Eras, 1789–1989   *Joel H. Silbey*   3

2. Like Waiting for Godot: The Uselessness of "Realignment" for
   Understanding Change in Contemporary American Politics
       Everett Carll Ladd   24

3. The Notion of an Electoral Order: The Structure of Electoral
   Politics at the Accession of George Bush   *Byron E. Shafer*   37

4. No More "Waiting for Godot": Comments on the Putative
   "End of Realignment"   *Samuel T. McSeveney*   85

5. Critical Realignment: Dead or Alive?   *Walter Dean Burnham*   101

Background to Debate: A Reader's Guide and Bibliography
       Harold F. Bass, Jr.   141

Index   181

Contributors

Harold F. Bass, Jr., *Ouachita Baptist University*

Walter Dean Burnham, *University of Texas*

Everett Carll Ladd, *University of Connecticut*

Samuel T. McSeveney, *Vanderbilt University*

Byron E. Shafer, *Oxford University*

Joel H. Silbey, *Cornell University*

Preface

Electoral "realignment," referring originally to a major shift in party preferences within the general public, is one of the great success stories of modern social science. Intellectually, the notion has been extended to provide the dominant conceptual framework for organizing, and studying, electoral politics—and increasingly, all of the politics which follows after elections. Practically, the phenomenon underneath the concept has been used not just to revise the presentation of American political history but even to shape contemporary journalistic accounts of major electoral events. Institutionally, there is now a veritable "industry" of interpreters who strive to bring more phenomena into the realignment framework, or more precision to those previously included.

Perhaps inevitably, there is also a more diverse group of students of electoral politics who are less enamored of the realignment approach and its scholarly product. Some argue that the central notion, while historically useful, has ceased to offer much explanatory power in the modern world. Others argue the reverse: that a notion based on comparatively recent history has been made to group earlier developments which are really quite distinctive, in their roots, in their evolution, and in their effect. Many in both camps agree that a dependence on realignment, at best, skews attention among the elements of electoral politics. At worst, such a dependence minimizes influences which, cumulatively, provide the more important part of any apt explanation.

This book is an attempt at providing a focus for—at outlining and structuring—this debate. The chapters, accordingly, reflect that intention in a painfully straightforward fashion:

In chapter 1, Joel H. Silbey, Professor of History at Cornell University, argues that electoral realignments are not useful for carving American history into grand political eras.

In chapter 2, Everett Carll Ladd, Professor of Political Science and Director of the Roper Center at the University of Connecticut, argues that the structural preconditions for a realignment have *disappeared* in our time.

And in chapter 3, I address the question, "If not realignment, then what?"

Samuel T. McSeveney, Professor of History at Vanderbilt University, follows in chapter 4 with a general overview and commentary on this debate, suggesting that the first three authors are at least overstated in historical terms.

In chapter 5, Walter Dean Burnham, Professor of Political Science at the University of Texas at Austin, argues that we are wrong, most especially wrong, in contemporary terms as well.

Harold F. Bass, Jr., Professor of Political Science at Ouachita Baptist University, then closes the book with a short bibliographical essay and lengthy bibliography on realignment and its alternatives, to provide the reader with a map to the literature itself, so as to permit further, independent judgments.

There is no denying—and if there were, chapter 3 would undo the pretense—that, as the originator of this project, I have to be placed solidly in the camp of the skeptics, or at least the grumblers. Yet it is testament both to the scholarly caliber and to the mix of dedication and detachment of all the others in this volume that each was the *original* choice for his portion of the project, and each assented to undertake it without hesitation. Joel Silbey and Everett Ladd were both extremely gracious in being willing to craft precisely the piece of the tripartite argument which was necessary to present that argument in full battle dress. Sam McSeveney and Dean Burnham were even more gracious in being prepared to undertake the "defense," when the "offense" had been created and coordinated first.

Originally, there were these five essays. And originally, they were planned as a panel for the special section on "Realignment" at the annual meeting of the American Political Science Association in 1989—though the possibility of a subsequent volume was certainly in our collective minds even then. As chairman of that special section, Hal Bass not only took an immediate interest in the proposed panel, by reserving it a slot on his crowded calendar; he also called it forcefully to the attention of the full program committee. That committee, under the leadership of Nelson W. Polsby, Professor of Political Science at the University of California at Berkeley, then moved to make this panel the Harold G. Lasswell Symposium, giving it a prime place on the program as the Friday evening session.

The response of that gathering—large, clearly engaged, and intermittently unsettled—did nothing to disabuse us of the notion that a volume might follow. *The End of Realignment?* is, of course, that volume. The first three chapters are thus revisions of papers presented at the Lasswell Symposium. Chapters 4 and 5 are largely new, richly developed responses, going well beyond what a panel discussant could conceivably do at the time. Hal Bass had already played key roles in the evolution of this project, but we all agreed that a new, extended bibliography, along with introductory notes, was an essential part of any published version and that Hal was the obvious person to undertake it. In a pattern which characterized the entire venture, he, too, agreed, and completed the volume.

The only other "revision," for the true student of the biography of projects, was the addition of the question mark at the end of the title. The Lasswell Symposium, in the spirit of its creation, had been titled, simply, "The End of Realignment." Dean Burnham argued, however, that if this was obviously so, then there was no need for a debate—and the final question mark thus became the final revision. Allen N. Fitchen, Director of the University of Wisconsin Press, was instantly responsive to a query about publishing the collection, and its practical fate was settled. He has been a constant supporter—and expediter—ever since. Raphael Kadushin, manuscript editor, and Jack Kirshbaum, copy editor, provided the very best of both technical *and* intellectual support along the way. As a result, the authors have allowed themselves to hope that the diversity of views collected within this volume will only affirm our unanimity in welcoming any and all readers into the debate.

The End of Realignment?

1 *Joel H. Silbey*

Beyond Realignment and Realignment Theory
American Political Eras, 1789–1989

Confusion and conflict over the precise nature of reality in contemporary American electoral politics abound. As usual, such confusion reflects a fundamental change in parameters of the field of study that has outstripped analytic capacity to order this change conceptually.[1]

Critical realignment theory has been the analytic common coin among students of American politics for more than thirty years. Since V. O. Key's seminal 1955 article, a great deal of effort has gone into trying to understand realignment's underlying dynamics and to catalogue the various marking points that characterize the nation's electoral universe over two centuries. These efforts have been rewarding and stimulating. But the theory has been an increasingly troubled one for some time as well. Critical realignments once provided precise markers signaling a profound shift in American politics. Scholars could readily catch those shifts by noting the onset of durable switches in voters' partisan preferences in a particular election or series of them, or by marking the partisan socialization of new voters.[2]

That precision no longer exists. The theory has not been able to account for what has happened over the past generation of American politics, despite the often frustrating search by scholars to locate the electoral realignment that was due in 1964, 1968, or thereabout. Attempts at fitting unlikely elements into the existing understanding have become increasingly cumbersome and, to many, more and more unconvincing. The occasional assertations that a realignment has, in fact, occurred in one election or another in the past twenty-five years have been met not only by challenge and denial, but also by an escalating criticism of the relevance of the theory to understanding the nation's current electoral situation.[3]

Existing political conditions appear to be clear-cut. There has been increasing electoral fragmentation since the 1960s, due to the decline of party loyalty among voters; the voters' commitment to either the Democrats or the Republicans no longer exists at levels that once defined the norms of the American political world; the number of independent voters has grown to levels previously unrecorded, as has the constant uncertainty of the people's choices on any election day. Certainly, much evidence has accumulated suggesting that the New Deal party system did not realign into a successor one; that the electoral universe dealigned instead; and, most critically, that our political system seems unable to have a realignment under present electoral conditions. All these are new conditions, and together they add up to a major deviation from the cyclical norms that have heretofore characterized our political history. As Vernon Bogdanor suggests, "the case for realignment sits uneasily with the 'decline of party' thesis."[4]

In response to these continued problems and ever sharper criticisms, reconsidering the reach and authority of critical realignment theory has become a scholarly growth industry. A massive literature of analysis, defense, and redefinition now exists, in which some scholars seek to save it, others to redefine it, or to change its focus. There have been suggestions that there has been an "incomplete realignment," or a "hollow realignment," or both. Some analysts, recognizing that the theory is troubled so long as it relies primarily on electoral behavior, have broadened its meaning to emphasize sharp and enduring policy transformations or critical changes in political "regimes." Much of the reconceptualization work is quite astute, and some of it is partially convincing. But, whatever scholars may accomplish by these efforts, at the very least, the theory's former tidiness is gone.[5]

If, in fact, a critical realignment has recently occurred on, or a little off, schedule, it has been quite unlike the hallowed and classic episodes of the 1850s, 1890s, and 1930s, which have been the foundation stones of the theory. Although the Republican party has been revived at the presidential level as it has won five of the last six elections, were the party's successive victories due to an electoral realignment? Some voters have switched parties. Others have joined the voting universe as committed partisans. But, as James Sundquist suggests, American presidential elections are now "decided by the independents attached firmly to neither party and by the partisans whose attachments are weak. They make up a majority of the electorate. . . ."[6] Further, as Walter Dean Burnham has recently written,

one key element has been omitted up to this point, and for good reason: It does not exist. This is a part of realignment that involves *general, comprehensive,* partisan shifts across the vertical and horizontal boundaries of the constitutional system connected with large-scale and durable shifts in electoral behavior. Traditional realignments, in whichever partisan direction, at whatever time, or over whatever issues, uniformly entailed the capture and control *by a single party* of all branches of the federal government and (usually) a preponderant majority of state legislative seats and control of state governments too.[7]

Such rather substantial differences from a previous norm and from supposedly similar political episodes have provoked much weariness in parts of the academy concerned with decoding American politics. That weariness has been compounded, in turn, by the constant, and apparently futile, attempts at rescuing realignment theory, by winning a consensus around some reformulated definitions. All of which has caused a certain amount of turning to other things among many scholars and a desire among not a few of them to take the logic of recent events to their natural conclusions and "bury the concept."[8]

Has, in fact, critical realignment theory had its day and should it now be buried as a major measuring and organizing tool alongside other, once promising but now obsolete, artifacts of the intellectual past? From the perspective of a historian who has regularly tried to understand the boundaries of, and the underlying impulses present in, two hundred years of electoral data, such a course seems premature. Critical realignment theory's essential logic can still be salvaged but only if its constraints are recognized and it is fitted within a different conceptual framework. Electoral realignments are an important part of the dynamics of American politics since 1789, but they are only one of several parts. They are time-bound in ways that have not always been fully appreciated. They have existed as the dynamic mechanism of American electoral change for one-half of the nation's political life under the Constitution—only from the late 1830s to the 1930s.

A great many American political historians have been much influenced by realignment theory and have used it to organize and illuminate their own research. Many of their findings have been in the literature for some time; others of their conclusions are more recent. In total, they add up to more than an interesting history lesson or two. This continuing work has clarified the nature of party choice and focused much attention on the realignments of the 1850s, 1890s, and 1930s as well as the stable periods in between. Although serious gaps remain in the record, all of this material is an important resource in efforts to clarify the nature of the critical realignment phenomenon in American politics. There is enough in it to contribute a great deal to our understanding, sketch the outlines of a broader landscape than is usually the case, and, as I have suggested, cast a very different light of the changing shape of the American political universe from the one we have enjoyed since V. O. Key.[9]

The First Century

In particular, scholars have to look quite closely at the first century of American political life under the Constitution, the years between George Washington's election as president in 1789 and the realignment of the 1890s, a period encompassing what Burnham once referred to as "the lost Atlantis" of our political history. The vibrant, rich, and complex political world before the 1850s is extremely significant in any efforts to explore and understand the way American politics has behaved, as Ronald Formisano's pivotal essay in the *American Political Science Review* first suggested in 1974.[10]

Some years ago Lee Benson, Phyllis Field, and I began to look at a much greater chronological reach of American electoral politics than had been the norm among students of realignment sequences. We also focused a certain amount of attention on voting behavior at the state level, as well as in the national contests which had been the focus of most realignment research. Others have done similar work since.[11] Although not as complete in coverage as research into more accessible periods, much of the post-Constitutional to Jacksonian world and beyond has been examined and measured enough to be incorporated into our analysis. As Burnham has reminded political scientists from time to time, Atlantis is now much less lost than it was.[12]

In our research, Benson, Field, and I concentrated on electoral behavior. We did so because realignment theory itself began there and elections continue to be the dynamic element in the process, their analysis providing the proper foundation stone for all else that may follow. As we probed further into political life after 1789, with its frequent election activity, we suggested that there were geographic and chronological constraints that substantially challenged the robustness of critical realignment theory. The more we pushed the chronological boundaries back, the more disorderly we found popular voting behavior to be, and the more problematic the periodicity of realignments as a normal condition of American electoral behavior. In fact, we argued, the rhythms of American politics were such that the notion of five party systems, each bounded by realignments, did not begin to catch the long-term pattern of American political realities. Instead, behavioral distinctions have existed across time which suggest a pattern that differs entirely from that postulated by the realignment perspective. The American political universe changed its shape not once—at the end of the nineteenth century, as another critic of the five-party system contract has suggested—but several times, not all of them coterminous with an identifiable critical realignment or party system.[13]

Since the work reported above, my own further research and elaboration have confirmed the usefulness of the particular direction of the earlier findings and the interpretative power of the alternative understanding of the American political universe. In particular, the nature and substance of the nation's political life in the half-century from the late 1830s into the 1890s—a block of years Richard L. McCormick has referred to as "the party period" of America's political experience—has become the focus of much additional research with realignment theory in mind. That fifty-year period can be mapped using a mix of quantitative data: state, county, and precinct election returns, along with anthropological probing into the remnants of a lost civilization through the range of traditional sources historians use. Both the usual quantitative measures of voter behavior and the systematic charting of the political organization, texture, and outlooks of these years, suggest how different the party period was from what went before and what came afterward. In Burnham's terms, ". . . in many ways, the democratized nineteenth century was of one piece, compared either with the deferential-participant era which preceded it or the demobilized, partisan-decomposed era which followed."[14]

What these findings demonstrate is, first, that the notion of a Federalist-Republican, first party system, followed by an Era of Good Feelings, and then by a second party system, beginning in 1828, oversimplified a more complex situation in these years, one quite different in its fundamental structure from what was to come. In an effort to organize and focus political life, two national political coalitions briefly appeared on the national scene in the 1790s. But their lives were short, their activities limited, their influence narrow, and their impress quite shallow. They did not develop organizations in any depth or complexity; they did not reach widely across states and nation; they did not greatly touch the hearts and minds of what few voters there were. Voter mobilization was limited. The extent of competition between the coalitions varied widely; there were many single candidate and multicandidate races. There was always an intermittent, ad hoc, impermanent, quality about the Federalists and Republicans, often a casual or, conversely, a quite hostile, attitude toward them. The essential character of this period in which they temporarily appeared, and for a generation thereafter, was individual, not collective; largely fragmented and volatile, not stable and patterned.[15]

All this was evident at the polling place throughout the half-century after 1789. As the careful work of Burnham and Kleppner convincingly argues, turnout at the polls in American presidential elections clearly marks significant political currents. It certainly did in these years. In the post–1789 period, for example, the percentage of those eligible voters who went to cast a ballot on election day was quite low by later standards. In 1800, 31.4% of those eligible to do so, voted for president; in 1816, just over 20% turned out on election day; and neither of these figures were at the low end of the sequence. By the late 1820s, voter participation reached its high plateau in this half-century, of just over 57%. In a reversal of later patterns, turnout for many state elections throughout the period was usually somewhat higher, but even at the state and local level, participation remained well below what was soon to become characteristic on the American political scene as a whole.[16]

At the same time, this indifferent participation was matched by the volatility of those voters who came to the polls. Partisan alignments and behavior did appear at moments throughout this half-century, but they were rare, and uncharacteristic of the period as a whole, brief deviations from the larger picture of nonalignment. In sum, this period, "usually defined as containing the first American party system, did not have, except briefly, one of the major elements of such a system: a stable partisan electorate."[17] Furthermore, there was little relationship between voting patterns for one office and those for another. Voters were not consistently marshalled from one election to the next. There were different pools of electors coming to the polling places each time, each unpredictably drawn from the total voter pool from one election to another and from one office to the next.[18]

In the absence of specific institutional focus, apparatus, and effective means (or will) to develop and sustain commitments to a party, none of this is particularly surprising. Few American voters were socialized into the electoral system. The mechanisms for doing so did not exist. Formisano has suggested that the years before 1840 made up an evolutionary, developmental period, one of mixed forms, a transition period between the elite-dominated colonial political world and the more popular and organized world of two-party dominance. Another historian, Paul Kleppner, suggests characterizing the period as dominated by "a *preparty* party system." But, however one labels the mixture—as transitional, evolutionary, or otherwise—it did not fit the notion of party systems and their regularities. These years formed a distinct and unique pattern, in their central nature, unlike what was to come. Without pushing the similarities too far, since they are based on quite different elements, both those years and the most recent ones stand in sharp contrast to the century of American political life in between.[19]

Electoral realignments did not occur in this period, not in 1800 or in 1828 or in any other election. Categorization of the Jeffersonian or Jacksonian presidential election triumphs as critical realignments stretches the meaning of the concept and the electoral comparability much too far. In the fifty years before 1838, such realignments were impossible in the electoral universe because there was no alignment to realign from. In the cases of 1800 and 1828, the electoral movement of voters, or the mobilization of previous nonvoters, did not begin from an existing stable pattern of voter commitment. Nor is it surprising that, in such circumstances, there are few signs of maintaining, converting, reinstating, or even deviating elections throughout the period. (Deviation from what, reinstatement to what, would seem to be appropriate questions, given then-current electoral behavior.) One might argue that there is a realignment when the whole system moves from non-alignment to alignment. But this seems strained. Not to be too stringent, didactic, or purist, but only to be repetitious, the concept of realignment suggests that there was a previous alignment of some kind. It also suggests that certain institutional and behavioral conditions had to be normal parts of the political landscape in order to establish the prerequisites for both significant commitment and electoral change.[20]

"The Arrival of Party"

This volatile, nonparty situation was succeeded by a quite different behavioral pattern. Just as much more happened in the 1890s than McKinley's defeat of Bryan, much more happened at the end of the 1830s than the destruction of Martin Van Buren's political career and the "Hurrah" campaign that elected the Whig ticket of "Tippecanoe and Tyler Too." The decade after 1828 were years of tremendous turmoil and bitter confrontation in American politics. They also constituted a transforming political moment. True, persistent and elaborate political maneuvering and significant changes in political organization and style had been underway for some time. But all those efforts remained incomplete until the late 1830s. Only then, in Formisano's apt phrase, can we mark "the arrival of party," that moment when all of the elements we associate with a fully functioning party system came to dominate the landscape and also became locked into place as a distinct pattern of political life. What had never existed before, now did.[21]

But what happened was more than the birth of a new party system. American politics codified in a very particular way. The entire texture and structure of the political world shifted markedly. A new political universe, America's second under the Constitution, replaced the existing one. Its driving impulses were deeply partisan in ways never before known. The recent studies of the powerful antiparty tradition in early American politics underscore the depth and scale of the change. Where parties had once been condemned as an unacceptable threat to the republic, robust partisan organizations now matured and became normal aspects of the political scene—this, for the first time ever. Competition between them became formal and regularized. Unlike the earlier period, political conflict was accepted as normal rather than so divisive that it threatened the survival of the nation. Parties, partisan attitudes, and partisan perspectives all became legitimate, and dominant, in ways previously unknown.[22]

What finally cemented all these elements into the partisan dominance of American political life was the direct and constant participation of masses of the people—at least white, adult males—in marked and previously unknown ways. Elite involvement in the new partisan ways occurred first. As early as 1831–32, many of them had begun to behave in partisan fashion. By 1838, the American voter was also dramatically affected by the changes underway. As their numbers grew with the collapse of restrictive legal limits on participation, sustained attention had to be given to mobilizing voters over and over again, to keeping them interested and politically involved, not just once, or infrequently, but regularly. These partisanly directed efforts worked. By 1838, despite the constant and extraordinary levels of population movement in and out of American communities, voters everywhere began to flock to the polls in unusual numbers.[23]

The multitudes turning out at the polls after 1838 added up to many more participants, proportionately, than had voted at any earlier time, or compared to the numbers who did so in the years following the end of the period. In 1836, 57.8% of those eligible, nationally, turned out to vote for president, a figure congruent with the levels of the 1980s. In 1840, in contrast, 80.2% of those eligible to vote across the nation did so. And they kept coming, thereafter. Burnham has estimated that the national turnout for presidential elections between 1840 and 1896 averaged just under 77% (compared with about 60% between 1900 and the present, and just under 50% between 1824 and 1836).[24]

At the state level, similarly high turnouts also occurred. In 1840, for example, over 88% of those who were eligible came to the polls in Mississippi; in New York turnout was just under 92%. Participation rates averaging over 80% were not unusual, thereafter, in many states. Such high turnout was not a sectional phenomenon. Although northern voter participation was higher than southern, it was not so by much, and the seven top turnout states before the Civil War were a mix from across the country. Moreover, turnout for different offices varied much less from one another than had been the case earlier and would be the pattern subsequently. The turnout differential averaged about 12% less in off-year elections from what it was in presidential years after 1838.[25]

Most critically, in the years beginning with 1838, once at the polls, most voters began to behave in a stable, highly predictable fashion. As early as the presidential election of 1828, partial voter coalitions had begun to form behind party labels. But before 1838, such grouping remained incomplete. Off-year elections and contests for minor offices, in particular, continued to exhibit the same kind of voter volatility that had characterized the earlier period since the Constitution. At the end of the 1830s, this changed forcefully. As at other times, in the years 1853–54 and again in 1893–94, for example, significant electoral shifts first manifested themselves in off-year contests for Congress and state office. The elections of 1838, and those immediately following, made up the first *aligning* episode in the United States. For the first time, voters fell into line behind their particular party regardless of the office being contested. They stayed there, thereafter.[26]

Regardless of office, the way that voters behaved in each succeeding election, from 1838 to 1853, looked remarkably like the way they had done in the one before. Correlation coefficients of party voting above .90 were common, not only between elections for the same office, but across different offices as well. In North Carolina, for one example, the Democrats' vote for president in 1840 correlated at .97 both with the 1842 gubernatorial vote and with the 1844 presidential vote. In New Jersey, state legislative races in 1844 correlated with the vote for governor at .99 and for that of president at .97. Neither of these states were exhibiting unusual patterns. In contrast to what had been the case before, and what was to come afterward, the American electorate now contained few apathetic, poorly informed, or marginally involved voters. After 1838, each major party had a steady corps of loyal supporters, who turned out regularly to support their partisan community. (They were, of course, helped by the commonly used party ballot form, with its listing of many party candidates on one ballot, which ensured high correlations of voting for various offices.)[27]

Finally, the voting system became a highly competitive one at most levels of politics, unique in the extent and reach of its pattern of close contests. Presidential elections were usually narrowly decided in the popular vote. Most gubernatorial and many congressional contests were as well, certainly by margins unlike those in the earlier period or in the years after the 1890s. In the nine largest states in the Union, the Democrats averaged 48% of the vote in gubernatorial races between 1838 and 1853, the Whigs 48.4%. Indices of competitiveness further underline the point of the close character of the contest between the parties throughout the nation. Six of these crucial, large states were intensely competitive, two of them were moderately competitive, and only one, Massachusetts, lay on the border between dominant one-party and safe one-party. Their overall level of competitiveness was .95, right at the intensely competitive point. In congressional races, a similar pattern appeared, although with somewhat less competitiveness across the country.

As one example of the whole, in 1835, when Tennesseans voted for the members of the 24th Congress, two of the thirteen districts had three candidates. Each candidate won a substantial portion of the popular vote. In three other districts, there were uncontested walkovers for one candidate. In six of the rest the winner received better than 60% of the vote. Putting it another way, only two of the Tennessee "contests" were competitive two-party races. Four years later, in 1839, there were, in contrast, no multicandidate races, only one unopposed contest, and the number in the noncompetitive, 60% or better range, fell to four. Eight contests now were within the boundaries defining two-party competitiveness. The Tennessee pattern was not unique. Most states had a range of competitive seats, some that were consistently dominated by one party, and a few that were unopposed walkovers.[28]

It is not surprising that the American electoral structure had taken this shape. After 1838, parties were, and were accepted as, the key integrating mechanisms of all aspects of American politics. The political world's boundaries, organization, commitments, and constraints, as well as the behavior of its inhabitants, were deeply partisan in ways unique to our political life before or since. Parties organized all of the elements on the scene, framed meaningful choices for voters, and kept order in a potentially turbulent and fragmented situation. For most Americans, politics was not a separate sphere divorced from their socioeconomic and personal concerns. Rather, politics was woven into the fabric of the society at all levels. Parties reflected this. With their ideological bite, they enshrined traditional animosities between groups, reflected current differences in society, and provided clear ways of looking at the world.[29]

The partisan, integrative factors at work penetrated the entire system. Even the Whigs, often viewed as being more hesitant about adopting party norms than were the Democrats, became (with some heartburnings) all but totally enmeshed in the new structure and adopted it for their own purposes. Parties were salient objects in the voting universe for both Whigs and Democrats and brought a remarkable stability in voting behavior to that universe. Party loyalty affected more people, reached deeper, and extended over a wider field than had ever been considered possible, let alone existed as an American political reality. The intense mass loyalties to parties that had become characteristic were rooted deep in community relationships and understandings of one's best interests. These commitments were powerfully reinforced on a regular basis and became remarkably persistent to a degree strikingly unlike anything American politics had seen before, or would see again. Party organizations, symbols, issues, and cues were now powerful enough to catch, and keep loyal, the overwhelming number of American voters at every office level.[30]

On each election day, when they went to the polls, Americans voted for party labels, not candidates. Different elections were not viewed as separate contests involving new issues or new dominant personalities. Rather, they were seen as different opportunities to vote for, and reaffirm, support for one's party, its principles, its faith, and the community it embraced. All of that was due to the whole range of vigorous and active partisan political institutions which made such voting possible. Predictable, patterned voting existed because partisan-directed and -organized elections defined, articulated, stabilized, and made congruent all the issues in each election under specific party labels.[31]

Much of what occurred is familiar enough from the scholarly literature. But the reach and nature of the nineteenth-century political nation may not always have been fully appreciated. What I am trying to convey is how deep and penetrative party influence had become, how much it drove matters in this fifty-year period, how different the party-society relationship was then, compared to other times, how different parties themselves were, in the years between 1838 and 1893, to the way they operated and what they meant at other moments, and how much they then differed in their behavior, commitment, and appeals from the later, quite negative characterizations and interpretations of them. The party institutions, loyalty, and roles that existed after 1893 were a pale imitation of the situation in the half-century before. Whatever their individual problems, whatever their interests, commitments, and ideals, Americans found the route to solution and satisfaction through the organized political system, specifically through a life-long commitment to their particular political party.

Turning points, of course, are never as sharp as scholars make them. The ongoing process of partisan political development and involvement that I have described did not finitely end but continued to unfold after 1838. Nor were all of the states fully involved in the emerging system at its very outset. (However, all but one soon were.) Nevertheless, as of 1838, the overwhelming weight of the political nation had shifted. In both North and South, parties had become, and then remained, strong enough to control the political nation, to resist attacks on them, and to hang on to their dominant position through subsequent voter shifts, a civil war, and, for some time, new socioeconomic realities as well.[32]

The consistent level of voter support for each party in the various geographic entities was significantly interrupted by the electoral realignment of the 1850s. That episode had a powerful impact on American politics, leading to the demise of the Whig party, the emergence of the Republican party, and a shift in national political power. But, its effect on the institutions and behavior of the political world was much more limited. Despite the electoral disruption, an essential continuity of the rocklike party loyalties and the strongly partisan ways of most American voters continued into the 1890s. As Formisano suggests, "the habit of partisanship ingrained by the Whigs and Democrats was not ephemeral." It remained the American norm. The political parties survived with great strength during the Civil War, not barely, but as an important, competitive force shaping policies and leadership calculations. They continued to hold the loyalty of their supporters. The dominant partisan impulse remained strong afterward as well. Partisan voting stability continued to be steadfast in the years between 1860 and 1892. Party discipline among legislators and other government officials remained comparably unremitting. The party period of American political life continued largely as before.[33]

"A Very Large Sea Change"

Despite the unique power and extent of the partisan imperative before the 1890s, the political universe was reshaped once again, this time at the expense of parties. The depression of the early 1890s, and its immediate political consequences, triggered changes that had far-reaching effect. Voting coalitions and the levels of party support shifted, as they had forty years before. This time, however, a series of forces were also unleashed which ultimately destroyed the central role of parties in American politics. Antiparty tendencies had revived earlier among some Americans and grew much stronger than they had been for half a century. The electoral disruption of the 1893–96 period, in combination with the new socioeconomic conditions coming to dominate the landscape, gave them their head.[34]

The successful attack on the parties had extraordinary consequences for the American political system. The changes unleashed in the mid-1890s led to a new and very different political pattern. What happened did not occur immediately, or all at once, but ultimately the full range of elements composing the system shifted in their activities, mix, relationships, and importance. The party period passed, never again to be revived as it had been. Popular voting patterns thus provided the same boundary marker at the end of the party period as they had at its beginning, but only because, as before, they were part of a larger set of sociopolitical processes.[35]

Crucial to the period beginning in the 1890s has been the increasing tendency toward declining voter turnout and the greater instability of mass voting patterns. After the McKinley-Bryan realignment, voter turnout fell sharply, ticket splitting increased, and the number of strong, consistent, partisan voters decreased significantly, in a long, downward slide. The hallmark of the previous system, party identification, began to weaken over the course of the twentieth century, first slowly and then at an accelerated pace in the past generation. Electoral stability has become episodic and increasingly rare. In Congress and state legislatures as well, there has been a similar, major, falling off in partisan voting—a clear-cut, long-range, downward trend in partisanship. As Burnham has observed,

It is quite clear [that] a very large sea change in the political culture occurred around the turn of the century: the collapse of intense partisanship, its replacement by widespread hostility to political parties and political machines, and a parallel shift of campaign styles from the typical militia-drill model of the nineteenth century to the advertising-oriented techniques of the twentieth.[36]

As in the years after 1838, a new dominant force emerged as the balance among influences and determining elements shifted significantly and took hold in a new configuration. Yet, at first, the American political universe still contained strong voter alignments, and then, another significant realignment sequence still occurred in the 1930s. How was it possible for the cycle of alignment-realignment to continue after 1893, with the onset of the powerful forces undermining parties? It seems clear that, as in the years before 1838, certain changes took place first at the elite level and only then penetrated throughout the rest of the system. Popular party identification was the last element to go, just as it had been that last to develop in the 1830s. Yet, it was early evident that significant changes had occurred in the way that the political world was functioning. The New Deal party system was not just an echo of the earlier system. To be sure, it had many of the same electoral attributes. But the nature, reach, and texture of party loyalty was already shifting—and weakening. Nevertheless, parties remained powerful enough *in the electorate* for there to be another major realignment, the last of three.[37]

The 1890s into the 1940s was a mixed era where, amid the signs of party decay in government affairs, policy making, and the particular structuring of popular involvement in politics, partisanship was still able to anchor much voter choice, as it had in the past. But the New Deal episode was an end of a cycle, not its continuation. That partisan honeymoon, no matter how powerful and dramatic it was for some years, was only a deviation from the long-range pattern of party collapse. The partisan decline was only delayed, not ended. And when it began again, the many disintegrative factors at work attacking the basic substance of party power penetrated throughout the system.[38]

Over time, the behavior of voters has shifted dramatically. It has moved further and further away from, and then traveled outside of, the alignment-realignment sequence. Turnout has dropped sharply, as has the partisan loyalty of voters. By the 1980s, to quote Everett Ladd, we are in a political world where partisan commitments among the half of the potential electorate that bothers to vote "count for less . . . than at any point since a mature party system took shape in the United States in the 1830s." The largest bloc of those voters consider themselves to be independents and vote, in Demetrios Caraley's words, "without feeling any emotional pulls of party loyalty to anchor them. . . ." Their behavior leads to an electoral situation dominated by a "performance-oriented, what-have-you-done-for-us-lately mood of an electorate that no longer considers voting for 'my party' a sociological or psychological imperative."[39]

American Political Eras

Putting the data from 1789 to the present together, I believe that we can now get a better purchase on the nature of the American political pattern during the past two hundred years. The nation's electoral universe under the Constitution came into being in 1788–89; a political party system matured within it by the late 1830s. The universe's first realignment was in 1854–60. The American electoral universe remains with us in 1990, having shifted its basic character—away from parties—in the 1890s. It seems to have had its last realignment in the 1930s. Stretching the notion of critical realignment to cover elections before 1838, those of 1800 or 1828, for example, is to distort what happened then. So would stretching it to cover the election of 1964 or some other recent contest. Critical realignment theory cannot bear the weight of the sytemic differences present and the conditions, such as sturdy pre-existing voter alignments, *not* present. As remarked earlier, if the elections of 1800, 1828, or 1964 were realignments, they were, at the very least, quite unlike the classic three episodes on which the theory rests.

Whatever regularities have existed over the course of American electoral history, they have done so in a form different from that proposed by critical election theory. The phenomenon of critical-elections/realignments appears to be only one, among several, elements composing the structure of America's political experience. What we have identified as five similar party systems are not

readily comparable. The two labeled the third and fourth such party systems
had a unity to them. They were not alike, but individually or together, they
differed significantly from those that came before them and those that came
later. The distinctive qualities of the 1838–90s period stands out as an unparalleled political phenomenon. David Mayhew, some years ago, grasped much
of this in his review of Chambers and Burnham's classic work on party periods.
"It may be useful," he wrote, "to speak of *two* successive American party
systems rather than five (or two and a half if one counts the evanescent Jeffersonians and Hamiltonians): a *Jacksonian system,* extending from the 1830s
through about the first decade of the twentieth century, and a *Progressive system,* extending roughly from that first decade to the present."[40]

Mayhew seems primarily to have in mind the organizational structures of the
parties. But bringing voting behavior, organizational components, and attitudes and perspectives about parties all together allows us to extend and clarify
his idea. In 1978, Benson, Field, and I suggested that scholars adopt the notion
of political eras as a replacement for the core idea of party systems, bounded by
realignments, succeeding each other in a regular rhythm. It seemed to be a very
useful notion when first presented. In light of another decade of research, it
still does. Although five party systems have existed since 1789, we argued that
there were three political eras, and perhaps an emerging fourth, each of them
having chronological boundaries that differed from the five party systems.[41]

Of course, the setting of chronological boundaries is difficult and conten-
tious. As noted, historical eras neither begin nor end abruptly, nor completely.
Nevertheless, the basic nature of American political life has changed markedly
into quite different patterns at moments that seem clear enough. The first political era stretched from 1789 to 1838; the second lasted from 1838 to 1893 and
included the onset of a voter realignment in the latter year; the third era came on
the scene after 1893. A fourth then began in the years around 1948–52 and has
encompassed the period since then, more than forty years now. The years
1948–52 seem to be an appropriate dividing point because the disintegration of
the New Deal party coalition was evident in both presidential elections, as was
the onset of candidate-centered voting behavior. At first, scholars considered
these elections to be examples of the voters' occasional, but temporary, idiosyncratic and anomalous behavior. But, in a longer view, it is now clear that the
"reinstating" election of 1960 was the anomaly in the new political era on the
scene.[42]

The crucial analytical issue lies not in the number of eras (or party systems)
but in the profoundly different qualities of each, and what those differences tell
us about the patterns of American politics over time. The justification for ar-
ranging political experience in this way relates to the kind of society that pre-
dominated in each era, and to the kinds of political institutions, norms, and
behavior, that were paramount in each. In each era, a distinctive consensus has

emerged as to what is at stake, what proper behavior is, what political resources and institutions are important, and how they are to be used. Differences exist about what is needed to manage political life, about how to define the political agenda, and how to advance the purpose of politics. There were specific political norms, rituals, and routines in each era that provided the constraints within which involved Americans went about their political activities.

Some of the active political elements present in each era were holdovers from a previous time; others were new. But they all cohered differently each time from the way they did in another era, behaved differently, and blended together into something quite distinctive each time, reflecting the larger socioeconomic forces at work in the society at a particular moment. This essay has primarily focused on electoral behavior as a major definer of the chronological boundaries of each era, but, to repeat the underlying point, popular voting behavior has been only one aspect of the situation. There were other major differences between each era as well, differences that encompassed the whole range, nature, and mix of all of the elements constituting the political nation at each distinct moment.

In summary, borrowing from, adding to, and moving beyond the vocabulary of critical realignment theory, each of the four eras that have existed over the course of American political history can be sequentially labeled, and characterized in this suggested synthesis as: (1) prealignment; (2) alignment-realignment; (3) realignment-dealignment; and, (4) postalignment (see table 1.1).

Table 1.1. American Political Eras, 1789–1989

Era	Description	Years
1	Prealignment	1789–1838
2	Alignment/Realignment	1838–1893
3	Realignment/Dealignment	1893–1948/52
4	Postalignment	1948/52–present

"No Historic Counterpart"

In conclusion, it seems useful to return to the starting point: the constraints on critical realignment theory. As one examines the accumulation of research on the subject by political scientists in the light of the available historical data on the same subject, it becomes evident that there are stringent chronological limitations on the possibilities of there being any more critical realignments. In the first place, realignments need alignments to undergird them. That seems logical. That point suggests, in turn, the crucial importance of political parties to realignment theory. Alignments need parties to focus and anchor them.

Thus, the cyclical pattern of realignment does not extend into nonparty, anti-party, or postparty periods.

Second, realignments are not the normal dynamic of the American political order. Whatever the underlying continuities in the nation's voting behavior, they do not include the particular kind of realignment cycle usually identified in the scholarly literature. The organizational scheme proposed here, and the elements on which it is based, suggest the unusual and central importance of the era between 1838 and the 1940s. On either side of the two alignment-realignment-dealignment eras were two eras totaling together about the same number of years in which realignment was not part of the pattern of electoral behavior. Granted that the differences between each of the two eras, the one before and the other after, along with the era of realignment, are extensive. Still, they share some things as well. Whatever the underlying dynamic and particular qualities of each of them, one of the eras bounding the realignment era was dominated by the absence of party; the era lying on the other boundary is dominated by the decline of party and its influence, leading toward the absence of party. In short, they were a prepartisan era and a postpartisan one. In both, the voters often have not participated; in both, voters have not been locked into party commitments, but have instead been up for grabs. The bounding eras have been of about equal duration; together they add up to about half of our political history under the Federal Constitution.

It seems, therefore, that not one but several dynamics have been at work over the course of American electoral history. The record is richer and more complicated than has been usually believed. There have not always been cycles of recurrent change based on repeated triggering of the same mechanisms and behavior but, rather, quite distinct and separate phenomena. The concept of critical realignments, as an organizing perspective, is not applicable to many of the changes that have occurred in American electoral behavior since 1789. They did not exist before 1838. Nor have they occurred since the 1940s. If scholars accept, as the evidence suggests that they should, Ladd's comment that "a transformed parties and election system is [now] firmly in place in the United States . . . [which] has no historic counterpart," let them also accept, in consequence, that realignment is an important, but quite bounded, phenomenon within the American political universe over two hundred years.[43]

Notes

This essay was written while I was a visiting scholar at the Russell Sage Foundation during the academic year 1988–89. I am grateful to two of my colleagues there, Michael Hechter and Robert Merton, for close, incisive readings of an earlier draft of this essay. They are, of course, not responsible for what I have written.

1 Walter Dean Burnham, "The Reagan Heritage," in *The Election of 1988: Reports and Interpretations,* ed. Gerald M. Pomper (Chatham, N.J.: Chatham House, 1989), 20.

2 V. O. Key, Jr., "A Theory of Critical Elections," *Journal of Politics* 17 (February 1955): 3–18; William Nisbet Chambers and Walter Dean Burnham, *The American Party Systems: Stages of Political Development* (New York: Oxford University Press, 1967; 2d ed., 1975); Walter Dean Burnham, *Critical Elections and the Mainsprings of American Politics* (New York: W. W. Norton, 1970); Richard J. Trilling, *Party Image and Electoral Behavior* (New York: John Wiley and Sons, 1976); Jerome L. Clubb, William H. Flanigan, and Nancy Zingale, *Partisan Realignment: Voters, Parties, and Government in American History* (Beverly Hills, Calif.: Sage, 1980); James L. Sundquist, *Dynamics of the Party System: Alignment and Realignment of Political Parties in the United States* (Washington, D.C.: Brookings Institution, 1983).

3 Everett C. Ladd with Charles Hadley, *Transformations of the American Party System,* 2d ed. (New York: W. W. Norton, 1978); Bruce A. Campbell and Richard J. Trilling, eds., *Realignment in American Politics: Toward a Theory* (Austin: University of Texas Press, 1979); Gerald Pomper, *Voters' Choice: Varieties of American Electoral Behavior* (New York: University Press of America, 1983); Everett C. Ladd, "A Rebuttal: Realignment? No. Dealignment? Yes." *Public Opinion* 3 (October–November 1980): 13–15, 54–55; idem, "The 1988 Elections: Continuation of the Post–New Deal System," *Political Science Quarterly* 104 (Spring 1989): 1–18.

4 Vernon Bogdanor, *Parties and Democracy in Britain and America* (New York: Praeger, 1984), xiii; Norman H. Nie, Sidney Verba, and John R. Petrocik, *The Changing American Voter* (Cambridge: Harvard University Press, 1976); Martin Wattenberg, *The Decline of American Political Parties, 1952–1984* (Cambridge: Harvard University Press, 1986); Everett C. Ladd, "On Mandates, Realignments, and the 1984 Presidential Election," *Political Science Quarterly* 100 (Spring 1985): 1–25.

5 Campbell and Trilling, *Realignment in American Politics;* Richard G. Niemi and Herbert Weisberg, eds., *Controversies in Voting Behavior,* 2d ed. (Washington, D.C.: Congressional Quarterly Press, 1984); Paul Allen Beck, "Incomplete Realignment: The Reagan Legacy for Parties and Elections," in *The Reagan Legacy: Promise and Performance,* ed. Charles O. Jones (Chatham, N.J.: Chatham House, 1989), 145–71; Martin Wattenberg, "The Hollow Realignment: Partisan Change in a Candidate-Centered Era," *Public Opinion Quarterly* 51 (Spring 1987): 58–74; Benjamin Ginsberg and Martin Shefter, *Politics by Other Means: The Declining Importance of Elections in America* (New York: Basic Books, 1990).

6 James L. Sundquist, "The 1984 Election: How Much Realignment?" *Brookings Review* 3 (Winter 1985): 15.

7 Burnham, "The Reagan Heritage," 16. Burnham goes on to suggest that "what has really been going on since the late 1960s has been a radical *recomposition* of the American political system. A chief, but by no means the only, empirical sign of this transformation is the accelerating decomposition of nominally partisan coalitions across office-specific and level-specific lines" (20).

20   *Joel H. Silbey*

Ladd, "The 1988 Elections," 18.
These efforts include historians' own contributions to "the end of realignment theory." Allan J. Lichtman, "The End of Realignment Theory—Toward a New Research Program for American Political History," *Historical Methods* 15 (Fall 1982): 170–88. See also Lichtman's "Critical Election Theory and the Reality of American Presidential Politics, 1916–1940," *American Historical Review* 81 (April 1976): 317–50.

Of course, political scientists are well aware of the historical record. Both Burnham and Sundquist have immersed themselves in that historical data bank and used it to develop realignment theory much further than anyone else has done. I am only suggesting that, in reopening and continuing a dialogue among Burnham, myself, and several others, which began some time ago before an audience of historians and which was unfortunately sidetracked on the historians' part by other concerns, there is an opportunity to go still further to clarify the much different scholarly place that critical realignment theory occupies now than it did then. If we do not settle all matters completely, at least ground can be cleared, the record further developed, and remaining differences narrowed. See Lee Benson and Joel H. Silbey, "The American Voter, 1854–1860 and 1948–1984" (Paper for the annual meeting of the Organization of American Historians, 1978); and Walter Dean Burnham, "Comment on Benson and Silbey, 'The American Voter . . . ,' " ibid. Burnham's masterly use of historical data begins with his "The Changing Shape of the American Political Universe," *American Political Science Review* 59 (March 1965): 7–28. See also Sundquist, *Dynamics of American Politics.*

10 Walter Dean Burnham, "The Problem of Turnout," in *Elections—American Style,* ed. A. James Reichley (Washington, D.C.: Brookings Institution, 1987), 98; Ronald P. Formisano, "Deferential-Participant Politics: The Early Republic's Political Culture, 1789–1840," *America Political Science Review* 68 (June 1974): 473–87.

11 Lee Benson and Joel H. Silbey, "American Political Eras, 1788–1988: Toward A Normative, Substantive, and Conceptual Framework for the Historical Study of American Political Behavior" (Paper for the Annual Meeting of the Social Science History Association, 1978); Lee Benson, Joel H. Silbey, and Phyllis F. Field, "Toward a Theory of Stability and Change in American Voting Patterns: New York State, 1792–1970," in *The History of American Electoral Behavior,* ed. Joel H. Silbey, Allan G. Bogue, and William H. Flanigan (Princeton: Princeton University Press, 1978), 77–105; David Bohmer, "The Maryland Electorate and the Concept of a Party System in the Early National Period," in *History of American Electoral Behavior,* ed. Silbey, Bogue, and Flanigan, 146–73; William G. Shade, "Political Pluralism and Party Development: The Creation of a Modern Party System, 1815–1852," in *The Evolution of American Electoral Systems,* ed. Paul Kleppner et al. (Westport, Conn.: Greenwood Press, 1981), 77–111; Marc Kruman, *Parties and Politics in North Carolina, 1836–1865* (Baton Rouge: Louisiana State University Press, 1983); M. Philip Lucas, "The Development of the Second Party System in Mississippi, 1817–1846" (Ph.D. diss. Cornell University, 1983); Ronald P. Formisano, *The Transformation of Political Culture: Massachusetts Parties, 1790s–1840s* (New York: Oxford University Press, 1983).

12 Most recently in "V. O. Key, Jr., and the Study of Political Parties," in *V. O. Key, Jr. and the Study of American Politics,* ed. Milton C. Cummings (Washington, D.C.: American Political Science Association, 1983), 3–23.

13 See the citations in note 11; Burnham, "Changing Shape."

14 Walter Dean Burnham, "Those High Nineteenth-Century American Voting Turnouts: Fact or Fiction?" *Journal of Interdisciplinary History* 16 (Spring 1986): 640; Richard L. McCormick, "The Party Period and Public Policy: An Exploratory Hypothesis," *Journal of American History* 66 (September 1979): 279–98; idem, *The Party Period and Public Policy: American Politics from the Age of Jackson to the Progressive Era* (New York: Oxford University Press, 1986); Joel H. Silbey, *The American Political Nation, 1838–1893* (Stanford: Stanford University Press, forthcoming 1991).

15 Ronald P. Formisano, "Federalists and Republicans: Parties, Yes—System, No," in Kleppner, *Evolution of American Electoral Systems,* 33–76; idem, "Deferential-Participant Politics"; idem, *Transformation of Political Culture.*

16 Burnham, "Problem of Turnout"; Richard P. McCormick, "New Perspectives on Jacksonian Politics," *American Historical Review* 65 (January 1960): 288–301; Paul Kleppner, *Who Voted?: The Dynamics of Electoral Turnout, 1870–1980* (New York: Praeger, 1982).

17 Benson, Silbey, and Field, "Toward a Theory of Stability and Change," 87.

18 Ibid.; Benson and Silbey, "American Political Eras"; Bohmer, "Maryland Electorate"; Shade, "Political Pluralism"; Formisano, *Transformation of Political Culture.*

19 Formisano, *Transformation of Political Culture;* Paul Kleppner, *The Third Electoral System, 1853–1892: Parties, Voters, and Political Cultures* (Chapel Hill: University of North Carolina Press, 1979), 19.

20 "The term *party system,* or *electoral era,* designates a set of maintaining, deviating, and reinstating elections bounded by realigning sequences" (Kleppner, *Third Electoral System,* 19). The categorization of elections comes, of course, originally from Angus Campbell, Philip Converse, Warren Miller, and Donald Stokes, *The American Voter* (New York: John Wiley & Sons, 1960); and idem, *Elections and the Political Order* (New York: John Wiley & Sons, 1966).

21 This paragraph sums up the argument in Silbey, *American Political Nation,* chap. 1–3. The Formisano quotation is in *Transformation of Political Culture,* 487. See also Joel H. Silbey, "Election of 1836," and William N. Chambers, "Election of 1840," both in *History of American Presidential Elections,* ed. Arthur M. Schlesinger, Jr., and Fred L. Israel (New York: Chelsea House Publishers, 1971), 1:577–640, 643–744; and Shade, "Political Pluralism."

22 Steven Watts, *The Republic Reborn: War and the Making of Liberal America, 1790–1820* (Baltimore: Johns Hopkins University Press, 1987); Drew R. McCoy, *The Elusive Republic: Political Economy in Jeffersonian America* (Chapel Hill: University of North Carolina Press, 1980); William Gienapp, " 'Politics Seems to Enter into Everything': Political Culture in the North, 1840–1860," in *Essays on American Antebellum Politics, 1840–1860,* ed. Stephen Maizlish and John Kushma (College Station: Texas A & M University Press, 1982), 14–69; Silbey, *American Political Nation.*

23 This was a nationwide phenomenon if not present in every political jurisdiction. The thrust and direction of the movement was clear-cut.

24 Burnham, "Problem of Turnout," and "Elections As Democratic Institutions," in *Elections in America,* ed. Kay Schlozman (Boston: Allen & Unwin, 1987) 27–60; Kleppner, *Who Voted?*

The issue of the inflation of voter numbers through corruption is often suggested when one presents these turnout figures. Current historical analysis suggests that the extent of turnout fraud has been greatly overstressed, although some believe it was an important factor in part of the half-century at least. Walter Dean Burnham, "Theory and Voting Research: Some Reflections on Converse's 'Change in the American Electorate,'" *American Political Science Review* 68 (September 1974): 1002–23; Philip Converse, "Comment on Burnham's 'Theory And Voting Research,'" ibid., 1024–27; Jerrold G. Rusk, "The American Electoral Universe: Speculation and Evidence," ibid., 1028–49; Howard W. Allen and Kay Warren Allen, "Vote Fraud and Data Validity," in *Analyzing Electoral History: A Guide to the Study of American Voting Behavior,* ed. Jerome M. Clubb, William H. Flanigan, and Nancy H. Zingale (Beverly Hills, Calif.: Sage, 1981), 153–93; Gienapp, "'Politics Seems to Enter into Everything,'" 25–33; Gerald Ginsburg, "Computing Antebellum Turnout: Methods and Models," *Journal of Interdisciplinary History* 16 (Spring 1986): 579–611; and Burnham, "Those High Nineteenth-Century Turnouts."

25 The seven top turnout states were, in order, New York, Indiana, Mississippi, New Jersey, Tennessee, Ohio, and Georgia. See, as an example, Lucas, "Development of Second Party System"; and Silbey, *American Political Nation,* chap. 9.

26 Benson, Silbey, and Field, "Toward a Theory of Stability and Change"; Kleppner, *Third Electoral System;* Kruman, *Parties and Politics;* Lucas, "Development of Second Party System."

27 Kruman, *Parties and Politics;* Philip C. Davis "The Persistence of Partisan Alignment: Issues, Leader and Votes in New Jersey, 1840–1860" (Ph.D. diss., Washington University, 1978); Silbey, *American Political Nation,* chap. 9.

Recent efforts to refine and sharpen these estimates by the use of ecological regression procedures fundamentally support the findings of a marked stability pattern. However, they do sometimes show more fluidity than do the correlations, resulting from voters moving in and out of the electorate in specific elections. See, among others, William Gienapp, *The Origins of the Republican Party, 1852–1856* (New York: Oxford University Press, 1987).

28 Silbey, *American Political Nation,* chap. 9. For the broader, longitudinal picture in regard to congressional elections, see David W. Brady, *Critical Elections and Congressional Policy Making* (Stanford: Stanford University Press, 1988).

29 Gienapp, "'Politics Seems to Enter into Everything'"; Michael F. Holt, *The Political Crisis of the 1850s* (New York: John Wiley & Sons, 1978); Richard Jensen, *The Winning of the Midwest: Social and Political Conflict, 1888–1896* (Chicago: University of Chicago Press, 1971); Joel H. Silbey, *The Partisan Imperative: The Dynamics of American Politics Before the Civil War* (New York: Oxford University Press, 1985).

30 On the Whigs, see Kruman, *Parties and Politics;* and Lucas, "Development of Second Party System." For the broader picture, see Silbey, *American Political Nation.*
31 Silbey, *American Political Nation,* chaps. 9–10 and passim.
32 The major exception to the pattern was South Carolina before the Civil War.
33 Formisano, *Transformation of Political Culture,* 280. For the vigor of two-party politics during the Civil War, see Joel H. Silbey, *A Respectable Minority: The Democratic Party in the Civil War Era, 1860–1868* (New York: W. W. Norton, 1977); Allan G. Bogue, *The Congressman's Civil War* (New York: Cambridge University Press, 1989); on the later period, Kleppner, *Third Electoral System;* and McCormick, *The Party Period.*
34 Jensen, *Winning of Midwest;* Samuel T. McSeveney, *The Politics of Depression: Voting Behavior in the Northeast, 1893–1896* (New York: Oxford University Press, 1971); Kleppner, *Third Electoral System;* Richard L. McCormick, *From Realignment to Reform: Political Change in New York State, 1893–1910* (Ithaca, N.Y.: Cornell University Press, 1981).
35 Burnham, "Changing Shape"; Michael McGerr, *The Decline of Popular Politics: The American North, 1865–1928* (New York: Oxford University Press, 1986); McCormick, *From Realignment to Reform.*
36 Burnham, "Problem of Turnout," 117; Paul Kleppner, *Continuity and Change in Electoral Politics, 1893–1928* (Westport, Conn.: Greenwood Press, 1986); David W. Brady, Joseph Cooper, and Patricia A. Hurley, "The Decline of Party in the U.S. House of Representatives, 1887–1968," *Legislative Studies Quarterly* 4 (August 1979): 381–407.
37 Kristi Andersen, *Creation of A Democratic Majority 1928 to 1936* (Chicago: University of Chicago Press, 1979); John R. Petrocik, *Party Coalitions: Realignments and the Decline of the New Deal Party System* (Chicago: University of Chicago Press, 1981).
38 Ladd with Hadley, *Transformations of the Party System.*
39 Everett C. Ladd, "Elections 1988: The National Election," *Public Opinion* 11 (January–February 1989): 60; Demetrios Caraley, "Elections and Dilemmas of American Democratic Governance: Reflections," *Political Science Quarterly* 104 (Spring 1989): 25.
40 David Mayhew, "Party Systems in American History," *Polity* 1 (Fall 1968): 139.
41 Benson, Silbey, and Field, "Toward a Theory of Stability and Change."
42 Angus Campbell et al., "Stability and Change in 1960: A Reinstating Election," *American Political Science Review* 55 (June 1961): 269–80.
43 Ladd, "Elections, 1988," 18.

2 *Everett Carll Ladd*

Like Waiting for Godot
The Uselessness of "Realignment" for Understanding Change in Contemporary American Politics

Estragon:	"Charming spot. . . . Let's go.
Vladimir:	We can't.
E:	Why not?
V:	We're waiting for Godot.
E:	Ah! You're sure it was here?
V:	What?
E:	That we were to wait.
V:	He said by the tree. Do you see any others?
E:	What is it?
V:	I don't know. A willow.
E:	Where are the leaves?
V:	It must be dead.
E:	No more weeping.
V:	Or perhaps it's not the season.
E:	Looks to me more like a bush.
V:	A shrub.
E:	A bush.
V:	A——. What are you insinuating? That we've come to the wrong place?
E:	He should be here.
V:	He didn't say for sure he'd come.
E:	And if he doesn't come?
V:	We'll come back to-morrow.
E:	And then the day after to-morrow?
V:	Possibly.
E:	And so on.
V:	The point is—
E:	Until he comes.
V:	You're merciless. . . ."

Samuel Beckett,
Waiting for Godot

The cover to my copy of Samuel Beckett's *Waiting for Godot* assures us that a "battle of interpretation still rages" around the play. Has the author penned a bleak existential metaphor for mankind's search for God? At the very least, *Waiting for Godot* is a stark description of *human futility*. Estragon and Vladimir are waiting for something that never comes and that, even if it did, the reader is told, could not really help them.

Since the phrase, "like waiting for Godot," has become a casual allusion, I should stress that I do not intend it casually. For political scientists, "Waiting for Realignment" has been as bleak an experience as waiting for Godot was for Estragon and Vladimir. I argue in this chapter that political science's preoccupation with "realignment" over the past thirty-five years has been mostly unfortunate. The "realignment focus" is vastly too confining. It has in fact served to deflect attention from the rich variety of changes that have transformed the contemporary party system.

What Is "Realignment?"

Three sets of definitions of the phenomenon have been in circulation: The "dictionary" meaning, which is the most general; the understanding common in media discussions; and the predominant political science usages, which are the most elaborate and hence the narrowest. The *Random House Dictionary of the English Language* (2d ed., unabridged) defines "alignment" as "a state of agreement or cooperation among persons, groups . . . with a common cause or viewpoint." "Realignment" occurs, then, when such an alliance is significantly changed or, inferentially, when conflict among competing alliances is transformed. This simple construction would have provided a far better starting point for disciplinary research than those that have in fact held sway.

Journalistic definitions pivot on the idea of a new majority party. The question the press has posed untiringly after every Republican victory since Eisenhower's first—"But is it a realignment?"—in fact asks: Has the GOP supplanted the Democrats as the majority party? Since in every instance the correct answer has been "No," these press accounts have for the most part concluded complacently. In effect: "The Republicans won, but the long-awaited realignment has yet to occur. Whether the GOP will succeed eventually, or the Democrats' New Deal coalition will be revitalized, remains to be seen." Already a bit silly in 1972, this perspective had become ludicrous by the 1980s.

V. O. Key, Jr., the discipline's "Father of Realignment," wrote three key realignment pieces in the 1950s, not just the two *Journal of Politics* works so often cited. His first was an essay in *The Virginia Quarterly Review,* published during the 1952 campaign.[1] In it, he introduced the term "party realignment" (p. 166) and described some of what realignment entails. His starting point was the pivotal role that had been played historically by "catastrophe." "For almost a hundred years," Key wrote, "catastrophe has fixed the grand outlines of the partisan division among American voters." First, it was the Civil War that "burned into the American electorate a pattern of partisan faith that persisted in its main outlines until 1932." The Depression was the second great realigning catastrophe.

But Key immediately went beyond this formulation, arguing that in fact it was not the Depression itself that established a Democratic majority, nor even the opportunity the collapse gave them to show they could govern well that was decisive. The Democrats became the majority party when they developed convincing answers to problems long manifested but hitherto addressed only in part. Thus, party competition was transformed by "the New Deal's fulfillment of the hopes of these many streams of progressive agitation . . ." (p. 164). Here, a decisive reformulation of policy is the key element in realignment.

Key also introduced "secular realignment": "The New Deal should not be credited with the entire accretion to Democratic strength. In part the Democrats merely recruited potential converts who had been accumulating under the effects of long-term demographic trends and were awaiting political activation" (p. 166). The sources he cited were industrialization, urbanization, and the gradual political incorporation of the last great wave of European immigration.

Key's initial formulation in "The Future of the Democratic Party" was a promising start. The U.S. party system was seen to have been permanently reshaped by a few massive sociopolitical events which left deep imprints on Americans' collective memories. But realignment has also involved the emergence of new social needs and breakthroughs in partisan responses to them, as well as demographic shifts that gradually transform the electorate. These diverse developments surely help determine winners and losers, and in certain periods they have come with special force. But in his first formulation of realignment, Key did not envision any fixed pattern or singular model.

By itself, Key's next piece in the series, "A Theory of Critical Elections," need not have been a step backward conceptually. It was, as he stated, "an attempt to formulate a concept of one type of election . . . *which might be built into a more general theory of elections*"—not a mature theory of partisan change.[2] Key discerns "a category of elections in which voters are . . . unusually deeply concerned, in which the extent of electoral involvement is relatively quite high, and in which the decisive results of the voting reveal a sharp alteration of the preexisting cleavage within the electorate. Moreover, and perhaps this is a truly differentiating characteristic of this sort of election, the realignment made manifest in the voting in such elections seems to persist for several succeeding elections" (p. 4).

Unfortunately, as we know, American political science proceeded to build on this modest foundation an elaborate conceptualization of realignment as the centerpiece of a more general theory of partisan change. Many things besides Key's suggestions caused this to happen. The New Deal's burst of partisan change was alive in analysts' minds. It was the one such occurrence political scientists of the time had experienced personally. The vividness of the specific instance helped it masquerade convincingly as the general rule. With more perspective, we can now see that the massive shifts in the party system and voting alignments in the 1930s were in fact *sui generis*. In many essential structural regards, nothing like the New Deal transformation had ever occurred before—nor has it since.

For other reasons, a discipline seeking the neatness, precision, and predictability it naively attributed to "science" could not resist realignment's beguiling simplicity. We were highly "susceptible." I remarked in a convention paper fifteen years ago that "it is truly a case of Key sneezing and political science catching a cold."[3]

The Odyssey

There is no need to review the labyrinthian developments whereby a narrow model of partisan change, based on a historically unique circumstance, became a discipline's absorbing focus. Others have done that.[4] Three key ideas are common to the varied disciplinary statements of the realignment model: that certain elections are of special importance to partisan change; that these critical elections occur with a rather precise frequency or periodicity—usually, every 32 to 36 years; and that with realignment, a decisive, unidirectional shift occurs in partisan control over the agencies of government, as a new majority party appears at all levels and relegates its predecessor to the dustbin of history.[5] "The problem with this prevailing account," Edward Carmines and James Stimson write, is that "it is clearly incomplete."

The New Deal–derived critical-elections model of partisan change, known as realignment, is too tight a box, too crimped conceptually to guide us productively. Carmines and Stimson have nicely stated why this is so. "Change is a brute, stubborn fact of contemporary society; it is especially pervasive in the political arena. Candidates change, issues change, and, on occasion, even the parties change." The realignment literature does not reject this, of course, but "its theory is problematic at its core. It fails to provide a *general account of change* in the party system."[6]

Approaches to the party system that start from a bigger, more catholic sense of change have long been available. A good example is Charles E. Merriam and Harold F. Gosnell's *The American Party System*. In the last edition of this classic work, which they published in 1949, Merriam and Gosnell never use the word "realignment." They certainly have an idea, though, of political parties as central institutions changing in response to a complexly changing society.[7] They begin their description of each era in American party competition with a brief account of decisive features of the societal setting which surrounded and animated it. The social structure of each period is seen as producing distinctive needs, interests, and social and policy cleavages. Parties develop in response to these conditions and seek to build popular majorities upon them. At various points, society has changed so much that the parties, as mediating institutions, are substantially transformed. Within any given era, party coalitions are fairly stable, which means among other things that electoral victories and defeats are not randomly distributed.[8] Merriam and Gosnell would have had little difficulty seeing today's party system as greatly different from those of earlier eras, or explaining why it is.

The fact that a contemporary account of partisan change accepts the confining and misleading realignment perspective need not doom it. For example, in *The Emerging Republican Majority,* Kevin Phillips submits to a notably simplistic version of realignment's periodicity. He writes that, "to structure a mathematical perspective reaching back to 1828, political history divides into four cycles: 1828–60, 1860–96, 1896–1932, and 1932–68. All four cycles lasted 32 or 36 years, and all four included steady rule by one party with an interregnum of just 8 years when the lesser party held power. . . . The Nixon Administration [elected in 1968] seems *destined by precedent* to be the beginning of a new Republican era."[9]

Phillips' model told him that every era had to have its own unequivocal majority party. So, with the Democratic coalition experiencing ferocious strains in the late 1960s in the face of massive social change, a new Republican majority had to be emerging. Yet transcending this crude perspective, which sweeps all manner of complexity and variability in partisan change under the rug in the interest of analytic neatness and ideological fulfillment, Phillips went on to write a fine book. Earlier than most, he described the passing of the New Deal era—and, what is more, he explained why it was now "history." Ideological conflict had been vastly transformed from what it was in the Depression years and just after, he argued, because new groups and interests had become engaged. His account of complex social change mocks the simplistic question: "Is it a realignment?"

In similar fashion, I take issue with Walter Dean Burnham's obeisance to the idea of critical realignment and its centrality to American sociopolitical change. I think, among other things, that he has set for himself a wholly unnecessary problem in trying to explain why the realignment that was "predicted" for 1968 or so did not materialize, at least in anything approaching the "classic" form. Nonetheless, Burnham's accounts of the contemporary American societal setting and its political requirements are splendidly big-minded and full of insight. The first ten pages or so of his essay on the context for the 1988 election are a monument to forceful and imaginative scholarship.[10]

The test of an analytic perspective is not, of course, whether bright people can manage to transcend it, but whether it can guide research to more elaborate understanding. It is in the latter that the failure of realignment is manifest. The failure is not that of a once-useful concept that has been passed by; "realignment" was always too confining a vision, and it was always guilty of over-generalizing from a unique historical circumstance.[11]

A New Starting Point

A more useful perspective, I think, derives easily from a simple question: What do we want to know about the party system and its changes? I would submit that the following further questions are among the most important:

1. What are the major issues, policy differences, etc., and how do these cleave political elites and the public? Do some partisan elites have special problems articulating the concerns of their copartisans within the general public or in reflecting majoritarian values? If they do, why?
2. What is the social and ideological make-up of each party, at both the mass public and the elite levels? What are the key groups and interests within each coalition? How faithfully does each of these support its party? How stable are the coalitions from election to election? How similar or different are they from office to office, or from one level of government to another?
3. What are the principal features of party organization, nomination procedures, and campaign structure?
4. In each of the above areas, are major shifts currently taking place? What kinds? What are their sources?
5. Overall, how well is the party system performing? Answering this requires, of course, explicitly stating objectives in democratic representation and elaborating standards by which such performance can be judged.

Together, answers to these questions would provide a robust description of the party system and its current evolution. Were they securely established for the entire span of U.S. history, we would have all the raw material needed to form and test generalizations. It is unlikely that the generalizations which have grown out of the realignment perspective would loom very large or seem very persuasive.

Throughout its history, the U.S. party system has displayed certain enduring attributes. These are the products of persisting features of American society and its polity. As many analysts have recognized, an American ideology, derived from classical liberalism, has shown extraordinary strength and staying power—the "Lockean solidarity of the nation," Louis Hartz called it.[12] To be successful, American political parties have had to operate within boundaries set by this ideology. The breadth of popular adherence to these ideas has helped sustain a two-party system, while the greater ideological fracturing of other democracies has encouraged multipartyism.

The need to seek support within an overarching ideological consensus has historically imposed certain characteristics on the major American parties— social group inclusiveness, accommodationism, a "non-ideological" stance vis-à-vis their principal opponents (which, after all, accept the same ideology). Turning to political institutions, separation of powers and federalism have also left deep imprints on the U.S. party system. Other lesser institutional characteristics, such as the prevalence of winner-take-all electoral arrangements, have had persisting influence.

Within the boundaries set by these ideological and institutional constraints, however, the American party system has evolved, in response to broad social changes, in a fundamentally unpatterned way. Each succeeding *partisan era* has differed significantly from each of its predecessors because in important regards each succeeding *societal era* is unique.

Consider, for example, one characteristic of the current party system much commented on and obviously consequential politically—the persistence of "split-level" results, in which the Republicans have done well in presidential balloting over an extended period while the Democrats have controlled Congress. Identifiable features of the contemporary sociopolitical setting have established these split outcomes as a recurring, predictable though not precisely inevitable, feature of party competition.[13] The realignment perspective finds split outcomes "unnatural," because the periodic realignments are supposed to culminate in a majority party's becoming ascendant across the several levels and institutions of American government.

In fact, split results are a perfectly natural response within a polity whose defining feature is the elaborate separation of political institutions and authority. That other social and political conditions necessary to produce split results on a sustained basis, not in place in earlier periods, have taken form in recent years is surely important; some analysts believe their appearance is fraught with practical problems.[14] But there should not be any problem theoretically. Major social change typically entails the appearance of historically unprecedented conditions.

Change and the Contemporary Party System

I have argued for some time that, by focusing on the emergence of a new majority party in the New Deal model, the concept of "critical realignment" detracts attention from other changes in parties and elections which are of fundamental imporatnce. Anyone who hazards to write about current political developments will receive ample training in the need for humility. I assert this confidently, as the author of a summer 1980 article titled, "Why Carter Will Probably Win."[15]

Nonetheless, I will insist that the general outlines of a new party system, fundamentally different from that of the New Deal era, have been evident for some time. This system is really not envisioned by the realignment perspective. As the Watergate election balloting was taking place, in the fall of 1974, I attempted the following summary of the new system's notable features:

1. The Democrats have lost the presidential majority status which they enjoyed during the new Deal era, as new lines of conflict have decimated parts of the old coalition, but the Republicans have not attained presidential majority status. There is no majority party in the presidential arena.
2. There has been an inversion of the old New Deal relationship of social class to the vote. In wide sectors of public policy, high socioeconomic-status (SES) groups are now more supportive of equalitarian (liberal) change than are the middle to lower SES cohorts (within white America); and as a result, liberal (often, although not always, Democratic) candidates are finding higher measures of electoral sustenance at the top of the socioeconomic ladder than among the middle and lower rungs. This inversion follows from very basic changes in the structure of conflict in American society, and is likely to be long term.
3. The Republican coalition has experienced serious erosions and is weaker now than at any time since the days of the Great Depression, probably weaker, in fact, than at any time since the party's rise during the Civil War era.
4. A "two-tier" party system has emerged, with one set of electoral dynamics operating at the presidential level, and yet another at sub-presidential contests.
5. The electorate is far more weakly tied to political parties now than at any time in the past century, and as it has been freed from the "anchor" of party loyalties, it has become vastly more volatile.
6. The communications function—whereby party leaders communicate with the rank and file, and the latter in turn send messages up to the party leadership- —has historically been a great raison d'être for political parties in egalitarian systems; but this function has increasingly been assumed by other structures, notably those organized around the mass media of communication.
7. A major new cohort of activists has assumed vastly increased importance in the electoral arena, a cohort whose position is closely linked to the growth of the intelligentsia in postindustrial America.[16]

The second observation was an overextrapolation from certain tendencies then evident in public opinion data. The third either did not belong at all, if taken simply as a commentary on short-term conditions (where the Republicans were besieged); or, it was flat-out wrong, if seen as a long-term projection. Point seven was too limited; the changes in elite composition and outlook extended far beyond the element identified.

Still, much of the formulation seems about right. A new party system had appeared, though it did not include the emergence of a new majority party. Voter ties to political parties were weaker than they had been in the past, a factor which had important implications throughout the system's operations. The composition and outlook of party elites had shifted markedly from what they were in the New Deal years. Split outcomes were not accidental occurrences in the new system but an inherent feature of it. The Democrats had lost their presidential majority status (to which we would now add that the Republicans have secured majority status presidentially, though by no means elsewhere). The structure of campaigning had been transformed, especially by the dramatic enlargement of the mass media's role in political communication—a role played out independent of the political parties and even in opposition to them institutionally. By no means a realignment, these developments surely reflected whopping, highly consequential, largely irreversible change.

Each succeeding U.S. party system has been ushered in by the dynamics of a new societal era; the current system is no exception. Although no one term can ever adequately identify an era's distinguishing characteristics, for the present one, "postindustrial" is very helpful.[17] Many, though by no means all, of the important social changes experienced by the United States in recent decades are captured by the idea of postindustrialism's emergence.

Influences of the postindustrial setting on the party system are varied and profound, and easily traced. For example, an electorate with high levels of formal education, which receives its political information largely through national communications media of great institutional autonomy, must be far less dependent on political parties for cues and direction than were its predecessors.

Similarly, vast growth in occupations involved in creating, manipulating, and disseminating ideas, as opposed to producing things, has transformed the labor force. Organized labor, which developed in the industrial era, became a major economic and political force during and immediately following the New Deal as union membership soared. In 1989, however, after much of postindustrialism's transformation had been completed, unionized workers were scarcely half the proportion of the labor force they were thirty-five years earlier; inevitably, labor had become a far more feeble element in national politics generally, and in the Democratic coalition specifically.

Other important changes in the larger society are related more tangentially to postindustrialism's coming. For example, the collapse of the "Jim Crow" system of racial separation and gross discrimination in the South since World War II has had enormous political implications. Of special importance given our focus here, the enfranchisement of black Americans and their entry en masse into the Democratic coalition transformed party competition in the South.

Such features of the postindustrial setting as greatly expanded affluence and extended access to higher education undoubtedly contributed to the growing perception of categoric discrimination as illegitimate. But, obviously, many other things were at work: For example, the development of a political base for blacks in large northern states, which gave them new leverage; the population shift within the South itself from rural to urban areas, where black political organization could be achieved more easily and extralegal violence against blacks with greater difficulty; and initiatives of the civil rights movement.

Similarly, changing generational experiences only partially attributable to postindustrialism have reshaped the party system since the New Deal era. Those who came of age politically at the time of the Great Depression, when the immediate comparison of presidential leadership centered on Republican Herbert Hoover and Democrat Franklin Roosevelt, remain even today notably Democratic in their party attachments. Once the youngest cohort in American politics, the Depression Generation is now, however, the oldest. The Republicans fare much better among those who have come of age politically in the late 1970s and 1980s, for whom the most vivid comparison is that of Democrat Jimmy Carter to Republican Ronald Reagan.[18]

Quite apart from how we categorize their sources, we can see massive shifts in social needs, problems, and interests in the contemporary era, which have in turn transformed the ideational substance of political conflict. The intense conflict over abortion is only the latest manifestation of the high salience social or moral issues have attained in the past quarter-century. Social issues had been relatively submerged in the New Deal years, though they had loomed large in earlier eras. Now, they have not only again come to the fore, but have taken new form and derive from new sources. Historically, immigration loomed large as a source of cultural tensions, but it is little implicated in the ascendance of social issues today. Cultural class conflict, organized around different levels of formal education and attributable to jarringly different world views thus transmitted, forms the core of today's moral disputation.

When the New Deal parties were taking form, Adolf Hitler was just coming to power in Germany, and Soviet communism seemed to many, including some idealistic Americans, a system rich in promise. The world has changed much since then, and so has how we view it. Quite apart from the arguments over specific programs and policies, the intellectual climate has changed enormously. Not many, in the United States or abroad, are now inclined to see the road to economic salvation running through increased interventions of the state. Call it capitalism, free enterprise, or market-centered economy, the idea has a following whose breadth and depth would have been unimaginable fifty years ago.

In the United States during the New Deal, "more government" seemed to be linked to "progress." Committed to the expanded state, the Democratic party thus derived enormous political sustenance. Today things have changed greatly

The suggestion sometimes advanced in the late 1970s and early 1980s that Americans had swung philosophically *against* government was nonsense—but certainly they had become and still are far more *uncertain* about the merits of expanding it. The exceptional ambivalence of today's public on many policy questions, but especially on those of government's proper role, deeply influences the parties' present status.[19] It is a major source of the Republican revival.

Systematic attention to the many dimensions of social change and their partisan consequences lies beyond the reach of this chapter. But there is little real dispute that, in the last quarter-century, a new societal era has become manifested in the United States. The "New Deal coalitions" and other features of the party system of the preceding era could not possibly have survived this transformation. They have not—save for the fact that residues of earlier systems always remain in their successors.[20]

The realignment perspective requires us to ask why the partisan "Big Change" has not occurred—and when it will. Thus it continues to tease us with the promise that an enormously complex reality will submit to a very simple and highly parsimonious theoretic organization. But the political world stubbornly refuses to comply. It requires of us the task—laborious and prosaic—of charting the many shifts that have occurred in the party system, and seeking their diverse sources and implications.

Notes

1 V. O. Key, Jr., "The Future of the Democratic Party," *Virginia Quarterly Review* 28 (Spring 1952): 161–75. Key's other two early realignment articles are better known. See "A Theory of Critical Elections," *Journal of Politics* 17 (February 1955): 3–18; and "Secular Realignment and the Party System," *Journal of Politics* 21 (May 1959): 198–210.
2 V. O. Key, Jr., "A Theory of Critical Elections," 3 (emphasis added).
3 Everett C. Ladd, "Pursuing American Voters: V. O. Key, Jr., and the Modern Political Science Odyssey" (Paper delivered at the annual meeting of the Southern Political Science Association, New Orleans, November 9, 1974).
4 See, for example, David G. Lawrence and Richard Fleisher, "Puzzles and Confusions: Political Realignment in the 1980s," *Political Science Quarterly* 102 (Spring 1987): 79–92; Jerome M. Clubb, William H. Flanagan, and Nancy H. Zingale, *Partisan Realignment: Voters, Parties, and Government in American History* (Beverly Hills, Calif.: Sage, 1980), esp. 19–45; and Edward G. Carmines and James A. Stimson, "The Dynamics of Issue Evolution: The United States," in *Electoral Change in Advance Industrial Democracies,* ed. Russell J. Dalton et al. (Princeton: Princeton University Press, 1984), 134–58.

5 I exclude the idea of secular realignment, because it has never loomed large in orienting disciplinary research.

6 Carmines and Stimson, "Dynamics of Issue Evolution," 51 (emphasis added).

7 Charles E. Merriam and Harold Foote Gosnell, *The American Party System*, 4th ed. (New York: Johnson Reprint Corporation, 1969; the 4th edition was first published in 1949).

8 Ibid., 37–53.

9 Kevin P. Phillips, *The Emerging Republican Majority* (New Rochelle, N.Y.: Arlington House, 1969), 37 (emphasis added). Looking for patterns in elections is tricky business. Different starting points and assumptions lead to vastly different interpretations of what the patterns really are. Phillips sees 4 distinct one-party-ascendent cycles in the years since 1860, each with a brief interregnum when the other party held the White House. From another perspective, though, the striking pattern involves the Democrats' persisting problems with the presidency. In the 34 elections the Democratic and Republican parties have together contested—beginning in 1856—Franklin Roosevelt (four times) and Lyndon Johnson (once) are the only Democrats to win as much as 52% of the popular vote. Jimmy Carter (50%) and Samuel Tilden (51%) are the other party nominees to have won majorities. In contrast, 11 Republicans from Lincoln to Bush surpassed 52% of the popular vote, and the party won an absolute majority in 16 contests. Eleven Republicans had victory margins of 8 points or more, something only 4 Democrats achieved. Indeed, in 130 years of competition, the Democrats have had a sustained presidential majority only during the New Deal and under just one man—Franklin Delano Roosevelt. It would, of course, be silly to suggest that the Democrats' problems with the presidency have been fixed and unchanging over a century and a third. Still, other than under Roosevelt, they have in fact never had more than episodic success in their presidential battles with Republicans. So deep and persisting a pattern is, almost certainly, not due to chance.

10 Walter Dean Burnham, "The Reagan Heritage," in *The Election of 1988: Reports and Interpretations,* ed. Gerald M. Pomper (Chatham, N.J.: Chatham House, 1989), 1–32.

11 It is true, of course, that much in even the New Deal transformation is distorted by the critical realignment perspective. As a number of scholars have noted, many of the changes manifested in the New Deal years began long before the Great Depression. Some had already produced major shifts in party strength, elite make-up, etc., a decade or more before the economic collapse. Lee Benson, Joel Silbey, and Phyllis Field have shown, for example, that by the end of Alfred E. Smith's first term as governor of New York, a new alignment of Empire State voters had been realized that "has remained with us until at least very recently." "Toward a Theory of Stability and Change in American Voting Patterns: New York State, 1792–1970," in *The History of American Electoral Behavior,* ed. Joel H. Silbey, Allan G. Bogue, and William H. Flanigan (Princeton: Princeton University Press, 1978), 97. Still, if U.S. partisan politics had in fact experienced every 32 years or so developments closely resembling those of 1930–36, the realignment perspective would look much better than it in fact does.

12 Louis Hartz, *The Liberal Tradition in America* (New York: Harcourt, Brace, 1955), 30.

13 I have tried to describe some of the sources in "The 1988 Elections: Continuation of the Post-New Deal System," *Political Science Quarterly* 104 (Spring 1989): 1–18. Walter Dean Burnham's view (expressed in *Critical Elections* and other writings) of realignment as temporary redemption from system failure—and hence its absence in our present era as troubling—seems to me a purely ideological formulation. I see no persuasive empirical evidence that our separation-of-powers-dominated system has been comparatively unsuccessful—compared to other existing institutional arrangements—in producing satisfactory policy responses to changing social needs. Every society confronts especially difficult problems from time to time; ours is no exception. But our institutional structure is not the culprit. Ladd, "Party Reform and the Public Interest," *Political Science Quarterly* 102 (Fall 1987): 355–69.

14 See, for example, James L. Sundquist, *Constitutional Reform and Effective Government* (Washington, D.C.: Brookings Institution, 1986).

15 Ladd, "Why Carter Will Probably Win," *Fortune,* July 28, 1980, pp.86–89.

16 "Pursuing American Voters," mimeo (November 1974), 16–17. Charles Hadley and I reiterated this summary, and expanded on it, a year later in *Transformations of the American Party System* (New York: Norton, 1975; 2d rev. ed., 1978).

17 In the large literature describing postindustrialism, Daniel Bell's *The Coming of Postindustrial Society* remains the seminal work (New York: Basic Books, 1973).

18 For analysis of survey data on changes in generational experience, see Ladd, "Alignment and Realignment: Where Are All the Voters Going?" *Ladd Report* 3 (1986), 10–15; and "The 1988 Elections," 10–13.

19 I have set forth some thoughts on this subject in a number of articles, including "Politics in the 80s: An Electorate at Odds with Itself," *Public Opinion* (December–January 1983): 2–6; "The Reagan Phenomenon and Public Attitudes Toward Government," in *The Reagan Presidency and the Governing of America,* ed. Lester M. Salomon and Michael S. Lund (Washington, D.C.: Urban Institute Press, 1984), 221–49; and, regularly, in the "Opinion Round-Up" compilations of public opinion in *Public Opinion* over the past decade. The latter data round-up is now appearing in two new magazines that replaced *Public Opinion* in January 1990: *American Enterprise* (Washington, D.C.: American Enterprise Institute), and *Public Perspective* (Storrs, Conn.: Roper Center for Public Opinion Research).

20 The party system "swims" in a much larger body, the society. In the American case—involving political democracy and limited government—the flow of influence has always been disproportionately from the latter to the former. This does not mean, however, that political parties in the United States are merely passive, that they only respond to social changes occurring outside them rather than contribute to these changes. Actions of party leaders clearly influence social and political change. A democratic party system that is performing its representative functions poorly can contribute to political system failure—with profound implications for the entire social order. Nonetheless, understanding transformations of the party system in the United States must always begin with chartings of relevant change in society at large.

3 *Byron E. Shafer*

The Notion of an Electoral Order
The Structure of Electoral Politics at the Accession of George Bush

Notions in political science which offer conceptual clarity, historical reach, and contemporary explanation have a right to be cherished—they are few and far between. One thinks, for example, of the "balance of power" in international relations, despite all its problems. One thinks of "political culture" in comparative politics, problematic but resilient since the day of its elucidation. And one comes just as quickly to the concept of "realignment," along with its epiphenomenon "dealignment," in American government and politics. One suggests alternatives to such concepts only with the greatest hesitation—and care.

Nevertheless, Joel Silbey has set out all the reasons why realignment can obscure more than it clarifies in addressing the successive epochs of American history.[1] Some sort of periodization *is* helpful; realignments, alas, do not provide it. Moreover, in our time, the search for the possibility of a realignment in the results of the most recent election—producing little more, repeatedly, than discovery of its absence—is a particularly poor approach to understanding what *has* just happened. Everett Ladd is not alone in noting this phenomenon, but he has made a real contribution in explaining *why* classical realignments are so unlikely to be present in those results in the late twentieth century.[2]

What remains is the need for something to fill the void. This is not just because of the enduring truth of the old folk wisdom that "something beats nothing." Rather, it is because the periodization of American electoral politics *is* a

useful intellectual device—and the ability to say something about current electoral outcomes in relation to those extended electoral periods even more so.
The necessary enterprise, then, is empirical political theory. It must begin with
a number of disparate pieces of understanding, pieces which have gained a
certain consensual character when treated individually. And it must proceed by
connecting them—into a larger framework which aspires to describe a larger
portion of the political world, of course, but into a framework which almost
inevitably produces additional, unexpected, and often provocative assertions
about that world.[3] The short-run purpose of this enterprise is to organize
knowledge concisely. Its long-run purpose is to generate researchable questions—questions of apparent social consequence.

In an ahistorical world, this process might begin by introducing the notion of
an "electoral order" in its full abstraction, as a composite of those political
structures which shape the outcomes of elections and provide their pattern.
Exposition could then move back and forth between abstracted notions and real
political behavior. There is no point, however, in ignoring the way in which the
"realignment framework" has shaped contemporary perceptions of electoral
politics, and this primacy—temporal *and* intellectual—makes it the obvious
starting place. By the same token, there is little point in trying to introduce in
advance the empirical perceptions which arise in the course of an attempt at
escaping the realignment framework and at proceeding by way of an alternative
conception. Better just to outline the sections of the argument, save their details
for the appropriate section, and hold a summary—not to mention a prognosis—
for the end.

Accordingly, this chapter begins with the rise of realignment, the concept,
and with the subsequent arrival, only a half-step behind, of some major associated anomalies. These anomalies lead more or less naturally to the notion of an
electoral order, presented first in its most abstract form. This abstract framework is then inserted back into electoral history, to help search for the key
political structures of the *preceding* electoral order. That "potted structural history" makes it easier to see the *break* represented by the current order when it
does arrive. And the search for a fundamental and continuing structure to this
order—our order—contributes not just the empirical essence of the chapter but
a "model" of contemporary electoral politics.

This model begins with a set of preferences, based on the grand issue-areas
of our time but tied to associated divisions within the social base for American
politics. These divisions find their expression in voting for the major institutions of American national government. The *differentiated* structure of this
institutional arrangement then produces a pattern—a continuing pattern, even
an institutionalized pattern—of electoral outcomes. Ironically, this pattern
empties the election of 1988 of most of its intellectual interest, reducing this
stereotypical product of the current electoral order to a means of making stray

refinements in an understanding of the targeting, and themes, of modern election campaigns.

The more intriguing question thus becomes why this electoral order, rendered so stereotypically in 1988, has become so *stable*. An answer rests with its intermediary structure, especially its party organizations, organized interests, and political elites. That answer leads almost automatically to the opposite, and closing, question: If the current electoral order can thus be reduced to a pattern of social divisions, falling across a structure of institutions, producing a recurring set of election outcomes, and sustained by intermediary organizations, can such a model nevertheless handle *change*? Indeed, can it go on to signpost specific possibilities for *further* change in the same, contemporary, electoral order?

Lest that seem just too abstract an introduction, to what must ultimately be a highly concrete analysis, perhaps a violently simplified summary of its product will serve as temporary compensation. Within this framework, contemporary American electoral politics appears to be characterized by *cross-cutting* majorities on the dominant concerns of its age—a liberal majority on social welfare, a nationalist majority on foreign policy, and a traditionalist majority on cultural values. For a host of reasons, old and new, the presidency is more amenable to concerns about foreign policy and cultural values; the House of Representatives is more amenable to concerns about social welfare and service provision; and the Senate is inherently biased toward the latter but can oscillate between the two.

Accordingly, the presidency should be—and is—reliably Republican in our time; the House should be—and is—reliably Democratic; and the Senate recurrently leans Democratic but can go Republican. Ironically, relevant partisan elites in *both* political parties work, in effect though surely not by intent, to sustain this arrangement—by championing the very issues which will lose them one or another of these offices. The key to short-run reversals in this pattern, then, lies in the contradictions intrinsic to cross-cutting majorities, while the key to any long-run reversals lies in a changing international order, in rising cultural tensions, and in growing economic dislocation.

Realignment and Political Structure

For a concept which was to achieve such intellectual centrality and such substantive reach, the notion of realignment had a remarkably precise and consensual origin. The currently dominant mode of thinking about electoral politics began with a piece by V. O. Key, Jr., in the *Journal of Politics* in February of 1955, entitled "A Theory of Critical Elections."[4] This piece really set out the essence of "realignments," as "critical elections" in which large segments of the general public shifted their partisan preferences, more or less permanently.

Hal Bass only suggests the extent of its progeny, in the rich but still stringently edited bibliography which closes this volume.[5]

In the beginning, however, not just the seminal piece but its path to dominance—via other central items in the realignment canon—were also unusually clear and consensual. Three subsequent works in fact converted this idea into a full-blown framework for understanding electoral politics—and for organizing research. In the first, "A Classification of the Presidential Elections," published as chapter 4 of *Elections and the Political Order,* Angus Campbell took Key's central insight and made realignments only the most dramatic classification in a small typology of election outcomes, whose categories were intended to be mutually exclusive and jointly exhaustive.[6]

In hindsight, it is clear that two major books then ensured the consequence of Campbell's realignment category, while setting off the chain of elaborations and permutations to follow. The first of these was *Critical Elections and the Mainsprings of American Politics,* where Walter Dean Burnham put the phenomenon of realignment at the operative center of American politics *and* gave it an inherent periodicity. The second was *Dynamics of the Party System: Alignment and Realignment of Political Parties in the United States,* where James L. Sundquist added not just comprehensive detail to Burnham's dynamic but further theoretical explanation as well.[7] And from there, the notion simply exploded, so that neat and simple summaries are much less easily accomplished.

Some scholars focused on the precise mechanics of the archetypal critical election, the realigning contest of 1932. Kristi Andersen, with *The Creation of a Democratic Majority, 1928–1936,* is an excellent example. Some scholars applied the perspective with similar rigor to earlier instances of the same general phenomenon. Samuel T. McSeveney, in *The Politics of Depression: Political Behavior in the Northeast, 1893–1896,* is probably the outstanding case. Some took this originally electoral notion, more dramatically, into the operations of government itself. Jerome M. Clubb, William H. Flanigan, and Nancy H. Zingale, with their *Partisan Realignment: Voters, Parties, and Government in American History,* are surely among the most comprehensive. Others, inevitably and naturally, took the notion (and its full array of applications) to the politics of other, non-American nations. A rich and fruitful introduction to this transportation is David Butler and Donald Stokes, *Political Change in Britain: Forces Shaping Electoral Choice.*[8]

Perhaps the greatest tribute to the apparent organizing power of the concept of realignment, however, lay not with this gargantuan scholarly progression, but with its conquest of the intelligent *popular* world. The seminal book here was *The Emerging Republican Majority* by Kevin P. Phillips, appearing in the early days of the new, Republican, Nixon administration.[9] After Phillips, some scholarly cross-over was never again to be absent. Accordingly, after each succeeding election, not just political scientists and historians but journalists were to ask diagnostically, "Has there been an electoral realignment?"

The fact that the answer was reliably "no" is a reasonable, short-hand introduction to the problems inherent in this otherwise impressive success. For in the modern era, extension to an ever-greater range of political phenomena has proceeded in tandem with an apparent *constriction* of explanatory power in the realm of original application, the realm of interpreting election outcomes. Diagnostically, and for now nigh onto sixty years, there has been no classical realignment. This "finding," of course, is also painfully self-evident, and in the absence of the long-awaited new alignment, realignment partisans moved to refine their framework additionally. For all those periods when a new realignment was waiting to be born, gradual erosion of the old alignments at every level—"dealignment"—was to be the expected outcome.

Dealignment landmarks were the logical scholarly result. Burnham's *Critical Elections and the Mainsprings of American Politics* really prefigured this approach as well. It was elucidated by John R. Petrocik, for example, in *Party Coalitions: Realignments and the Decline of the New Deal Party System,* and by Martin P. Wattenberg, in *The Decline of American Political Parties, 1952–1980.* This approach, in turn, spilled out into all the previous avenues. It touched the international arena with, for example, Russell J. Dalton et al., eds., *Electoral Change in Advanced Industrial Democracies: Realignment or Dealignment?* It achieved a new popular interpretation, and perhaps the ultimate extension of the notion, in an argument that a realignment had occurred *without a partisan shift,* in John F. Stacks, *Watershed: The Campaign for the Presidency 1980.* [10]

Seen from inside the realignment framework, such work was only further evidence of the organizing power of the original concept—of its ability to sustain elaboration, underpin research, and reassemble the results. Seen from *outside* the framework, however, it was increasingly possible to believe something different: that as closer examination revealed more and more phenomena, obviously of consequence, which the original notion could not handle, disciples felt compelled to extend the framework in ever-more-elaborate contortions, rather than to look for some alternative approach. Yet if the reality of the major factors which collectively shaped an electoral order was such that they were as often overlooked as emphasized by realignment/dealignment—if sixty years of elections appeared to have consequences even in the absence of a realignment, and if earlier presumed realignments proved to be dissimilar upon examination—then the search for some alternative was not just reasonable but necessary.

It would be possible to try to steal this point rhetorically, by listing all the twists on realignment which political life appeared to require—as with secular realignments, partial realignments, rolling realignments, aborted realignments, regional realignments, hollow realignments, and on, and on. Yet if the realities of politics, when examined, are such as to require the extension of realignment/dealignment to an expanding array of major shaping forces—to additional issue-areas, to further social divisions, to the character of political intermediaries, and to the institutional structure of government itself—then perhaps all that need be said is that an alternative course should be explored. In this, it might be better to begin with these fundamental building blocks; to define, apply, and link them carefully; and then to see if they can be reassembled into a continuing "electoral order."

Political Structures and Electoral Orders

Such an effort must move back, very temporarily, to a much higher level of abstraction. For this, a "political structure," so as not to overdevelop the definition, is anything which shapes behavior related to the role of government. Those political structures which, together, shape electoral outcomes are thus the essential components of any given electoral order. The specific factors qualifying as political structures, at least in the United States, can range from things formal and fundamental, as with the conformation of national offices established in the Constitution itself; through things equally tangible but more private and informal, as with the operational character of political parties; to things intangible but equally potent in their impact, as with continuing party or policy attachments within the general public.

The notion of political structure does presuppose some minimal level of continuity and effect. In some hypothetical society with policy preferences randomized among individuals, with complete ease in formation (and dissolution) of intermediary organizations, and with numerous and diverse public offices which could shift their substantive responsibilities as desired, the notion of political structure would make no sense. On the other hand, a disbelief in the likelihood of any such society, and thus a hope that the political structures constituting an electoral order can be unearthed, are not the same as insistence either on some single leading element within that structure or on a set of elements which demonstrate impressive continuity. Those are, so to speak, empirical questions.[11]

Such a conception, ideally, permits continuing structure; it permits individual actors to create, sustain, *or alter* that structure; and it permits change in a composite of political structures—in an electoral order—as well. The activities of mass or elite participants, for example, while those activites are presumed to be aimed at securing their own wishes in politics, can also, if they assume recurring patterns, *themselves* become part of the political structure to which other actors respond. At the other extreme, even the formal institutions of national government, despite their Constitutional definition and continuity—

even the presidency, the Senate, and the House of Representatives—can function quite differently as electoral targets when the preferences of large parts of the social base for electoral politics, or when the universe of interest groups or the character of political parties, change around them.

At a somewhat less exalted level of abstraction, there are three general locations—three strata of political life, if you will—which together encompass the possible sites for political structures. There is the societal base for politics, that is, the nature of the general public upon which it is grounded. There are the intermediary organizations for politics, that array of organizations which stands between the individual citizen and the institutions of government. And there are those governmental institutions themselves, normally a complex of institutions in the full conformation of their organization, rules, and procedures.

Two key aspects of the *social base* for electoral politics seem particularly likely to generate elements of political structure which in turn shape electoral politicking and its outcomes. The first of these are the inherent divisions of group identification within that social base, four of which have received particular attention across American history. In the American context, race and ethnicity, religion and culture, social class, and region, each have been treated as central social divisions at various points. The second of these key aspects of the social base are those values and orientations which are usually collected in the term "political culture." These include not just attitudes toward the proper behavior of various public officials, but also, in the electoral context, the (varying) propensity to turn out and vote, so as to operationalize those attitudes.[12]

In the same way, two grand characteristics of the array of *intermediary organizations* seem particularly likely to generate—indeed, to constitute—key elements of political structrue. The configuration and vitality of political parties and organized interests are the first of these grand characteristics. Although the number of major political parties has remained effectively stable in the United States since at least the Civil War, their operational character has varied enormously. The contents of the universe of organized interests has surely varied even more, as has the character and vitality of individual interests within it. The second key characteristic of intermediary organizations, one not tautologically a product of the first, is the nature of elite-mass linkages within them. Some subset of members inevitably do the more specialized labor of intermediation. This elite, while formally "representing" its membership, can actually be tied to it in a host of ways.[13]

Finally, at the level of *governmental institutions* themselves—at the level of those public offices which will be filled by way of electoral politics—there is the most self-evident sort of political structure. This includes the conformation of those positions, with their individual terms of office, their distribution across the nation (with the associated nature of their formal constituencies), and the substantive responsibilities which inhere (formally or informally) in them. This is "structure" at its most elemental, though even this invites some variety across time. Yet since the combining of political structures into an *electoral* order is in fact the focus of this examination, the institutional arrangements for attaining those offices—for seeking them, for being nominated and then elected to them, and for holding them through subsequent reelection—promise additionally and critically relevant aspects of political structure.[14]

What ties these elements together, and hence what ultimately drives the political change or stability which results, is an array of policy preferences. It is perhaps more common to think of these as the grand issues of an era, the organizing conflicts which bend and are bent by a general public, intermediary elites, and governmental officials. Yet these concerns need not in any given election be "large" in programmatic terms, nor do they need to possess narrowly programmatic—much less formulaic—qualities. The "policy preferences" intrinsic to an electoral order may be for a tougher bargaining "attitude" toward the outside world, for example, for "moral leadership" at home, or for "social justice" in both locales, without much further operational definition. These preferences, too, are hardly static, though they do acquire some force of inertia when they are already in place to shape subsequent activity.

It is also common to cede these concerns, effectively, to historians. Political scientists get the "nuts-and-bolts" of contemporary politicking; historians get the "great issues" of a subsequently perceivable era. Yet there is no inherent reason why, if such conflicts were organizing politics in most prior eras, they would not be organizing it *now*—and thus be the simultaneous responsibility of political scientists. Just as there is no inherent reason why, if such conflicts operate through, and thus are shaped by, contemporary politicking, they would not have operated this way in the past—and so be the responsibility of historians to unravel in *any* preceding era.[15]

The same point can be made differently by noting that if central policy preferences can be argued to *drive* the interaction of the elements of political structure, they are just as much a *product* of that interaction. But it is perhaps more useful to make the point by noting that such an electoral order, with its political structures, their specific location in three general areas, and a set of policy preferences linking them together, contains one further supposition embedded within it: that policy preferences are unlikely to acquire much political reality—to move beyond the most sterile sort of paper-and-pencil response to questions—if they are not themselves attached to continuing features of social structure.

Again, it is most common to think of these features as involving *group* divisions within the body politic, and that may well be their most usual location. But it is also possible for these features—and their divisions—to involve attachments to (different) intermediary organizations instead, or even to involve elite-mass tensions within those organizations. Just as it is possible for such divisions to find continuing institutional reinforcement in a differential attach-ment to various public offices within government itself.

Antecedent Electoral Orders

A search for the antecedents of the current electoral order must begin well over a hundred years ago. Or, more precisely, it must begin over 130 years ago for the American South, over 60 years ago for the nonsouthern part of the nation. The great event establishing the first of these benchmarks—perhaps still the "great event" of American history since the Revolution—was, of course, the Civil War. The central policy concern of its aftermath was, inevitably, how to respond to that great national conflagration. And the central social division which resulted was ineluctably regional, pitting the non-South (the former Union) versus the South (the former Confederacy). The non-South was to move on to other political concerns—and a very different political order—within a few generations; the South was not.

It is common to summarize the politics which resulted there as the emer-gence of a "Solid South"—solidly Democratic at every time and every level—but there was much more to the electoral order than that. The Civil War did remain a formative experience—and then an explosive symbol—for all sorts of perceived differences from the rest of the nation. These experiences (and that symbol) did appear to counsel regional integrity, unity against a hostile outside world, above all else. And politics was to be organized around that central fact from the 1860s into the 1960s. Yet the classic further elements of an electoral order were all simultaneously present and operative.[16]

Thus at the social base for politics, almost everyone considered themselves Democrats, with the noteworthy exception of black southerners, who were quickly disfranchised. Among intermediary organizations, a Democratic party which was organized around courthouse rings and dominated by local notables transferred basically conservative demands into the institutions of government. The conformation of public offices within that government, finally, did nothing to introduce differentiation into this pattern: it was Demo-cratic presidentially, Democratic congressionally, Democratic gubernatorially, Democratic state-legislatively, and so on. Into the 1960s, it was also customary to assert that this was an additionally conservative Democracy, courtesy of the disfranchisement of lower-income *whites* which came simultaneously with the disfranchisement of blacks.

For the rest of the nation, the search for antecedents to the contemporary electoral order leads back to a different great event. That event was the Great Depression, and the central policy question was, again inevitably, how to respond. The central social division which accompanied the alternatives was along lines of social class. Across that divide, blue-collar America, the poor, and certain demographic minorities faced white-collar America, as joined subsequently by farmers. Here, too, the resulting divisions were powerfully formative, lasting well beyond direct memories of the critical event itself. Yet here, too, there was further, consequential differentiation to the accompanying electoral order.[17]

The Democratic party as an organization was an amalgam of urban machines in the North, volunteer activist branches throughout the country, and the old courthouse rings in the South. These were joined principally by unionized labor among the organized interests, but also by the civil rights organizations. The Republican party retained some rural rings of its own in the Midwest and West, but it actually moved much earlier than the Democrats—more from necessity than from choice—to become what would now be recognized as a contemporary, activist-based, political party. Its organized allies were big and little business, though never as distinctively as for labor and racial minorities within the Democratic party.

National institutions of government both responded to these other elements and contributed further distinctiveness to the composite electoral order. *Democrats* were the statistical preference to win the presidency, and to bring both houses of Congress along with them. As a result, the unity and vitality of the Democratic coalition was often the central story of electoral politics. Yet even in their successful years, substantial geographic areas still contributed Republican majorities. Republicans could potentially build upon these to secure the presidency, whenever they had an especially attractive candidate; when that happened, he could hope to pull Congress along as well. Nevertheless, these Republican presidencies—and even more these Republican Congresses—were individually based and short-lived. Republicans could not (at least in hindsight) really hope to *hold* the presidency beyond the tenure of a single, successful incumbent, and their congressional reach, in such an environment, was all the more tenuous.[18]

A Break without a Realignment

This composite order broke apart in the 1960s, and the current electoral order came into being. The details, the sequence, and the connectedness of the events leading up to this break are subject to numerous (inherently reasonable) disputes. Yet most are also easily summarized—and subsumed: During the 1960s, a previous national consensus on both foreign policy and cultural values disintegrated, and the resulting lines of conflict did not parallel those on social welfare and direct economic benefit. The working out of these new conflicts, as they fell differentially across the institutions of national government and as they worked additionally through altered intermediary organizations, came to constitute the new electoral order.

The roots of a change of this particular sort—a change in the grand issue-*areas* of an age—permit of nearly endless extrapolation. Yet for purposes of separating distinct electoral orders, the timing of this break can be specified with some precision. Or at least, the *outcomes* of the election of 1964 still largely conformed to the old electoral order, whereas the *outcomes* of the election of 1968—again, with the tremendous advantage of hindsight—testified to a new electoral era. At the time, after thirty years of rough continuity, 1968 was assured only of raising anomalous possibilities.[19] Now, after twenty years of subsequent (and different) continuity, 1968 stands divided from 1964 as an incipient—and ultimately real—break.

In the same way, the ultimate substantive composition of that break was actually visible to scholars at the time. Or at least, intensified splits over foreign affairs and cultural values were not just filling newspaper headlines of the day; they were beginning to acquire attention in scholarly journals as well. What was missing was the knowledge that these splits were not transitory. Yet again, hindsight through the lens of an electoral order does suggest that the changes which were to combine in characterizing a new era—the breakdowns of consensus on foreign policy and cultural values—were already being studied in their individual pieces.[20] Accordingly, the necessary further contribution of hindsight, when placed in the service of empirical theory, is the linking of these individual findings—and the pursuit of implications inherent in this link.

It is difficult to say which consensus died first, especially since the most dramatic harbinger of their demise, the Vietnam War and protests about it, intimately blended the two concerns. The incipient cultural division may have achieved this peculiar pride of place, most proximately through civil rights agitation and most especially in the South. Yet cultural concerns were soon to encompass more issues and to reach wider areas, and they were soon to proceed in the company of foreign policy disputes. In any case, the impact of the two dissolutions effectively coincided, and that was to be the crucial operative fact.

Disputes over basic cultural values may ultimately trace to certain grand and gradual changes in American society, touching everything from metropolitan land use to family composition. These disputes may initially have been given focus by civil rights conflicts, or by the more general protest *style* brought to prominence with those conflicts. Yet these cultural disputes were really to be crystallized around an entire set of issues propelled to prominence by the Supreme Court. On criminal rights, on the public role of religion, on private morality, on community prerogatives, on questions literally of life and death, the Court enunciated policies which were clearly not shared by majorities of the American public.[21]

Moreover, divisions on this complex of "cultural issues" did not coincide with divisions on social welfare and economic benefit. That is, the progressive position on cultural values—the position being enunciated by the Court—did not coincide, *socially,* with the liberal position on economic well-being. Just as the traditionalist side on cultural values did not coincide, again socially, with the conservative side on economics. Those favoring liberalism on social welfare were as likely to favor traditionalism on cultural values; those favoring conservatism on social welfare were as likely to favor progressivism on matters of culture.

The situation on foreign policy was roughly similar. From an era of comparative disengagement with the outside world, the United States emerged after World War II with clear (and ultimately effective) pressures toward world leadership. For roughly a generation, in responding to these, there was also consensus—favoring international involvement, negotiation and humanitarian aid, but military intervention as necessary, especially in opposition to communist expansion. In the 1960s, this consensus, too, disintegrated. The Vietnam War was the obvious and immediate catalyst. Orientations toward nationalism and patriotism became the electoral touchstones thereafter.[22]

Once again, the line dividing those emphasizing accommodationism and international self-restraint from those emphasizing nationalism and the pursuit of American values did not coincide, socially, with the line dividing those supporting expanded social welfare and an active domestic government from those preferring limited social welfare and limited government as well. Said differently, the accommodationist side on foreign policy did not coincide with the liberal side on economic issues, just as the nationalist side on foreign policy did not coincide with the conservative position on domestic economics. More critically, and to jump a step ahead of the argument, *majorities* favoring policies tied to nationalism and anticommunism in the international arena did not coincide with *majorities* favoring policies of governmental insurance against the vicissitudes of the economic marketplace at home.[23]

Issue Areas and Institutional Attractions

At the social base for electoral politics, then, there were to be cross-cutting positions on *three* great issue-areas: economic welfare, foreign affairs, and cultural values. The institutions upon which the new pattern of public division fell would not, of course, change in their basic conformation. Yet the way in which the new array of public preferences fell across an existing structure of public offices did create the *potential* for a new electoral order. For it became clear, in the aftermath of the rise of new and cross-cutting issue divisions, that the individual institutions of American national government already possessed a certain inherent and latent—and distinctive—relevance to the grand issue-areas of an incipiently new political order.[24]

This, too, was a fact long recognized in other contexts. Thus the presidency had long been the logical focus for those concerned with foreign policy. Congress was almost always secondary in this realm, but within Congress, the Senate was still more relevant to foreign affairs than was the House. The presidency had likewise become more relevant to cultural values than was Congress. And again, within Congress, the Senate was to prove more relevant to cultural issues than was the House. Yet Congress did not have to give up its previous focus—and primacy—on social welfare policies generally, and it did not. So that Congress was to give more emphasis to social welfare than was the presidency, and the House more so than the Senate within it. Moreover, Congress remained more relevant to direct governmental benefits than was the presidency, and the House more so than the Senate within it.

Again, the extended complex of reasons for this, both formal and informal, was very familiar from a basically institutional literature. In foreign affairs, the Constitution itself gave the president primacy, through his place as commander-in-chief and through his responsibility for negotiating international treaties. This was powerfully reinforced by extra-Constitutional developments in the modern era, by World War II, the Cold War, the rise of a standing military establishment, and America's evolving role in a bipolar world. Congress was actually to reassert itself, comparatively, in the Vietnam period and after, yet it was never to be more than an augmented influence on essentially presidential initiatives.[25]

Nevertheless, within Congress, the same basic shaping factors applied. Constitutionally, the Senate was more relevant than the House, thanks to its ability to approve most of the (presidential) personnel of foreign affairs and to pass upon any (presidentially negotiated) international agreements. Practically as well, it was, for example, the Senate Foreign Relations Committee, not the House Foreign Affairs Committee, which was intermittently the crucial site for assaults on executive power in the postwar period. There could still be grand congressional challenges to the presidency in foreign affairs, as with the War Powers Act of 1973. Yet these were widely understood to be dramatic exceptions, while even such exceptions followed a second pattern, of being principally Senate, not House, products.

The institutional situation in the realm of cultural values was less immediately obvious, but that may have had more to do with the lesser inclination of policy analysts to think of cultural issues in institutional terms, rather than with anything intrinsic to those issues. For once again, the presidency blended inherent, formal and informal, advantages over Congress. The fact that the Constitution combined the role of head-of-state and head-of-government in one office made a president singularly able to symbolize desired national values and to personify "moral leadership." No individual member of congress could approximate this symbolic potential; Congress collectively was even less able to do so. Beyond that, to the extent that the *Supreme Court* became the ultimate custodian of policy outcomes on these issues, a single national executive was inherently advantaged over a 535-headed legislature when it came to commenting on—articulating either opposition to or endorsement of—Court rulings.[26]

Again, Congress did not have to abandon the field entirely, as occasional, reliably ineffective insurrections over rulings on such issues as metropolitan busing could still attest. But again, there was a crucial secondary distinction within Congress. Because so many of the cultural issues of the modern era were initiated within (or at least critically propelled by) the Supreme Court, the constitutional powers of the Senate to advise and consent on Supreme Court nominations kept it inherently closer to these issues. So, probably, did the greater comparative diversity of constituent views on these matters in the average Senate (versus the average House) district, making Senators more inherently exposed to *conflict* on them.

The situation was radically different when it came to issues of social welfare and economic well-being. Here, too, differing institutional predispositions had always been incipiently present, at least through the preceding electoral order. Yet here, the actual institutional attractions for issues of social welfare and service provision produced the exact opposite pattern to that involving foreign affairs and cultural values. Congress had always—again, for at least the preceding electoral era—been deeply invested in the making of social welfare policy. But as the modern era emerged, Congress found that it did *not* have to surrender primacy in this area. As a result, for another complex of formal and informal reasons, Congress retained an advantage over the president here, as the House retained an advantage over the Senate within Congress.[27]

Constitutionally, the very structure of Congress meant that its members were charged with the general well-being of a specifically demarcated locale, a locale in which their individual constituents necessarily had more access to a single member of Congress than to a president—and more still to a member of the House than of the Senate. This, too, was reinforced by major, informal developments. The coming of the welfare state during the preceding electoral order—that was, after all, what the New Deal was about—had produced very practical links between welfare administration and congressional organization, as members of congress targeted their institution on building ties to the new social-welfare bureaucracy.

Seen from the other side, if an individual district relied heavily upon a particular program or needed a particular change in the formula for such a program, Congress was likely to be a better bet than the presidency, as the House was likely to be a better bet than the Senate. Accordingly, if the coming of a standing military establishment had sealed the constitutional primacy of the executive in foreign policy, in a vary practical fashion, then the coming of a "standing" social-service bureaucracy had sealed the institutional primacy of the legislature on issues of domestic welfare, in the same way. Moreover, what was true of social welfare as a policy realm was even more true of the direct provision of services—though the line between them was sometimes hard to draw.[28]

Nevertheless, if congressional representatives viewed social welfare programs and their formulae principally in terms of their effect on—their servicing of—individual districts, they were even more alert to possibilities for the extraction of concrete, individualized, divisible benefits. Indeed, one of the major stories on Congress in the modern era is the discovery by individual members of the tremendous *personal* rewards inherent in good constituency service. What had long been an institutional predisposition verged on becoming a collective obsession, with augmented staff and reorganized committees to pursue it. Naturally, when seen from the other side, if an individual citizen wanted a particular benefit, Congress was that much more a logical target than the presidency, as the House was that much better a target than the Senate within it.

The Shape of the Contemporary Electoral Order

What produced a new electoral description out of this model, and a new electoral order out of the situation from which it was abstracted, was a further set of simple propositions about majorities in public opinion, propositions destined to be tested and (re)affirmed in the real world of politics, election after election. The general public, as it turned out, was *liberal* on economic welfare, *nationalist* on foreign policy, and *traditionalist* on cultural values. There were individual issues within each of these issue-areas which ran against the trend, but for the clusters as a whole, these were to prove remarkably durable propositions.[29] When they were reimmersed in the real political world, that is, when continuing majorities on the major issue divisions of our time were sorted electorally to their relevant institutions, the partisan shape of a new electoral order came into view: the presidency *should* be Republican in such an order; the House *should* be Democratic; and the Senate should be capturable by *either* political party, while retaining an instrinsic Democratic bias.

That these are in fact the dominant contours of contemporary American electoral politics—its most dramatic surface manifestations and its most consequential recurring outcomes—is hardly at issue. For the period from 1968 through, at least, 1992, observers are agreed on the simplest outline of the pattern: Republicans *tend* to control the presidency. Democrats *tend* to control the Senate. And Democrats *always* control the House.[30] Moreover, these same observers would nearly all agree that this understates the phenomenon. For the one presidential exception in this period, the election of (Democrat) Jimmy Carter in 1976, is widely viewed as the aberrant product of the accumulation of peculiar political circumstances—the Watergate crisis, the Nixon resignation, the Ford pardon, and so on—a view reinforced by *the voters* at their first opportunity, when they returned the White House to Republican hands.[31]

The advantage of the notion of an electoral order, then, is in taking this most generally perceived and easily measured aspect of contemporary elections— this peculiar but lasting pattern of (split) partisan control of different public offices—and tying it back to the political structures which produced it. Most fundamentally, this means tying the *composite* characteristics of this order to a set of divisions within the social base for electoral politics, on one side, and to continuing (structural) predispositions by governmental institutions, on the other. In passing, such a (theoretically disciplined) enterprise eliminates the all-too-frequent argument that a pattern of election outcomes which is precise, intricate, and sustained—for what is now a quarter-century—is somehow the accidental sum of disconnected pieces.

The resulting pattern only gains affirmation (and authenticity) from the ability to specify, courtesy of *two* electoral orders and their political structures, how one order became distinctive from the other. Or at least, before 1968, the differential contribution of foreign affairs and cultural values had remained latent, because there was a general, public consensus on these matters, so that there was no reason for institutional differences to surface. Similarly, before 1968, the differential contribution of social welfare and economic well-being had remained latent *for precisely the opposite reason:* These were the grand issue-areas around which political conflict was organized, and this very fact— the fact of one major area reaching into all the institutions of national government—meant that incipient institutional differences on these issues, too, had been largely irrelevant.

After 1968, all this was different, and the character of electoral *campaigns,* too, necessarily reflected the change. Or at least, foreign policy issues were most likely to be a staple of presidential contests, least likely to be a staple of House contests, with the Senate in-between but closer to the House. Likewise, cultural policy issues were most often central to presidential contests, least often central to House contests, more intermittently characterizing contests for the Senate. Social welfare issues gained a contrasting prominence in campaigns for Congress rather than the presidency, and for the House more than for the Senate. Last and inevitably, direct service provision was most closely tied to campaigns for Congress rather than the presidency, even more closely tied to campaigns for the House than the Senate.[32]

Accordingly, in the modern era and indeed for the last quarter-century:

- The presidency was about foreign affairs and cultural values. There were nationalist and traditionalist majorities in the nation on these issues. The Republicans were the party of nationalist foreign policy and traditionalist cultural values. And Republicans won the presidency.

- The House was about social welfare and service provision. There were liberal majorities in the nation on both of these related concerns. The Democrats were the party of welfare and service liberalism. And the Democrats won the House, time after monotonous time.
- The Senate, finally, standing between the two bodies both institutionally and electorally, was amenable to *all* these issue-areas. Yet the Senate, as ultimately closer to the House than the presidency in powers, organization, constituency, and focus, was also ultimately more like the House than the presidency in electoral matters, so that it could be captured by the Republicans, but was a better bet to be found in the hands of the Democrats.

The Election of 1988

Ironically, an integrating concept which can thus make sense of an entire, extended period of electoral history—ours—simultaneously reduces the analytic interest of its most recent incarnation, the election of 1988. Indeed, seen as the latest link in an established electoral order, 1988 is effectively standard, almost stereotypical. That fact still serves as crucial if implicit confirmation that the contemporary electoral order is as this model—and this description—would suggest. But otherwise, 1988 must serve principally as one more occasion to see the concrete expression of an abstract order through its specific details—and thus perhaps to refine an understanding of that order.

Once again, the bare facts are familiar enough. George Bush won the presidency for the Republicans, solidly—a margin of 54%–46%, which although smaller than the landslide margin for the Reagan reelection of 1984, was actually larger than the original Reagan margin of 1980. At the same time, the Democrats captured the House of Representatives, with a slightly expanded margin despite their large and continuing edge, to produce the disastrous balance *against* the new president of 260–175. Finally, the Senate moved very slightly in the Democratic direction as well, producing the additionally difficult margin of 55–45 against the new president there.[33]

By the standards of an established electoral order, however, the key point was not the superficial disjunction apparent in these individual outcomes but the fundamental continuity which their composite pattern represented:

- In a year when there was no incumbent president, when an outgoing administration was beset by problems, when early opinion polls showed a general public ready for change, and when the most likely Republican nominee was consensually seen as lackluster, the presidency fell into line with a pattern established from 1968.
- In a year when the general public gave Congress only secondary attention by comparison to the presidency, when the winning presidential nominee roared

back from a deep deficit in public preferences, and when he then held this dominant status throughout the fall campaign, Congress, too, fell into line with a pattern established from 1968—deviating only slightly, and then in the "wrong" (the Democratic) direction.

- The composite outcome was thus effectively as it had been for the entire previous generation: The Republicans won the presidency again, solidly. The Democrats reaffirmed their grip—apparently their "lock"—on the House. And the Democrats resecured their hold on the Senate, a hold which nevertheless bore watching.

A student of electoral orders, in turn, was entitled to be unsurprised. When persisting conservative majorities on foreign policy and cultural values had begun to elect Republican presidents, persistently, that outcome was in effect "institutionally appropriate." When persisting liberal majorities on domestic welfare and service provision kept electing Democratic congressmen to the House of Representatives, *that* outcome was institutionally appropriate, too. Finally, when the Senate approximated the House more than the presidency in institutional predisposition and thus in ultimate partisan balance, that outcome only completed an interlocking structural picture. When the election of 1988 fell in with (and reflected) this continuing structure, despite all the surface perturbations of this peculiar, particular year, there was little analytic curiosity in such a result.

As a consequence, all that was left to the election of 1988 in intellectual terms—besides reaffirmation of the contours of a patterned electoral order and disposition of some of the world's most critical public offices—was a set of elaborations and refinements on the character of the current order itself. On the other hand, two of these further specifications, the identity of the critical subgroups within this order and the nature of the thematic appeals elicited by its contours, were at least dramatically displayed in 1988. Because they also achieved so much attention from analysts who did *not* connect them up to any larger pattern, they may merit some further, special attention.

Before that, however, even this partially elaborated vision of the contemporary electoral order dismisses another, frequently heard, summary assertion about the contest of 1988. Perhaps the most easily available and widely used postmortem on *any* election, one with powerful attractions for both winners and losers, is the argument that the comparative quality of the two campaigns was crucial. In such an argument, naturally, better campaigns win, and worse campaigns lose. The presidential year of 1988 was destined to draw (more than?) its share of this type of analysis.[34]

The most immediate flaw in all such arguments is their tendency to reason backward: The winner had the best campaign, of course, and the best campaign, accordingly, won. The more serious flaw, however, when the argument is applied to the election of 1988, is that it can hardly be the explanation of a stereotypical outcome forming part of a pattern *stretching back a quarter-century.* In analytic terms, if 1988 is indeed part of a continuing electoral order, the most that can be said about the contribution of its two campaigns is that the balance was not *so* extreme as to disrupt an established electoral logic.

1988 as Elaboration and Refinement

All of which does not mean that the details of these two campaigns do not provide further insights into—and hence further specification of—a continuing electoral order. Indeed, in some sense they must. An abstracted electoral order, providing a summary description of an entire era by way of its most influential political structures, must still be immanent in—made objective by—the specific details of the electoral contests alleged to fall within that order. Not all of the details of any given contest can, or need to, meet this standard; some of them must be genuinely idiosyncratic to the year in question. But if the most politically central (and thus potentially diagnostic) characteristics of a given contest do not meet this standard, that fact would begin to call the order itself into question.

Two such centrally diagnostic characteristics seem inescapable. One is the crucial *subgroups* for a given electoral contest, those social groups which successfully command the attention of *both* campaigns. A second is the central *themes* of those campaigns, the arguments crafted to capitalize upon (or suppress) the dominant characteristics of an electoral order. In the first of these, for example, if the general public in the contemporary electoral order is indeed centrally characterized by cross-cutting majorities in the major issue-areas of our time, then the campaigns of 1988 had to be focused, most centrally, on those social groups which most pointedly embodied this cross-cutting character. In 1988, these subgroups were actually the self-described partisan independents and the so-called Reagan Democrats—and the campaign was indeed specifically targeted toward them.

The partisan independents were those who, when asked "Generally speaking, do you think of yourself as a Republican, a Democrat, an Independent, or what?" chose the category "independent."[35] They tended to be above the median on measures of social class, measures of education, occupation, or income. More pointedly, they tended to be *conservative* on social welfare, *accommodationist* on foreign policy, and *progressive* on cultural values. The Reagan Democrats were their opposite numbers. When asked the same question, they overwhelmingly answered "a Democrat"—despite having voted for Ronald Reagan for president, in many cases twice.[36] These Reagan Democrats tended to be below the median on measures of social class. But again more pointedly, they tended to be *liberal* on social welfare, *nationalist* on foreign policy, and *traditionalist* on cultural values.

The usual explanation from campaign operatives for why their campaigns concentrated disproportionately on these groups was that they were the ones most clearly "up for grabs."[37] Yet when these groups are put back within the context of a continuing electoral order, it becomes possible to see that if this is the best proximate explanation, it is operationally true because these two groups best exemplify the cross-pressures inherent in public preferences on the major issue-areas of our time. This is not the same as saying that these groups are a microcosm of society, which clearly they are not. Nor do they necessarily, as individual groups, put the same internal priorities on issue-areas within the total cluster. But if major national cross-pressures are at the heart of electoral politics in the contemporary order, these groups should have been at the focus of national electoral campaigns—and they were.[38]

In the same way, the *themes* of the 1988 presidential campaign should provide further specification of an electoral order. For if the overall structure of contemporary opinion within that order is correctly described, then the realms of foreign affairs and cultural values within it are inherently more central to campaigns for president—and the campaigns of 1988 *had to be* focused on emphasizing (or displacing) those particular realms. Once again, campaign details attest precisely to this. Or, said differently, it is precisely an awareness of the structure of the contemporary order which makes its detailed embodiment so straightforward and comprehensible. Moreover, in this case, such a "structural translation" only gains credibility from the otherwise peculiar, almost bizarre, nature of this embodiment.

This is probably best exemplified with those peculiar and controversial themes, "the Pledge" and "the '1' word." "The Pledge" was, of course, the Pledge of Allegiance, an oath of loyalty to the American flag and, by implication, to the nation behind it. On its face, the Pledge was thus an odd campaign gambit. Familiar to generations of American schoolchildren and repeated intermittently by their elders at public occasions, it was distinguished by nothing so much as the *unanimity* of its normal applications and the *absence* of any partisan overtones. Despite that, its recitation became the closing act of the acceptance speech by George Bush at the Republican Convention, and its repetition continued through the fall campaign.[39]

Once again, however, what was peculiar in isolation gains meaning in the context of an existing electoral order. For in an order characterized by divisions on issues of foreign affairs and cultural values, what the Pledge managed to do was *join* these two grand concerns—along with the two grand majorities for traditionalism in cultural values and nationalism in foreign affairs—through a superficially odd but still universally familiar symbol. Indeed, the emotive power of that symbol was probably enhanced not just by the obvious discomfort of the Democratic campaign in addressing it, but by outraged complaints from other commentators that this was a "non-issue," obscuring "real concerns."[40]

What the Pledge did, in other words, was to activate the latent structure of a continuing electoral order, reminding the general public that there were continuing divisions on important matters here, and reminding the majority where it stood on these divisions. On the other hand, this electoral order, as a framework, suggests that the importance of the Pledge itself could easily be overstated. If there were major and continuing divisions on these fundamental concerns, and if they were especially relevant to campaigns for the presidency, then if the Pledge had not been successful in activating these divisions, some other gambit would probably have done so. Indeed, "crime" (for cultural values) and "defense" (for foreign policy) were obviously available, and simultaneously in use.[41]

The other great thematic example from the 1988 presidential campaign, the other great detail which packed so much structural import into a highly concentrated symbol, was known as "the 'l' word." That word, in turn, was "liberal," and together with "the Pledge," it probably generated as much anguished, outraged, and ultimately uncomprehending commentary as any item in a long and winding presidential campaign. Yet here, the roots of the analytic problem stemmed from an insistence that meanings and implications tied directly to an earlier electoral era remained constant in its successor—despite apparent public perceptions, *voter* perceptions, to the contrary.[42]

In the preceding electoral order, after the New Deal and into the 1960s, "liberalism" was a designation rooted in the realm of social welfare. Liberals thus favored melioration of the lot of the economically disadvantaged, along with social insurance programs to protect all citizens against market vagaries and market failings. In such a world, Democrats were liberal, the general public was liberal, and Democrats won the presidency. By the late 1960s, however, as cultural values and foreign affairs joined social welfare as organizing concerns in electoral politics, the definition of liberalism began inevitably to shift. Liberals now also favored progressivism on cultural values and accommodationism in foreign affairs. In this world, Democrats were still liberal, the general public was now *conservative,* and Republicans won the presidency.

While this fact became variously an asset and a liability for the Bush and Dukakis campaigns, the situation had been institutionalized long before either George Bush or Michael Dukakis were presidential nominees. The Bush campaign, of course, needed principally to *emphasize* the new definition of "liberal." The Dukakis campaign inherited the more unenviable task of redirecting that emphasis—a task which was at least actively addressed. Indeed, the campaign began by asserting that Dukakis was *not* a liberal, in contemporary understandings; he was instead moderate, forward-looking, and competent.[43]

When this did not work—when it could not avoid the institutionalized connotations of the revised definition of "liberal"—the campaign changed tactics. It asserted that since liberalism meant concern for economic well-being and service provision, *as it always had,* then Dukakis was, of course, a liberal—*as were most Americans.* These were highly reasonable, tactical adjustments. If they were ultimately unable to circumvent a continuing strategic environment, that was less a matter of campaign skill, more an inevitable product of a continuing electoral order, which might in its application be personally unfair but which constituted the electoral context nevertheless.

Forces for Stability

The election of 1988, then, attests principally to the continuity of an established electoral order, with its diagnostic details as little more than concrete embodiments—at best, further refinements—of the contours of that order. On the other hand, this very argument, so dismissive in one sense, raises its own central, implicit, theoretical question: If the main analytic use of the 1988 election is as evidence of the stability of the current electoral order, then how *has* that order become so stable? Said less theoretically, if the contours of an existing order have been in existence for more than a generation, and if the partisan highlights of this order are consensually recognized, then why have major political actors not moved to "correct" the situation? Or rather, why *did* they not so move when the pattern began to emerge, before it became institutionalized?

Within the framework of an electoral order, the answer can lie in only three places, that is, in the three general strata of political structures. In principle, it could lie within the institutions of government themselves. Yet although these institutions *responded* very differently in a new electoral era, they did not change in their basic conformation and thus cannot provide a direct explanation either of change or of stability. An answer could lie instead within the social divisions of politics, and these did in fact both change and then stabilize—around a new, integrated set of opinion majorities. But while it is precisely these changes which also made the institutions of government function differently, they cannot simultaneously explain what drove an old order in a new direction *and* what prevented other actors and other forces from responding to them, to counteract this change.

For that, conceptually, the focus must be on the intermediary organizations and intermediary elites of an electoral order, which is to say, on political parties, on interest groups, and on key actors within them. Practically, and in much more explicitly empirical terms, this focus leads directly to the changing organizational character of modern American political parties, to the changing universe of interest groups around those parties, and to the changing values of activist figures within both.[44] Translated into these terms, the stability of the contemporary electoral order does indeed appear to depend crucially on its (supporting) intermediary organizations and intermediary elites—though the character of their "support" is in other ways arguably perverse.

Regardless, in our time, *both* major American political parties have come to be built around independent, issue-based activists. Indeed, this trend actually began earlier on the Republican side. By the late 1950s, the Republican party was already an activist-based operation, featuring officeholders who were motivated principally by ideological positions or policy concerns, rather than by pecuniary goals or partisan attachments. Ideology and policy are hardly negligible incentives, and the Republican party has hardly withered. But such incentives did produce a party more characterized by elite actors who moved in and out of party politics with the passing parade of candidates and issues of the day. When the same tendency conquered the Democratic party, by the late 1960s, the reconstruction of a party *system* was effectively complete.[45]

That system, in turn, had further implications. Into the 1950s, it was not just that there was a societal consensus on economics and social welfare as the major dimension of electoral politics. There was also serious party organization, especially in the dominant (Democratic) party, to see that politics remained centered on economic well-being. Now, not only has the larger public consensus broken down. That *sort* of party organization has also largely disappeared, so that it is literally not there to respond. The first contribution to the stability of the current order, accordingly, was the disappearance of the organizations best able, in principle, to countervail it.[46]

In practice, however, the possibility of such resistance—an elite insistence that an electoral order stay focused on social welfare and economic well-being— was being undermined by much more than party organizational change. For in fact, these parties were increasingly surrounded by and allied with organized interests which were dedicated to movement in exactly the opposite direction. Said differently, a further, striking aspect of political change in the modern era has been the rise of new interest groups inside the party coalitions—interest groups which were themselves motivated by (and provided further reinforcement to) the new social divisions on foreign affairs and cultural values.[47]

An older electoral order, centered on social welfare and service provision, had been buttressed, symbiotically, by fundamentally economic interest groups: by organized labor on the Democratic side and by organized business and farm organizations among Republicans. By the late 1960s, this arrangement, too, was passing. The Democratic party had long been inclined to describe itself as a coalition of diverse interests, so that a burgeoning group phenomenon was hardly apostate there. Yet by the late 1960s, that self-confessed diversity was further expanding *and shifting* in its content. The shift first came to public attention by way of the various groups protesting the Vietnam War. But it became institutionalized, more effectively if less dramatically, in a larger array of organizations centered on such matters as feminism, peace, environmentalism, homosexuality, and freedom-of-choice (proabortion).

Less widely recognized—and perhaps less extreme but clearly moving in the same direction—was the same shift inside the Republican party.[48] Notwithstanding claims by party leaders that theirs was a party undivided into "special interests," the Republican party, too, expanded and diversified in its associated groups, a process led—indeed, dominated—by groups centered on cultural values and foreign affairs. In fact, the organizations which came to symbolize this trend for the nation as a whole were principally allies of the *Republican* party. Foremost among these was the Moral Majority, perhaps the quintessential cultural-value group, but the tendency extended to numerous other incarnations, like the Eagle Forum, a stereotypical blend of traditionalist and nationalist concerns—not to mention perhaps the most active of all, the variety of right-to-life (antiabortion) groups increasingly collected on the Republican side of the aisle.

Institutionalizing the New Order

Even this investigation of political parties and interest groups still seriously understates the forces for stability in a new electoral order, forces which would eventually allow that order to pass the quarter-century mark. For it was not just that an older type of organized party had passed from the scene. Nor that a newer, activist party was under a different set of pressures from (newer) organized interests, from a universe of interest groups tilted, increasingly, away from simple economics and toward cultural values and foreign affairs. Rather, part and parcel—indeed, integral—to both developments was the fact that, in a world where cultural values and foreign affairs were the emergent issue concerns, it was *precisely those issues* which were motivating individuals to put themselves forward—and do the work of the parties.

In other words, as issues and ideology came necessarily to motivate party officials, and as a shift in the issue concerns of the public was both expressed and exaggerated by a shift in the nature of the organized interests associated with the parties, party officials themselves, necessarily and indeed naturally, came to embody these issue concerns.[49] Grand changes in the issue divisions in society, proceeding in tandem with the demise of old-fashioned party organizations and the rise of new-fashioned organized interests, in fact went a long way toward guaranteeing that new entrants to party office on both the Democratic and Republican sides would automatically share the values (and associated policy preferences) of newly ascendant issue elites.

As a result, part of *being* a Democrat (at the level of partisan elites) would increasingly involve being progressive on cultural values and accommodationist on foreign policy. Just as part of being a Republican (again, at the elite level) would involve being traditionalist on cultural values and nationalist on foreign policy.[50] This was, of course, not at all true in the general public, where there were plenty of Democrats who were traditionalist on cultural values and nationalist on foreign policy, plenty of Republicans who were progressive on cultural values and accommodationist on foreign policy. That was, after all, one of the implications of cross-cutting majorities in the nation as a whole. But at the level of partisan elites, this issue filtering was not just real but the defining characteristic of a fundamental shift in elite orientations and preferences.

This fundamental shift, in turn, was to be central to the institutionalization (and hence the stability) of a new electoral order. In fact, all that remains to make this stabilizing role clear is to reintroduce the *old* partisan issues—economics and social welfare—into the model (and now the picture) of elite preferences. For at the elite level, it was not the case that as new issue-areas assumed a central role in motivating partisan activists, old areas began to lose their partisan distinctiveness; if anything, these previous partisan distinctions became sharper as well. In other words, at the elite (but not at the mass) level, new issues divisions were effectively "grafted onto" (rather than "laid across") the old.[51]

Once, Democratic party elites were liberal on economics and social welfare, Republican party elites were conservative. In the new world, this *remained* true. What was new was that Democratic elites were also progressive on cultural values and accommodationist of foreign policy, while Republican elites were traditionalist on cultural values and nationalist on foreign policy—and *these* were the dominant concerns in their mobilization and recruitment. Seen in the light of the search for the political structures of a new electoral order, however, the implications of all this can be summarized not just succinctly but somewhat perversely as well: The activist base of each political party had become effectively committed—energetically, consciously, even desperately committed—to precisely those positions on which their party would necessarily *lose* one or another major public office.

This situation is most widely recognized in the case of the Democrats, where a flood of published analysis (and complaint) has highlighted the way in which a focus on cultural values and foreign affairs—which is to say, on the *wrong side* of cultural values and foreign affairs—has impaired the party in pursuit of the presidency for more than a generation.[52] But the argument is as apt, if less acknowledged, on the Republican side. Indeed, here, too, it can be plumbed quickly: Perhaps the only subgroup left in American society which has not accepted the basic outlines even of the New Deal, the fundamental tenets of the welfare state, is *Republican party activists*—thereby making the House of Representatives probably unattainable.[53]

And in these continuing commitments, of course, lies the explanation for the lack of countervailing action by elites, action contrary to the structure of the current electoral order. It is not that partisan elites do not desire a government reunited in one set of partisan hands; they *want* to see such an outcome, far more than the public.[54] It is just that they are not prepared to gain this reunification at the cost of sacrificing their most central values—the very values, after all, which brought them into politics. Accordingly, cross-pressures among the rank and file may have been essential to *creating* a new electoral order. Yet the party elites ostensibly representing that rank and file were effectively committed to *maintaining* those cross-pressures, and thus to the stability of the new order, by consciously refusing to come into line with majority preferences across three main issue-areas.

Realignment/Dealignment and the New Electoral Order

The contemporary electoral order in American politics, then, can be modeled very simply. That order features a social base for politics which is characterized by overlapping and cross-cutting divisions—overlapping and cross-cutting majorities, actually—on the grand issue-areas of social welfare, foreign policy, and cultural values. These patterned and recurring divisions, in turn, fall across an institutional arrangement—a structure of offices—which taps these issues very differently. Foreign affairs and cultural values are focused on the presidency; social welfare and service provision are focused on the House of Representatives; the Senate is amenable to all four concerns, but leans more toward the House than the presidency. Finally, a set of intermediary organizations—political parties and interest groups—along with their intermediary elites are effectively dedicated to perpetuating, rather than meliorating, this composite situation.

The electoral hallmark of this arrangement—the original signal that there was something new to be explained, and then the recurring confirmation of a new order—is a peculiar and distinctive set of (split) partisan outcomes. The Republicans, being the party of cultural traditionalism and foreign nationalism, control the presidency. The Democrats, being the party of economic liberalism and service delivery, control the House. And both parties can reasonably bid for the Senate, though its greater priority for social welfare and service provisions does give the Democrats an inherent edge. Those are the fundamental contours, in a very few sentences, of the current *electoral order.* It does no disrespect to a powerful and historic, alternative organizing notion to observe that the coming of this order *was not a realignment.*

By extension, realignment, the concept, has little to say about it, an intellectual situation which cannot apparently be salvaged through the further notion of dealignment. What has been in existence in the United States since the mid 1960s—first registered at the election of 1968 and most recently reregistered in the election of 1988—is an intricate but stable pattern of outcomes, rooted in public preferences, institutional predispositions, and intermediary reinforcements, no part of which is captured by "dealignment." Said more forcefully, the contemporary electoral world is *not* the New Deal political order. But it is just as clearly *not* a classical realignment from that order. And the concept of dealignment, when faced with the specifics of this order, effectively compounds the conceptual problem by branding it "not realignment," and then stopping.

Such an argument naturally returns the analysis to the basic conceptual questions with which it began.[55] These questions could be ducked, of course, by falling back on a truly minimalist definition of realignment, as implying that there may well be another massive shifting of public partisan preferences *sometime*. Yet such a scaled-back definition is, even of itself, a dull analytic tool—and one which would devalue most of the theoretical elaborations which have come after the systemization of Key's original "critical elections" into "realignments." More concretely, it must also confront the empirical fact that there has been no such subsequent realignment for approximately 60 years, while there *has* been a major, subsequent, and stable shift in the contours of the electoral order.

The initial effort at rescuing the notion of realignment from this theoretical morass—suggesting an implicit awareness of the problem even as realignment was moving to the intellectual fore—was to assert an inherent *periodicity* to these major events.[56] Realignment would thus not be like a weather forecast which confined itself to reporting either "tornadoes" or "no tornadoes." Instead, periodicity—temporal regularity—would be added to the notion, with specifics deduced from the preceding historical pattern, so that the analyst could expect a full-blown realignment every twenty-eight to thirty-six years. History, alas, caught up with this revision quickly. A realignment was already "overdue," in these terms, as this further argument was formulated. Now, when there has not been a classical realignment for some sixty years and counting, any inherent periodicity, if once tenable, must apparently be discarded.

The more elusive, and much more widely used, effort to rescue the concept of realignment, however, came with the associated notion of dealignment. For all those periods when the old realignment was no longer a sufficient explanation for the patterns of politics but when a new realignment had just as clearly not been born, "dealignment" would be the guiding concept.[57] But again, a superficially straightforward notion came with its own immediate problems: stated this way, it is effectively a name, not a concept. Indeed, in its unelaborated usage, "dealignment"—the period when an old alignment does not hold but a new one has not yet appeared—means only "not realignment." "No tornadoes," of course, is still not absolutely empty as a weather report. But it does not say anything about what is happening or will happen.

The obvious solution is to give "dealignment" a more precise implication, one which could actually be applied to, and tested against, a recurring partisan pattern in elections. Curiously, this has not been a major focus of realignment theorists. Yet if dealignment *is* to mean something other than "not realignment," such a further specification can only lie in one of two clear and distinctive directions. Either it must imply a gradual *but general* shift away from the beneficiary of the last realignment, with partisan outcomes becoming gradually less favorable to the old majority party as the old realignment ebbs. Or it must imply that partisan attachments, as registered in partisan electoral *outcomes,* will become increasingly random.

Any other implication is confused, ambiguous, and, worst of all, shifting; it describes everything by specifying nothing. Rather than giving the concept precise analytic refinements, and thus precise empirical extrapolations, any other elaboration returns it, in effect, to "not realignment." On the other hand, these two very sensible elaborations of dealignment—a roughly unilinear decline or growing randomization—have also proved, in our time, to be *false.* The presidency has obviously become more Republican, the House has obviously become more Democratic, and the Senate has clearly become more changeable than the situation prevailing in the late New Deal order. This is not at all "unilinear decay"; it is almost the opposite to random partisan movement.

Realignments, Electoral Orders, and Political Change

It is tempting to drive such an argument back into electoral history as well. Or at least, if the notion of an "electoral order" (rather than the notion of a "realignment") is to provide the needed theoretical perspective across history, then the "critical elections" leading into each alleged realignment—not to mention the patterns of politics in each extended electoral era—do look powerfully different from one another. Those differences appear to be most easily addressed by looking at *composite* partisan outcomes. They appear to be most easily *explained* through the dominant political structures which together characterize each period—including most especially, in an analysis built around the notion of an electoral order, that period which begins most clearly in 1968, but which does *not* begin with a classical realignment.

These are, however, deep waters for the amateur historian. Better just to say that the notion of an electoral order appears to encompass—to isolate and to explain—a set of important changes (and then continuities) in the modern world, which the notion of realignment does not address. These changes, through their particular structural details, go on to suggest that classical realignments are increasingly unlikely, for a set of very familiar reasons. Growth in the sectors of society which have long been most inclined toward independent participation in politics; expansion in the reach of mass media of information, as alternative channels of communication about politics and its issues; and especially, the (related) decline of political parties as extended electoral organizations, the organizations which would historically have "cemented" any new social divisions accompanying newly consequential issue-areas: All these surely make a classical realignment less likely.

On the other hand, they do not make it impossible. Especially if new and major issue-divisions were to coincide with deep and continuing features of *social structure,* or if newly dominant issue-areas resulted from the kind of divisive *crisis* which could not, in principle, be resolved quickly, then a classical realignment might presumably still occur. The evidence from the modern era, however, does suggest that such an occurrence would still best be interpreted by way of the notion of an electoral order. Or at least, a break without a realignment produced the modern electoral era, and that era is also likely to change, when it does change, without a classical realignment. Yet the concept of an electoral order remains capable of integrating even a good, old-fashioned, "critical election"—even a classical realignment—should one actually occur.

Those appear to be the elementary propositions, both analytic and empirical, in favor of the notion of an electoral order. They could be further embroidered. Thus one further implication of an ability to handle changed situations which are clearly not classical realignments lies in the array of additional elements—apart from massive, consistent, and incipiently permanent shifts in public partisan preferences—which are allowed to reenter the analysis and shape the contours of an era. At one end of the continuum, these include the quintessentially political details of *campaigning* for public office, including the shaping of campaign themes and the targeting of social groups. At the other end of the continuum, they include the operation of political *institutions,* especially that most apparently nonelectoral institution, the Supreme Court. Such an analysis—and the place of the Court makes this point forcefully—also emphasizes the ways in which electoral change need not be (initially and directly) *electorally driven.*

Taken by themselves, these are relatively uncontroversial benefits. Yet at this same comparative analytic level, one must also inevitably ask: If the conceptual analysis were reversed, that is, if one were coming to realignments by way of electoral orders rather than the opposite, would the picture of intellectual assets and liabilities really look the same? Said differently, if one were searching for flaws in the notion of electoral orders by way of the advantages of realignment, rather than addressing problems in the concept of realignment by way of the virtues of electoral orders, would this not tilt the analytic balance in the other direction? Or, to put the question even more pointedly—to unpack its real implication—would the notion of an electoral order, apparently successful in boiling the details of contemporary politics to their existing structural essence, really prove as successful in handling *change*?

The notion, through its associated political structures, does appear to isolate the modern era as a distinctive period, and to permit an interlocking set of explanations for its *stability*. When the notion of realignment is confronted with the same empirical product, it appears to have little to say. Yet the great conceptual strength of "realignment," in turn, has always been its alleged ability to handle change—indeed, to focus on the central changes of politics, the ones with the most significant and lasting impact. From these "electoral earthquakes" have arisen all the further elaborations on the realignment/dealignment framework, along with all the subsequent phenomena of politics which true realignments are alleged to reach.[58] Accordingly, it seems necessary to ask: Can "electoral orders," apparently capable of explaining their own stability, also handle change?

As ever, it would be possible to respond by attacking the question, rather than providing an answer. The concept of realignment has actually had a very mixed record of dealing with change-in-progress—witness all those articles asking whether the first Reagan election, and then the second Reagan election, were really "realignments."[59] The concept itself asserts—especially now that the associated notion of periodicity has died—that one cannot, in principle, *foresee* the nature of the next realignment. Moreover, even when an electoral tremor of some scale has been registered, the empirical demands which define a classical realignment suggest that it cannot be *confirmed* until a number of subsequent elections have passed. Worse, those very characteristics which make a classical realignment a particularly demanding category, before such a major change can be confidently asserted, are the same characteristics which militate against discovering consequential changes in less global outcomes. Thus a "mere" shift of the presidency into Republican hands for five of the last six elections (and counting) is, in these terms, "not a realignment."

Still, all these complaints, even if justified, are not the same as demonstrating—even suggesting—that the notion of an electoral order can manage the same problems. That, of course, requires actual demonstration; it requires both abstract reasons which could improve upon the analysis of change *and* some concrete applications in the current, empirical, political world. Ideally, these abstract sources of change would be intrinsic to the concept of an electoral order. Ideally, subsequent concrete applications—possible contours for the *next* American electoral order—could be derived by focusing these abstract sources on the empirical content of the current order.

Abstract Sources of Change

In the most abstract terms, the comparative advantage of the concept of an electoral order in handling political change should lie in two related, defining characteristics. In the first, the concept provides more analytic foci, more cumulative *sources* for change, by way of its array of political structures. Not only that, but it goes on to organize these so as to facilitate the search. Yet in a second, related characteristic, the concept is still an effort to integrate this expanded array of potentially consequential sites into a simple model, reduced to its basic elements and recognizing priorities among them.

In this, an electoral order and its political structures do not just expand the foci for potential change, the points of examination in an election campaign and its outcome. They also specify three general areas where any such change must manifest itself—in the social base for politics, in its intermediary organizations and intermediary elites, and in the institutions of government and the institutional rules for securing them. Moreover, they go on to permit very pointed specifications within these—for example, *racial* divisions within the social base, interest group *deteriorations* among intermediary organizations, shifts in *ballot form* for the filling of elected institutions.[60]

In fact, the notion of an electoral order also offers a very precise starting point for such an analysis, in the *partisan pattern* of outcomes from an election. Thus in our time, should Democrats recapture the presidency or Republicans make even serious inroads in the House, a student of electoral orders would quickly move on to search for changes in social divisions, intermediary organizations, or institutional biases. Indeed, the current electoral order emphasizes the way in which even a continuing order—one, therefore, with presumed major elements of stability—can nevertheless encompass major *contradictions*. Such contradictions, especially if they do continue, are an inescapable point of examination in the search for prospective change.

In this case, of course, these contradictions consist of the major and continuing tensions inherent in major, *cross-cutting* policy preferences. If those tensions, from one side, are essential for explaining the structure of a continuing order, they are also, from the other, a very evident place to begin looking for change—even before there has been a shift in the partisan pattern of electoral outcomes. This will be attempted more concretely below, but even in the abstract, a shift in social divisions around a diagnostic issue-area, a shift in public priorities for the issue-area, or a shift in the composition of those leading, specific issues which comprise the composite area—all these become, instantly, potential catalysts for substantial further change.

The notion of an electoral order also appears to have the advantage of permitting deliberate and conscious *alterations* in political structures, alterations which then shift the contours of an entire electoral order, often inadvertently. The more dramatic and self-consciously structural among such alterations are ordinarily characterized as "reforms," and there are many prospective examples already visible on the American political landscape.[61] The move to a national primary for nominating presidents, for example, or changes in the disposition of congressional campaign funds—even in the tenure of congressmen themselves—are the sort of reforms which would almost inevitably have implications for the structure of an electoral order. The same can be said of intermittently bruited reforms in selection to, jurisdiction of, or membership on the Supreme Court—despite their formal distance from electoral politics.[62]

It is not at all necessary to insist that such reforms be *aimed* at shifting an electoral order (though it is worth remembering that they can be) in order to see them as plausible sources of major change. Reforms can be justified, or not, in terms of electoral change; they can produce outcomes representing, or even contraverting, their original justifications.[63] In such a situation, of course, facing the implementation of major, new, political reforms, it is precisely the array of political structures which can compose an electoral order that provides specific places to look for additional effects—even specific places through which to attempt to *estimate* those effects in advance.

The same is true with the major, truly external "shocks" of politics, those consensual crises forced upon any political system, occasionally, in ways which could not in principle be foreseen or prevented. These are, by definition, the core—conventionally the only core—of "realignments." Yet they can easily enough be introduced within the framework of an electoral order. Whether even these—depressions, wars, climatological or epidemiological disasters, and so forth—would elicit a classical realignment within the contemporary electoral order presents an interesting, theoretical and ultimately empirical, question. But the framework of an electoral order does not dismiss them, and in fact provides numerous *structural points* through which to gauge their specific impact.

The greatest potential gain in the notion of an electoral order, then, may actually lie at the boundary between abstractly conceptual and rigorously empirical approaches to politics. Viewed from the empirical side, the notion of an electoral order aspires to reintroduce politics *and politicking*—"politics" as we, and others, normally know it—back into the study of elections. For this, an expanded array of potential structural changes, producing significant practical consequences, must be derived from observation of the specifics of electoral politics in its broadest sense. Seen from the theoretical side and simultaneously, investigations conducted within the framework of this notion—searching for an electoral order and its crucial, determining, political structures—aspire *not* to reduce the outcomes of those elections to a mere aggregation of idiosyncratic events, influences, and ultimately results. The outline of an order, not the sum of all votes cast, remains the analytic goal.

Clearly, such a framework can handle major changes of the sort represented by the shift away from the New Deal order, the shift to what constitutes the electoral order of our time. Indeed, this particular change is the empirical phenomenon which suggested the need for—and then initially validated—a conceptual framework involving electoral orders. Clearly as well, such a framework offers its own inherent theoretical reasons for believing that it can handle change as it happens. These involve most directly its surfacing of contradlitions, its search for grand issue-areas, and its focus on the three general strata for (changing) political structures. In closing, then, and granting all the slippage naturally associated with moving from theoretically based explanation toward pointed empirical projection, can this framework be used to speculate about sources for—even characteristics of—some successor to the current electoral era?

The Next American Electoral Order?

The contradictions intrinsic to the existing order must be the starting point for any such prospective investigation. And indeed, leaders of both political parties, while they may not phrase the matter in this vocabulary, have actually been trusting to one of two alternative resolutions of these contradictions to solve their continuing—their institutionalized—political problems. Thus the Democrats have been waiting for an economic downturn sufficient to drive public preferences on social welfare "upward," from the House through the Senate and into the presidency. Just as the Republicans have been waiting for less easily specified developments in the social order or in international affairs to put further emphasis on cultural values and foreign relations, so that these are driven "down" from the presidency, through the Senate and into the House.[64]

Within the current electoral order, as described, both outcomes are certainly possible. On the other hand, it is also worth noting that this order is sufficiently institutionalized, more than a generation later, that a single election with the desired characteristics is not likely to work permanent change on its basic contours. Sooner or later, it would seem, a normal economic cycle must present sufficient problems to return a Democrat to the presidency, and this Democratic president should even enjoy the luxury of (at least) a marginally Democratic Senate and a strongly Democratic House. Conversely, cultural and international issues, although perhaps never sufficient actually to give the House of Representatives to the Republicans, were sufficient as recently as 1980 to produce a Republican majority in the Senate and to allow a cross-party "conservative coalition" on major issues in the House.

Yet it must also be said that the scope of economic difficulties necessary to produce the Democratic scenario from these contradictions appears to have grown more demanding in our time. Or at least, there has been only one such interlude from 1968 through 1992; it required a rare cumulation of circumstances, including Watergate; and it still lasted only one term. Lest this seem like a rosy Republican picture, it must be noted that the most ideal concatenations of circumstances in the modern era—the Democratic implosion of 1968, for example, or the end of the Carter Administration in an atmosphere of stagflation at home and hostage crisis abroad—were *still* not sufficient to drag the Republican party to power in the House of Representatives.

Such an examination of existing contradictions, then, suggests that shifts in the actual, dominant issue-areas of our time would be necessary in order to produce a new (and newly stabilized) electoral order. On the other hand, as this is written, events both at home and abroad conspire to suggest at least the serious *possibility* of such shifts. An international order central to American foreign relations since the end of the Second World War is certainly in flux. Tensions within both parties—not just one—on issues of cultural values are evidently, if perhaps temporarily, rising. Even social welfare policy offers elements teasingly suggestive of changing partisan impacts, though these are the most speculative and hypothetical.

A changing international order could, of course, work its way through the contemporary American electoral world in any number of ways.[65] Most straightforwardly and directly, declining international tensions might devalue identification with a strong national defense and with nationalism as a public posture, thereby devaluing an institutionalized Republican asset and augmenting Democratic advantages in its place. At one extreme, a truly major reduction of hostilities toward the Soviet Union, in particular, might even change the identity of major international opponents—for example, to the *Japanese* in the *economic* sphere. This could actually make the Democrats, with their greater receptivity to protectionism in international economics and a greater dislike of foreign nationals among their mass identifiers, the beneficiary of foreign affairs as an issue-area.[66] At the other extreme, even the end of the Cold War may only reveal that what has really been at the core of this issue-dimension for more than a generation is patriotism and national identity, not defense and anticommunism—so that this particular Republican advantage does not need to decline at all.

Some variant of these outcomes seems likely to follow ineluctably from a sharply changed international environment. As this is written, many believe that a counterpart shift in partisan consequences from cultural values may also be underway. The catalyst in this argument is the Supreme Court decision in its 1989–90 term which reduced putatively constitutional guarantees of the right to an abortion—and thus moved the specifics of abortion policy back into electoral politics.[67] This may or may not, by itself, be sufficient to reorient an entire issue-area; it is worth remembering that there are many other specific items which make up this general cluster. Yet the shifting politics of abortion does serve to reinforce awareness that cultural values were—and remain—*cross-cutting* issues, so that the simultaneous shift of *several* of the major items within this issue-area can certainly, in principle, have the hypothesized effect.

It is more difficult to create an apparent, incipient shift in social welfare and economic policy, but there are at least obvious, alternative straws in the wind. Many analysts—and many Democratic activists—have been waiting for the American fiscal deficit to produce the severe and sustained economic downturn which could resolve existing contradictions in public attitudes. Con-

versely, many Republican strategists—and, more propitiously, the basic
environment for Republican candidates in local races—have been attempting to
reorient the party on matters of social welfare, so as to reduce the Democratic
advantage there.[68] Suffice it to say that Democratic analysts and activists have
been waiting for a *long time* for the other economic shoe to drop, while
Republican candidates and strategists have been struggling with their social
welfare problem for even longer.

Potential changes in major *individual* items of political structure are, of
course, the final elements in any examination of prospects for a new electoral
order. In principle, these provide the largest array of such possibilities. In practice, that very wealth of alternatives brings its own problem; no single analysis
could hope to examine the effect of all such possible changes in political structures. Moreover, an existing range of incipient structural changes is already
observable in contemporary American politics. A changing character to black-
white political coalitions; sharp alterations to the process of congressional
campaign finance; the completion of an older cycle of ballot reform—all these
are actively on the national political agenda, and all have implications for an
electoral order.[69]

Given such wide-ranging possibilities, perhaps one further example can
stand in for these others in slightly more detail. As this is written, the most
widely discussed of such imminent structural changes are probably those
promising a vastly expanded potential *electorate,* by way of sharply eased procedures for voter registration.[70] At one extreme, this might add a uniformly
Democratic tilt to the electorate, in the form of those most responsive to social
welfare concerns. At the other extreme, such a prospect might actually (and
somewhat perversely) succeed where Republican party activists have failed, in
moving those concerned with cultural traditionalism and foreign nationalism
into the Republican party, in reaction. And in-between, lower turnout rates
among the lower-status individuals who are the primary victims of current registration arrangements might be compensated by higher turnout rates within
the smaller set of higher-status individuals who are also disadvantaged, to produce almost no impact on the existing electoral order.

The Structure of Politics and the Two Georges

All of these potential developments, growing out of existing contradictions,
shifting issue-areas, or changing major elements of political structure, qualify
as plausible extrapolations. More to the point, all qualify as possible evolutions
from the current electoral order. As such, all appear as obviously appropriate
material for analysis through the general notion of an electoral order. Each
appears evidently consequential if it should occur. *None* appears to have much
to do with the classical notion—and phenomenon—of realignment.

And that note, which brings an empirical application back to the conceptual framework with which it began, also takes this chapter all the way back to its title. Sir Lewis Namier, in his classic analysis of *The Structure of Politics at the Accession of George III*—the structure of English politics at the time an independent American politics was beginning—could find such a structure only by investigating individual constituencies and individual alliances among their members in Parliament.[71] Indeed, he found the sum of these individual investigations to *be* the structure of English politics at the time. Many contemporary American analysts, for all the difference in historical era and in available investigative tools, come perilously close to the same conclusion.

In this, individual partisan decisions made long ago, as reinforced by the initiatives of individual elected incumbents, with an occasional twist from the further and specific events of the day, are allowed to become "the structure" of contemporary American politics. Almost as invidiously, those who find themselves frustrated by this approach are inclined to retreat to a kind of single-factor explanation—some variant of the barroom riposte, "It's all just money," or of its academic equivalent, "It's all just microeconomics." The first set of analysts thus adopt Namier's method but not his goal, summing outcomes without ever producing a structure. The second set present the goal but ignore the method, thereby producing a structure by ignoring most of what is actually happening in politics.

The argument here has aspired to be different. It centers on a simple model, involving cross-cutting social divisions, which fall across political institutions with differential relevance to these divisions, and whose effects are sustained by intermediary organizations and intermediary elites—all held together by an integrated *set* of dominant issue-areas. In one direction, the model itself becomes evidence for the utility of the *concept* of an electoral order, as elaborated by its associated political structures. In the other direction, the model points the way toward a much more concrete structure for the politics of our own time.

In this, in the current era, the presidency is about foreign policy and cultural values. The House of Representatives is about social welfare and service provision. And the Senate is amenable to both concerns, while leaning toward the latter. There is a conservative majority in the nation, in the late twentieth century, on issues of foreign policy and cultural values, and the presidency is accordingly Republican. There is a liberal majority in the nation on issues of social welfare and service provision, and the House of Representatives is accordingly Democratic. Either majority can reach into the Senate, but the tendency of that institution to focus more on welfare and services than on foreign relations and cultural values means that it is more often Democratic than Republican. Yet *both* political parties are dedicated to maintaining these arrangements, albeit in spite of themselves.

A structure this coherent is not the simple sum of disconnected, individual contests. Just as a structure this complex is not the product of some single, simple, creative force. Coherent and complex, it has been with us since the middle 1960s. And it should be with us until—and only until—changing social divisions, changing institutional predispositions, changing intermediary structures, or, most of all, changing grand issue-areas and public preferences within them produce something different. Presumably, when that time arrives, the notion of an electoral order will help to isolate the structure of this changed political era, just as it helped to isolate the structure of its predecessor—our own.

Notes

David E. Butler provided the initial impetus toward this piece, by urging me to write something about contemporary American elections which was "larger" than an orthodox postmortem. The Politics Group at Nuffield College then provided the first forum for its exposition. Once there was a draft document, Robert K. Merton was instrumental in focusing on the notion of an electoral order, and in demanding its elaboration. Richard F. Fenno, Jr., and J. Jens Hesse were then equally central to testing the links in this elaboration—and requesting more. David B. Truman examined the result in a far more skeptical fashion; if I have not satisfied him, that will come as no surprise. Robert E. Lane and David R. Mayhew provided subsequent encouragement. And three audiences were absolutely crucial to the evolving revisions: the American History seminar at Cambridge University, the Political Science seminar at Essex University, and the American Politics Group of the Political Studies Association at its annual meeting. I thank—and absolve—them all.

1 Joel H. Silbey, "Beyond Realignment and Realignment Theory: American Political Eras, 1789–1989," chapter 1 of this volume. A crucial predecessor is Lee Benson and Joel H. Silbey, "American Political Eras, 1788–1984: Toward a Normative, Substantive, and Conceptual Framework for the Historical Study of American Political Behavior" (Paper presented to the Annual Meetings of the Social Science History Association, 1978).

2 Everett C. Ladd, "Like Waiting for Godot: The Uselessness of 'Realignment' for Understanding Change in Contemporary American Politics," chapter 2 of this volume. Its crucial predecessor is Everett C. Ladd, Jr., with Charles D. Hadley, *Transformations of the American Party System: Political Coalitions from the New Deal to the 1970s,* 2d ed. (New York: W. W. Norton, 1978).

3 My own, highly tentative, previous effort at this is "The Election of 1988 and the Structure of American Politics: Thoughts on Interpreting an Electoral Order," *Electoral Studies* 8 (April, 1989): 5–21.

4 V. O. Key, Jr., "A Theory of Critical Elections," *Journal of Politics* 17 (February 1955): 3–18. A precise genealogist should note that this argument was prefigured,

in a much less deliberately systematized form and without supporting data, in V. O. Key, Jr., "The Future of the Democratic Party," *Virginia Quarterly Review* 28 (Spring 1952): 161–75.

5 Harold F. Bass, Jr., "Background to Debate: A Reader's Guide and Bibliography," following Chapter 5 of this volume. The predecessor to this, now effectively a decade old, is Bruce A. Campbell and Richard J. Trilling, "Bibliography," in *Realignment in American Politics: Toward a Theory,* ed. Campbell and Trilling (Austin: University of Texas Press, 1980), 329–52.

6 Angus Campbell, "A Classification of the Presidential Elections," in Campbell et al., *Elections and the Political Order* (New York: John Wiley and Sons, 1966), 63–77. This, too, is an elaboration and systemization of the earlier Angus Campbell et al., "A Classification of Presidential Elections," in Campbell et al., *The American Voter* (New York: John Wiley and Sons, 1960), 531–38.

7 Walter Dean Burnham, *Critical Elections and the Mainsprings of American Politics* (New York: W. W. Norton, 1970); James L. Sundquist, *Dynamics of the Party System: Alignment and Realignment of Political Parties in the United States* (Washington, D.C.: Brookings Institution, 1973).

8 Kristi Andersen, *The Creation of a Democratic Majority, 1928–1936* (Chicago: University of Chicago Press, 1979); Samuel T. McSeveney, *The Politics of Depression: Political Behavior in the Northeast, 1893–1896* (New York: Oxford University Press, 1972); Jerome M. Clubb, William H. Flanigan, and Nancy H. Zingale, *Partisan Realignment: Voters, Parties, and Government in American History* (Beverly Hills, Calif.: Sage, 1980); David Butler and Donald Stokes, *Political Change in Britain: Forces Shaping Electoral Choice* (London: Macmillan, 1969).

9 Keven P. Phillips, *The Emerging Republican Majority* (New York: Arlington House, 1969).

10 John R. Petrocik, *Party Coalitions: Realignments and the Decline of the New Deal Party System* (Chicago: University of Chicago Press, 1980); Martin P. Wattenberg, *The Decline of American Political Parties, 1952–1980* (Cambridge: Harvard University Press, 1984); Russell J. Dalton et al., eds., *Electoral Change in Advanced Industrial Democracies: Realignment or Dealignment?* (Princeton: Princeton University Press, 1984); John F. Stacks, *Watershed: The Campaign for the Presidency 1980* (New York: Times Books, 1981).

11 It would be presumptuous to assign such a deliberately general and flexible approach to "political structure" to a self-conscious school of "structural analysis" or to a particular study of the "structure of politics." Better just to note that it follows the observation of Reinhard Bendix—"You know, a little bit of theory goes a long way"—as quoted in the preface to Arthur L. Stinchcombe, *Constructing Social Theories* (New York: Harcourt, Brace & World, 1968), v.

12 A useful route into the question of inherent divisions in group identification in the United States is by way of the literature on "American exceptionalism." See, most centrally, Seymour Martin Lipset, *The First New Nation: The United States in Historical and Comparative Perspective,* rev. ed. (New York: W. W. Norton, 1979). See also Byron E. Shafer, ed., *Is America Different? A New Look at American Exceptionalism* (Oxford: Oxford University Press, 1991). The starting point for

thinking about political culture as a framework is often Gabriel A. Almond and Sidney Verba, *The Civic Culture: Political Attitudes and Democracy in Five Nations* (Princeton: Princeton University Press, 1963). A specifically American investigation is Donald J. Devine, *The Political Culture of the United States* (Boston: Little, Brown, 1972).

13 A classic framework for thinking about intermediation is David B. Truman, *The Governmental Process: Political Interests and Public Opinion* (New York: Alfred A. Knopf, 1951). On parties in the United States, see Leon Epstein, *Political Parties in the American Mold* (Madison: University of Wisconsin Press, 1986). On interest groups, see Kay L. Schlozman and John T. Tierney, *Organized Interests and American Democracy* (New York: Harper & Row, 1985). Most elite-mass analysis makes at least a ceremonial bow toward Vilfredo Pareto, *The Mind and Society,* ed. Alfred Livingstone, 4 vols. (London: Jonathan Cape, 1935). A seminal empirical work in this tradition is Herbert McClosky, Paul J. Hoffman, and Rosemary O'Hara, "Issue Conflict and Consensus among Party Leaders and Followers," *American Political Science Review* 54 (June 1960): 406–27.

14 One route into the comprehensive structure of American government is Paul Eidelberg, *The Philosophy of the American Constitution: A Reinterpretation of the Intentions of the Founding Fathers* (New York: Free Press, 1968). A text overview with an institutional focus is James Q. Wilson, *American Government: Institutions & Policies,* 3d ed. (Lexington, Mass.: D. C. Heath, 1986). On the potential influence of institutional rules for the *attaining* of public office, see Peter H. Argersinger, "The Value of the Vote: Political Representation in the Gilded Age," *Journal of American History* 76 (June 1989): 59–90; see also John H. Reynolds and Richard L. McCormick, "Outlawing 'Treachery': Split Tickets and Ballot Laws in New York and New Jersey, 1880–1910," *Journal of American History* 72 (March 1986): 835–58.

15 Two obvious, leading exceptions to this tendency are represented in this volume: Samuel T. McSeveney, with "No More 'Waiting for Godot': Comments on the Putative 'End of Realignment,'" chapter 4, and Walter Dean Burnham, with "Critical Realignment: Dead or Alive?" chapter 5. McSeveney also deals explicitly with the troubled relationship between the otherwise substantively linked disciplines of history and political science.

16 A single, comprehensive source which does attempt to convey this total sense is James M. McPherson, *Battle Cry of Freedom: The Civil War Era* (Oxford: Oxford University Press, 1988). The southern part of the political order which resulted, the part which endured for the next hundred years, is richly profiled in V. O. Key, Jr., *Southern Politics in State and Nation* (New York: Alfred A. Knopf, 1949), esp. part 3, "The One-Party System—Mechanisms and Procedures," 385–485. Central aspects of the creation of this order are covered in J. Morgan Kousser, *The Shaping of Southern Politics: Suffrage Restriction and the Establishment of the One-Party South, 1880–1910* (New Haven: Yale University Press, 1974).

17 The Great Depression and New Deal appear as comprehensive stimuli to this new political order in William E. Leuchtenburg, *Franklin D. Roosevelt and the New Deal, 1932–1940* (New York: Harper & Row, 1963). Further analysis on the

arrival, transformation, and decline of this order can be found in David Burner, *The Politics of Provincialism: The Democratic Party in Transition, 1918–1932*, and Richard Jensen, "The Last Party System: Decay of Consensus, 1932–1980," in *The Evolution of American Electoral Systems*, ed. Paul Kleppner (Westport, Conn.: Greenwood, 1981), 203–41. Central, of course, is James L. Sundquist, "The Realignment of the 1930s," in Sundquist, *Dynamics of the Party System*, 183–217.

18 The standard way of thinking about this process at the time, buttressed with data which themselves provide a description of the period, is Angus Campbell, "Surge and Decline: A Study of Electoral Change," in Campbell et al., *Elections and the Political Order*, 40–62, which had previously appeared in *Public Opinion Quarterly* 24 (Fall 1960): 397–418. As supplements, see especially, Philip E. Converse, "The Concept of a Normal Vote," and Campbell, "A Classification of the Presidential Elections," both in *Elections and the Political Order*, 9–39, 63–77.

19 These were certainly not missed by contemporary commentators, including Lewis Chester, Godfrey Hodgson, and Bruce Page, *An American Melodrama: The Presidential Campaign of 1968* (New York: Dell, 1969), and Theodore H. White, *The Making of the President 1968* (New York: Atheneum, 1969). Compare the latter with White, *The Making of the President 1964* (New York: Atheneum, 1965).

20 These developments were in fact at the center of such diverse works as John P. Robinson, "Public Reaction to Political Protest: Chicago, 1968," *Public Opinion Quarterly* 34 (Spring 1970): 1–9; Philip E. Converse et al., "Continuity and Change in American Politics: Parties and Issues in the 1968 Election," *American Political Science Review* 63 (December 1969): 1083–1105; and Bernard Crick, "The Strange Death of the American Theory of Consensus," *Political Quarterly* 43 (January–March 1972): 46–59, with its closing aphorism, "Ex unibus plures!"

21 The period leading into this change is covered—capsulized—in Eric F. Goldman, *The Crucial Decade—And After: America, 1945–1960* (New York: Vintage, 1960). Two attempts at making sense of an apparent, major cultural division as it emerged are Richard M. Scammon and Ben J. Wattenberg, *The Real Majority* (New York: Coward-McCann, 1970), and Samuel Lubell, *The Hidden Crisis in American Politics* (New York: W. W. Norton, 1970).

22 Most accounts focused on the Johnson presidency deal, necessarily, with this emerging division at some length; see Eric F. Goldman, *The Tragedy of Lyndon Johnson* (New York: Dell, 1968), and Doris Kearns, *Lyndon Johnson and the American Dream* (New York: Harper & Row, 1976). A larger framework is Seyom Brown, *Faces of Power: Constancy and Change in U.S. Foreign Policy from Truman to Johnson* (New York: Columbia University Press, 1968); an even larger perspective is William E. Leuchtenburg, *A Troubled Feast: American Society Since 1945* (Glenview, Ill.: Scott, Foresman, 1982).

23 Read retrospectively, with an eye toward such coincidence or divergence, each of the studies in note 20 (above) attests to this cross-cutting character. A more self-conscious effort to search for the pattern is Everett Carll Ladd, Jr., and Charles D. Hadley, "The Structure of Inter-Party Differences," in Ladd and Hadley, *Political Parties and Political Issues: Patterns in Differentation Since the New Deal* (Beverly Hills, Calif.: Sage, 1973), 13–40. Most explicit of all is James L. Sundquist, "Years

of Disruption: Cross-Cutting Issues Nationwide," in the revised edition of Sund-quist, *Dynamics of the Party System* (Washington, D.C.: Brookings Institution, 1983), 376–411.

24 The very beginnings of such institutional predispositions can be seen in Eidelberg, *Philosophy of the American Constitution.* Their formal evolution over time is con-tained in Louis Fisher, *Constitutional Conflicts between Congress and the President* (Princeton: Princeton University Press, 1985). A sense of the counterpart informal evolution is Wilfred E. Binkley, *President and Congress,* 3d ed. (New York: Vin-tage, 1962). See also Jeffrey L. Pressman, *House vs. Senate* (New Haven: Yale University Press, 1966), and Richard F. Fenno, Jr., *The United States Senate: A Bicameral Perspective* (Washington, D.C.: American Enterprise Institute, 1982).

25 An influential early approach to this is Aaron Wildavsky, "The Two Presidencies," *Trans-Action* 2 (December 1966), reprinted in Wildavsky, ed., *The Presidency* (Boston: Little, Brown, 1969), 230–43. See also Paula Stern, *Water's Edge: Domestic Politics and the Making of American Foreign Policy* (Westport, Conn.: Greenwood, 1979); Cecil V. Crabb, Jr., and Pat M. Holt, *Invitation to Struggle: Congress, the President, and Foreign Policy* (Washington, D.C.: CQ Press, 1980), and I. M. Destler, "Executive-Congressional Conflict in Foreign Policy: Explain-ing it, Coping with It," in *Congress Reconsidered,* ed. Lawrence C. Dodd and Bruce I. Oppenheimer, 3d ed. (Washington, D.C.: CQ Press, 1985), 343–63.

26 The full range of symbolic potential for presidents is examined in Samuel Kernell, *Going Public: New Strategies of Presidential Leadership* (Washington, D.C.: CQ Press, 1986), and Bert A. Rockman, *The Leadership Question: The Presidency and the American System* (New York: Praeger, 1984). A much more jaundiced overview is Theodore J. Lowi, *The Personal President: Power Invested, Promise Unfulfilled* (Ithaca, N.Y.: Cornell University Press, 1985). But perhaps the best implicit mea-sure of institutional priorities in this area is the shortage of work on cultural issues, and especially their symbolization, within Congress.

27 Different pieces of this particular slice of institutional predisposition are contained in Roger H. Davidson and Walter J. Oleszek, *Congress and Its Members* (Wash-ington, D.C.: CQ Press, 1981); Randall B. Ripley and Grace A. Franklin, *Con-gress, the Bureaucracy, and Public Policy,* rev. ed. (Homewood, Ill.: Dorsey, 1980); and Charles O. Jones, *The Trusteeship Presidency: Jimmy Carter and the United States Congress* (Baton Rouge: Louisiana State University Press, 1988). A thought-provoking introduction to these differences, though written for somewhat other purposes, is Nelson W. Polsby, *Political Innovation in America: The Politics of Policy Initiation* (New Haven: Yale University Press, 1984). Much of this distinc-tion was implicit in Richard F. Fenno, Jr., *The Power of the Purse: Appropriations Politics in Congress* (Boston: Little, Brown, 1966).

28 An overview of this propensity is Morris P. Fiorina, *Congress: Keystone of the Washington Establishment* (New Haven: Yale University Press, 1977). Its dynamics are covered in Bruce Cain, John Ferejohn, and Morris Fiorina, *The Personal Vote: Constituency Service and Electoral Independence* (Cambridge: Harvard University Press, 1987). From the service side, see John R. Johannes, *To Serve the People: Congress and Constituency Service* (Lincoln: University of Nebraska Press, 1984);

for the place of staff in this, see Michael J. Malbin, *Unelected Representatives: Congressional Staff and the Future of Representative Government* (New York: Basic, 1979).

29 The literature on American public opinion is so voluminous, especially if work with *some* opinion items is counted, as almost to defy citation. Apart from the books and articles scattered throughout these notes, recent surveys with particularly stimulating questions include *The Connecticut Mutual Life Report on American Values in the '80s: The Impact of Belief* (Hartford, Conn.: Connecticut Mutual Life Insurance Company, 1981); John E. Reilly, ed., *American Public Opinion and U.S. Foreign Policy 1987* (Chicago: Chicago Council on Foreign Relations, 1987); and *The People, the Press, & Politics* (Los Angeles: Times Mirror Company, 1987).

30 For example, James L. Sundquist, "Needed: A Political Theory for the New Era of Coalition Government in the United States," *Political Science Quarterly* 103 (Winter 1988–89): 613–35, and Seymour Martin Lipset, "The U.S. Elections: The Status Quo Re-affirmed," *International Journal of Public Opinion Research* 1 (Spring 1989): 25–44—two pieces which find many *other* points on which to differ.

31 Indeed, recast in the vocabulary of the contemporary electoral order, the 1976 presidential election was perhaps the one time after 1964 when the Republicans lost control of cultural values—the "social issue"—to the Democratic presidential candidate. They appeared to regain this issue-area in 1980, and, adding it to foreign policy, they regained the presidency as well.

32 The study of electoral campaigns for various offices is not usually organized in these terms. Nevertheless, elements of this particular focus can be seen in, for example, John H. Kessel, *Presidential Campaign Politics: Coalition Strategies and Citizen Response* (Homewood, Ill.: Dorsey, 1980); Marjorie Randon Hershey, *Running for Office: The Political Education of Campaigners* (Chatham, N.J.: Chatham House, 1984); and Richard F. Fenno, Jr., *Home Style: House Members in Their Districts* (Boston: Little, Brown, 1978). Much more pointed conclusions can be drawn by comparing Gerald M. Pomper, "The Presidential Election," with Ross K. Baker, "The Congressional Elections," both in *The Election of 1988: Reports and Interpretations,* ed. Pomper (Chatham, N.J.: Chatham House, 1989), 129–76.

33 "His First 100 Days," *National Journal,* November 12, 1988, pp. 2838–97, and "In Search of a Mandate," *Congressional Quarterly Weekly Report,* November 12, 1988, pp. 3239–3307.

34 For example, Robin Toner, "Dukakis Camp's Insularity Bemoaned," *New York Times,* October 28, 1988, p. 10; James A. Barnes, "What Went Wrong?" *National Journal,* October 29, 1988, pp. 2716–21; and Gerald Boyd, "How Bush Won: Picking the Right Fights and Getting the Right Opponent," *New York Times,* November 12, 1988, p. 8.

35 The question has been used in American National Election Studies since 1952. The original analysis is contained in Angus Campbell et al., "The Impact of Party Identification," in Campbell et al., *The American Voter,* 120–45. The extent of the change from this in the modern era, along with the main points of difference in interpreting this change, can be gained from Bruce E. Keith et al., "The Partisan Affinities of Independent 'Leaners,' " *British Journal of Political Science* 16 (April

1986): 155–85; and William G. Jacoby, "The Impact of Party Identification on Issue Attitudes," *American Journal of Political Science* 32 (August 1988): 643–61.

36 As a category, "Reagan Democrats" have less persistence, in principle, than "partisan independents." Nevertheless, their pursuit is integral to most work on the two Reagan elections, including Paul R. Abramson, John J. Aldrich, and David W. Rohde, *Change and Continuity in the 1980 Elections* (Washington, D.C.: CQ Press, 1982), and Abramson, Aldrich, and Rohde, *Change and Continuity in the 1984 Elections* (Washington, D.C.: CQ Press, 1986).

37 This comes through—along with additional analysis of the issue positions of these two groups—in "Pollsters on the Polls: Interviews with Vincent J. Breglio and Irwin 'Tubby' Harrison," *Public Opinion* 11 (January–February 1989): 4–7, 50–51, 58, 60. Also striking is the extent to which both sides saw their strategic dilemmas—and tactical maneuvers to address them—in essentially identical terms. All of this could be said about 1980 as well; see "Face Off: A Conversation with the Presidents' Pollsters—Patrick Caddell and Richard Wirthlin," *Public Opinion* 3 (December–January 1981): 2–12, 63–64.

38 See especially James A. Barnes, "The Comeback Trail," *National Journal,* August 13, 1988, pp. 2080–84. See also David S. Broder, "Dukakis' Big Gamble," *Washington Post,* July 24, 1988, p. C7; E. J. Dionne, Jr., "Crucial Bloc for Bush," *New York Times,* September 20, 1988, pp. A1, B7; and Dick Kirschten, "Reagan's Road Show," *National Journal,* October 1, 1988, pp. 2460–64.

39 "George Bush on the Pledge," *Washington Post National Weekly Edition,* September 5–11, 1988, p. 27; John Dillin, "Why the Flag, of All Things, Became an Election Issue," *Christian Science Monitor,* September 21, 1988, p. 5; Paul Taylor and David S. Broder, "Early Volley of Bush Ads Exceeded Expectations," *Washington Post,* October 28, 1988, p. A1. One who foresaw exactly this sort of possibility was Michael J. Robinson, "Can Values Save George Bush?" *Public Opinion* 11 (July–August 1988): 11–13, 59–60.

40 A book-length version of this argument, from the title onward, is Jack W. Germond and Jules Witcover, *Whose Broad Stripes and Bright Stars? The Trivial Pursuit of the Presidency* (New York: Warner, 1989). Two who did not fall into this trap were E. J. Dionne, Jr., "Issues, or Their Lack, Reflect Voter Concern, or Its Lack," *New York Times,* September 18, 1988, p. 18, and especially David S. Broder, "Symbols and Substance," *Washington Post National Weekly Edition,* October 24–30, 1988, p. 4. A less accepting affirmation of the same point is Kathleen Hall Jamieson, "Is the Truth Now Irrelevant in Presidential Campaigns?" *Washington Post National Weekly Edition,* November 7–13, 1988, p. 28.

41 Other issues could—and ultimately did—carry some of the same load, reinforcing the notion that simply "countering" the Pledge as an issue was largely beside the point. See E. J. Dionne, Jr., "Poll Shows Bush Sets Agenda for Principal Election Issues," *New York Times,* September 14, 1989, pp. A1, A29; Pat Towell, "Dukakis a Symbol of Democrats' Defense Dilemma," *Congressional Quarterly Weekly Report,* October 22, 1988, pp. 3045–49; and Louis Harris, "Bush Gaining Upper Hand on Who Can Best Handle Key Issues," *Harris Poll,* October 27, 1988, 3pp.

42 The *potential* for a shifting content to the terms "liberal" *and* "conservative" had

often been noted, as in James L. Sundquist and Richard M. Scammon, "The 1980 Election: Profile and Historical Perspective," in *A Tide of Discontent: The 1980 Elections and Their Meaning,* ed. Ellis Sandoz and Cecil V. Crabb, Jr. (Washington, D.C.: CQ Press, 1981), 19–44. Nevertheless, partisans of an older definition of "liberalism" remained very unhappy with the gradual (and still-ambiguous) shift; see the full-page ad from many such prominent, traditional liberals, "A Reaffirmation of Principle," *New York Times,* October 26, 1988, p. 21. Finally, a reconsideration of the problem afterward is Celinda Lake and Stanley B. Greenberg, "What's Left for Liberalism?" *Public Opinion* 11 (March–April 1989), pp. 4–7.

43 The first round of this maneuvering is captured in Maureen Dowd, "Dukakis and Bush Spar on Conservatism," *New York Times,* June 8, 1988, p. 14. For the general evolution of the issue, see especially Marjorie Randon Hershey, "The Campaign and the Media," in *The Election of 1988,* ed. Pomper, 73–102. See also Jean Bethke Elshtain, "Issues and Themes in the 1988 Campaign," in *The Elections of 1988,* ed. Michael Nelson (Washington, D.C.: CQ Press, 1989), 111–26.

44 I have tried my hand at an overview of these developments, for quite other purposes, in "Evolution and Reform: The Convention and a Changing American Politics," in my *Bifurcated Politics: Evolution and Reform in the National Party Convention* (Cambridge: Harvard University Press, 1989), 290–325.

45 The earlier arrival of an activist structure in the Republican party came into dramatic focus at the time of the 1964 presidential election; see Theodore H. White, *The Making of the President 1964,* and Robert D. Novak, *The Agony of the G.O.P. 1964* (New York: Macmillan, 1965). The arrival of the same structure within the Democratic party was called to public notice by the events of, and especially after, the 1968 presidential contest. See William J. Crotty, *Decision for the Democrats: Reforming the Party Structure* (Baltimore: Johns Hopkins University Press, 1978), and Austin Ranney, *Curing the Mischiefs of Faction: Party Reform in America* (Berkeley: University of California Press, 1975).

46 A richly developed framework for thinking about these developments is James Q. Wilson, *Political Organizations* (New York: Basic, 1973), esp. chapter 6, "Political Parties." A lament for the evolving situation is David E. Price, *Bringing Back the Parties* (Washington, D.C.: CQ Press, 1984). A more detached and wide-ranging look at the same situation within the Democratic party is Alan Ware, *The Breakdown of Democratic Party Organization, 1940–1980* (Oxford: Oxford University Press, 1985). A powerful summary statement about both parties is David S. Broder, *The Party's Over: The Failure of Politics in America* (New York: Harper & Row, 1971).

47 Two thorough overviews of the current American universe of interest groups, albeit organized quite differently, are Kay L. Schlozman and John T. Tierney, *Organized Interests and American Democracy,* and Allan J. Cigler and Burdett A. Loomis, eds., *Interest Group Politics,* 2d ed. (Washington, D.C.: CQ Press, 1986). See also Allan J. Cigler, "Interest Groups: A Subfield in Search of an Identity," in *Political Science: Looking to the Future* ed. William J. Crotty, (Evanston, Ill.: Northwestern University Press, 1990), and Frank R. Baumgartner and Jack L. Walker, "Survey Research and Membership in Voluntary Organizations," *American Journal of Political Science* 32 (November 1988): 908–28.

48 Both the coming of these newer groups to presidential nominating politics and a sense for their variety can be observed in Byron E. Shafer, "The Rise of the Organized Interests: An Alternative Base for Delegate Selection," in Shafer, *Bifurcated Politics,* 108–48. A more comprehensive listing can be found in Susan B. Martin and Karin Koek, eds., *Encyclopedia of Associations, Vol. 1: National Organizations of the U.S.,* 22d ed. (Detroit: Gale Research, 1987). Finally, lest these seem too purely a phenomenon of the modern world, it is worth consulting, for example, Peter H. Odegard, *Pressure Politics: The Story of the Anti-Saloon League* (New York: Columbia University Press, 1928).

49 This development is at the heart of the story in Byron E. Shafer, *Quiet Revolution: The Struggle for the Democratic Party and the Shaping of Post-Reform Politics* (New York: Russell Sage Foundation, 1983). It is just as central, and even more broadly sketched, in David S. Broder, *Changing of the Guard: Power and Leadership in America* (New York: Simon and Schuster, 1980).

50 I have tried to suggest some of the further dynamics of this process in Byron E. Shafer, "Recurring Struggles over Tangible Products: Traditional Activities in the Reformed Convention," in Shafer, *Bifurcated Politics,* 185–225.

51 National convention delegates have proved to be the population most amenable to systematic study along these lines. The serious inaugural effort was McClosky et al., "Issue Conflict and Consensus" (n. 13 above). Within the substantial literature that followed, a particularly suggestive and ambitious work, containing citations to much of the rest, is Warren E. Miller and M. Kent Jennings, *Parties in Transition: A Longitudinal Study of Party Elites and Party Supporters* (New York: Russell Sage Foundation, 1986). Investigations focused instead at the state level tend, quite naturally, to focus on individual states. Many of these are collected in Malcolm E. Jewell and David M. Olson, *American State Political Parties and Elections,* 3d ed. (Homewood, Ill.: Dorsey Press, 1987).

52 The argument probably began with Scammon and Wattenberg, *The Real Majority.* It is pursued in, among others, Everett C. Ladd, *Where Have All the Voters Gone? The Fracturing of America's Political Parties* (New York: W. W. Norton, 1977), and Nelson W. Polsby, *The Consequences of Party Reform* (Oxford: Oxford University Press, 1983).

53 Recognition of the essentially structural nature of the problem, along with its evolution—in a story where even the titles tell a tale—can be gleaned from: Phil Duncan, "House Vote: Major Midterm Setback for the Republicans," and Rob Gurwitt, "Redistricting Bitter Disappointment to GOP," *Congressional Quarterly Weekly Report,* November 6, 1982, pp. 2780–83, 2787–88; Phil Duncan, "Wealthy and Well-Organized GOP Panel Eyes 1984 Elections," *Congressional Quarterly Weekly Report,* July 2, 1983, pp. 1349–51; Diane Granat, "Deep Divisions Loom Behind House GOP's Apparent Unity," *Congressional Quarterly Weekly Report,* March 23, 1985, pp. 535–39; Janet Hook, "House GOP: Plight of a Permanent Minority," *Congressional Quarterly Weekly Report,* June 21, 1986, pp. 1393–96; Bob Berenson, "Once a Key Force in Elections, House Is Now Just a Sideshow," *Congressional Quarterly Weekly Report,* October 3, 1987, pp. 2379–82.

54 Indeed, the American public has begun, consistently, to report a preference for

split partisan control of government. Thus, in October of 1988, 54% of that public found it "better to have different political parties controlling Congress and the Presidency." Cited in "Opinion Outlook," *National Journal,* December 17, 1988, p. 3214.

55 Two other, different but intriguing attempts at doing this are Richard L. McCormick, "The Realignment Synthesis in American History," *Journal of Interdisciplinary History* 13 (Summer 1982): 85–105; and David G. Lawrence and Richard Fleisher, "Puzzles and Confusions: Political Realignment in the 1980s," *Political Science Quarterly* 102 (Spring 1987): 79–92.

56 Once again, Walter Dean Burnham and James L. Sundquist were instrumental in elaborating this part of the realignment framework. In *Critical Elections and the Mainsprings of American Politics,* Burnham introduced the element of periodicity as point number three in his opening theoretical formulation (p. 8), backed subsequently with an entire chapter on "The Periodicity of American Critical Realignments," 11–33. In *Dynamics of the American Party System,* Sundquist then provided numerous supportive explanations-propositions for the process, along with careful (and massive) historical detail to support them.

57 A rich array of international examinations under this banner is collected in the five chapters of part 4, "Patterns of Dealignment," in Dalton et al., *Electoral Change,* 240–396; see especially Paul Allen Beck, "The Dealignment Era in America," 240–66. An ingenious attempt at getting around the conceptual problems inherent in "dealignment" is Wattenberg, *Decline of American Political Parties.* A student of electoral orders would still find this treatment to be unduly rooted in social psychology rather than social structure, but it *is* self-consciously conceptual and internally consistent.

58 The metaphor is Burnham's (see n. 59 below). The argument is well made conceptually in Walter Dean Burnham, Jerome M. Clubb, and William H. Flanigan, "Partisan Realignment: A Systemic Perspective," in *The History of American Electoral Behavior,* ed. Joel H. Silbey, Allan G. Bogue, and William H. Flanigan (Princeton: Princeton University Press, 1978), 45–77. Concrete exemplification is added in Clubb, Flanigan, and Zingale, *Partisan Realignment.*

59 For investigations of the 1980 elections by two central figures in the realignment framework, see Walter Dean Burnham, "The 1980 Earthquake: Realignment, Reaction, or What?" in *The Hidden Election: Politics and Economics in the 1980 Presidential Campaign,* ed. Thomas Ferguson and Joel Rogers (New York: Pantheon, 1981), 98–140; and James L. Sundquist, "The Reagan Revolution—and After," in the revised edition of Sundquist, *Dynamics of the Party System,* 412–49. For the 1984 election, see Everett Carll Ladd, "On Mandates, Realignments, and the 1984 Presidential Election," *Political Science Quarterly* 100 (Spring 1985): 1–25; and William Schneider, "The November 6 Vote for President: What Did It Mean?" in *The American Elections of 1984,* ed. Austin Ranney (Washington, D.C.: American Enterprise Institute, 1985), 203–44.

60 Each of these examples has some place on the current landscape of American politics. On racial divisions, see Edward G. Carmines and James A. Stimson, *Issue Evolution: Race and the Transformation of American Politics* (Princeton: Princeton

University Press, 1989). On organized interests in apparent decay, rather than on the rise, see the suggestive but not conclusive Ronald Brownstein, "On Paper, Conservative PACs Were Tigers in 1984—But Look Again," *National Journal,* June 29, 1985, pp. 1504–9; and David L. Wilson, "The Winter of the Freeze Movement," *National Journal,* July 16, 1988, pp. 1874–75. Finally, on ballot reforms, see Jerrold G. Rusk, "The Effect of the Australian Ballot on Split Ticket Voting, 1876–1908," *American Political Science Review* 64 (December 1970): 1220–38. See also Walter Dean Burnham, "Communication," and Rusk, "Communication," *American Political Science Review* 65 (December 1971): 1149–57.

61 One contemporary collection is the President's Commission for a National Agenda for the Eighties, *The Electoral and Democratic Process in the Eighties* (Washington, D.C.: U.S. Government Printing Office, 1980). An evolutionary examination with an even wider focus is William J. Crotty, *Political Reform and the American Experiment* (New York: Thomas Y. Crowell, 1977). Finally, my own, more thematic interpretation is " 'Reform' in the American Experience," *Reform and Corruption* 5 (forthcoming).

62 All of these examples have received some discussion; only the rule setting a limit on diversion of campaign contributions for personal purposes has actually become law. On the national presidential primary, see Byron E. Shafer, *Bifurcated Politics,* 343–47. For speculation on the consequence of allowing congressmen to keep their campaign warchests if they retire by 1992, see Janet Hook, "New Milieu for Republicans Doesn't Bring More Power," *Congressional Quarterly Weekly Report,* March 3, 1990, pp. 641–42. On a proposed limitation of congressional tenure, see Janet Hook, "New Drive to Limit Tenure Revives an Old Proposal," *Congressional Quarterly Weekly Report,* February 24, 1990, pp. 567–69. And on reform of judicial caseloads, see Joan Biskupic, "Congress Cool to Proposals to Ease Load on Courts," *Congressional Quarterly Weekly Report,* April 7, 1990, pp. 1073–75.

63 The framework for thinking about such (always partially anomalous) developments traces at least to Robert K. Merton, "The Unanticipated Consequences of Purposive Social Action," *American Sociological Review* 1 (1936): 894–904. See also Raymond Boudon, *The Unanticipated Consequences of Social Action* (New York: St. Martin's, 1982).

64 Presidential election years make this brand of thinking/hoping more self-evident among campaign strategists and political analysts. See James A. Barnes and Dick Kirschten, "Exchanging Jabs," *National Journal,* May 7, 1988, pp. 1180–83; James A. Barnes, "Back to the Future," *National Journal,* July 16, 1988, pp. 1848–51; Ronald Brownstein, "Now the Dukakis Campaign Really Begins," *National Journal Convention Special,* July 23, 1988, pp. 1913, 1936–37; James A. Barnes, "The Comeback Trail," *National Journal,* August 13, 1988, pp. 2080–84; idem, "Reagan's Spirit Drives Bush's GOP," *National Journal Convention Special,* August 20, 1988, pp. 2135, 2147.

65 The first stirrings of this process may even be visible in "When Peace Breaks Out," *National Journal,* January 13, 1988, various articles at pp. 56–68. See also James A. Barnes, "Cashing a Dividend," *National Journal,* January 6, 1990, p. 41; and Wilson, "Winter of the Freeze Movement" (n. 60 above).

66 Some speculations along these lines are Bruce Stokes, "Running on Nationalism," *National Journal,* March 3, 1990, pp. 513–17; and Ronald D. Elving, "Targeting Japan: Trade Mood Turns Hawkish as Frustration Builds," *Congressional Quarterly Weekly Report,* March 31, 1990, pp. 965–71.

67 The decision itself was *Webster v. Reproductive Health Services,* no. 88-605, announced July 3, 1989. For potential electoral fall-out, see "Abortion Politics: High-Voltage Issue Haunts Candidates as Pressure Builds to Take a Stand," *Congressional Quarterly Weekly Report,* March 10, 1990, various articles at pp. 765–75.

68 For variations on the economic theme, see Paul Starobin, "The Next Recession," *National Journal,* January 13, 1990, pp. 69–73. For Republican thinking about party prospects, see "Casting for Power: House GOP Fishing for New Strategies After Decade of Seats That Got Away," *Congressional Quarterly Weekly Report,* March 3, 1990, various pieces at pp. 641–42 and 687–94.

69 For speculation on black-white political alignments, see James A. Barnes, "The End of Black Politics? Into the Mainstream," *National Journal,* February 3, 1990, pp. 262–66. An assessment suggesting that finance reform may *not* arrive as early as many have predicted is Chuck Alston, "A Wide Gulf Still Separates Parties on Election Laws," *Congressional Quarterly Weekly Report,* February 17, 1990, pp. 517–19. Finally, the late stages of one long round of ballot reform were marked in the state of Connecticut during the 1988 elections. For that year, Connecticut finally dropped the *party lever* from its voting machines, a reform long since accomplished in most other states. In partial response, while George Bush was carrying the state solidly at the top of the ticket, Lowell Weicker, Jr., incumbent Republican Senator, was losing very narrowly farther down—without the benefit of that lever. The missing lever thus joined numerous other potential explanations for Weicker's narrow defeat. In so doing, it served as a reminder of ballot (re)form, an influence now buried in the histories and voting procedures of so many other states.

70 Basic background on the issue is Raymond E. Wolfinger and Steven J. Rosenstone, *Who Votes?* (New Haven: Yale University Press, 1980). One expansive argument about the effect of reform is Frances Fox Piven and Richard A. Cloward, *Why Americans Don't Vote* (New York: Pantheon, 1988). The variety of possibilities, some mix of which seems likely to succeed as this is written, can be found in John Schachter, "Low Voter Turnout Prompts Flurry of Reform Bills," *Congressional Quarterly Weekly Report,* March 25, 1990, pp. 664–65.

71 Sir Lewis B. Namier, *The Structure of Politics at the Accession of George III,* rev. ed. (London: Macmillan, 1957).

4 *Samuel T. McSeveney*

No More "Waiting for Godot"
Comments on the Putative "End of Realignment"

The volume's three initial chapters fit well together. Each in its own way asserts the end of realignment and questions realignment theory. According to Everett Carll Ladd, not only has Political Science's "preoccupation with 'realignment' over the past 35 years . . . been mostly unfortunate," "it is unlikely that the generalizations which have grown out of the realignment perspective would loom very large or seem very persuasive" in any solidly based treatment of the party system over "the entire span of U.S. history."[1] (One comes away from the essay hoping that Estragon and Vladimir are not political scientists, although Beckett's characters, one bearing a name suspiciously like Valdimer, did begin their stage wait in 1953.)

Byron Shafer makes clear that "the periodization of American electoral politics *is* a useful intellectual device," but that "realignments, alas, do not provide it." He readily accepts Joel Silbey's setting out of "all the reasons why realignment can obscure more than it clarifies in addressing the successive epochs of American history."[2] Silbey himself appears to be the most cautious of the three essayists. He accepts that "the New Deal party system did not realign into a successor one"; that instead "dealignment" occurred; and that "under present . . . conditions," the "political system seems unable to have a realignment." Still, he goes on, it would be "premature" to bury "critical realignment theory," though to salvage "its essential logic" will require recognizing its "constraints" and fitting it "within a different conceptual frame-

85

work." Realignments are ". . . an important part of the dynamics of American politics. But they are only one of several parts. They are time bound . . .," providing "*the* dynamic mechanism of American electoral change . . . only from the late 1830s to the 1930s."[3]

Largely leaving to Walter Dean Burnham the discussion of realignment or the absence thereof during the 1960s and since, I shall deal with aspects of the three chapters as viewed from the perspective of a political historian. If each essayist challenges realignment as a way of understanding change in American politics, all reveal sensitivity to the importance of periodization and of explicating fundamental changes in the political order. In this respect, Silbey ambitiously paints the broadest canvas, for in moving "Beyond Realignment," he depicts two full centuries of "American Political Eras," a term that, consistent with his analysis, he employs in preference to "party systems."

Building on the work of other scholars and on his own earlier and current research, Silbey makes the case that our understanding of American political eras can best be advanced by appreciating the centrality of political parties to one—and only one—political era, which ran from the late 1830s into the mid-1890s, and by understanding the contrasts between that party era and the earlier preparty political era, c. 1789–c.1838, and the subsequent postparty era (c. 1893 to the present).[4] Scholars who conceive of past (and present) politics in terms of party systems will recognize Silbey's "party era" as composing the second, stable phase of the second party system along with the third party system.

Given the significance Silbey assigns to the emergence of the party era, one is struck that his chapter does more to make the case for the coming into existence of a party era than to explain why the late 1830s witnessed this portentous development. On this point, a recent essay by Michael F. Holt strikes me as of particular relevance. Holt contends that the period from the election of Martin Van Buren (Democrat) in 1836 through the election of William Henry Harrison (Whig) in 1840 involved

. . . far more than the hardening of voters' partisan identities and the mobilization of new voters. It was also marked by the elaboration of party machinery and by the emergence of impressively high levels of internal party cohesion and inter-party disagreement or conflict on roll-call votes in both Congress and the state legislatures. For the first time, moreover, the parties articulated coherent and contrasting platforms regarding proper governmental policy at the state and national levels. . . . [These], in turn, primarily reflected the parties' divergent responses to the panic of 1837 and the subsequent depression that gripped the country for most of the period betwen 1837 and 1844.[5]

The very scattering of state and congressional elections from March through November and the holding of annual, as well as biennial, elections enable Holt to take frequent readings of the body politic's temperature and to link rises and falls in Whig strength to fluctuations in the economy.

To Holt, "an intensification of voter interest, a widening of issue differences between rival parties, and an increase in ideological polarization," meant that 1836–40 "shared most of the characteristics historians and political scientists ascribe to periods of critical voter realignments, such as the 1850s, the 1890s, and the 1930s." The nation had experienced "a *realignment* that *should* have made the Whigs the majority party during the stable phase of the second party system." Yet the Whigs failed to consolidate their gains, failed to achieve "a *permanent realignment*" because once in national power, the party did not enact the program for economic recovery on which it had campaigned and won, this due largely to the vetoing of Whig congressional measures by President John Tyler ("his accidency"), who had succeeded to the presidency upon the death of William Henry Harrison soon after the latter's inauguration.[6]

In making his case, Holt draws on the argument of Jerome Clubb, William Flanigan, and Nancy Zingale, that electoral-political realignments owe more to the successful actions of the ascendant party once in power than to the earlier electoral shifts that gave it its opportunity to govern—a point well taken. I do not wish to quibble with Holt's fine essay, but I would characterize only lasting electoral shifts as "realigning." All "realignments," then, are lasting (if not "permanent"). I would regard the Whig upswing of 1836–40 as a realignment in the making, but one that was aborted. In effect, the failure of the Whigs to translate electoral gains into a political realignment by decisively changing federal economic policy resulted in the undoing of their initial electoral gains. That the depression that had provided the Whigs with their opportunity to govern dragged on until the fall of 1843 likely added to the governing Whigs' electoral difficulties during September 1841–September 1843, for they now bore responsibility for hard times as well as their own failure to enact their program.[7]

Given the characteristics of the party era as spelled out by Silbey, it follows that electoral-political realignment would have figured in that era as in no other. Indeed, Silbey fits commentary on the realignments of the 1850s and 1890s into his discussion of the broader party era with which he deals. I would make only one suggestion and add a single point regarding the earlier realignment. In understandably stressing political continuity on various levels, Silbey may inadvertently play down the effect of the disruptions involved in the realignment of the 1850s.[8] In addition, from the beginning of the study of realignments and the elaboration of the realignment model, scholars have had to confront the many differences between realignments in context and course. Any expanded discussion of the realignment of the 1850s should make clear its unique qualities.

Alone of the three classic realignments, that of the 1850s did not involve the triumph of the prerealignment second major party. As is well known, during 1852–60 that party, the Whigs, lost ground in the slave states and all but disappeared in the free. In 1852, the Whig national ticket polled 44.2% of the vote in the South and 43.6% in the North. In 1856, the Whigs-Americans received 43.4% and 13.6% in the respective regions; four years later, the Constitutional Unionists, Whigs campaigning under another banner, won 39.2% and 2.3%. (The 1860 percentages are somewhat deflated by Constitutional Unionist fusion with Douglas Democrats in Texas and with Douglas *and* Breckinridge Democrats in New York, New Jersey, and Rhode Island, but they still capture the central trend, 1852–60.) No later disintegration of one party system and emergence of another involved third and lesser party activity, including fusion campaigns, truly analogous to those that challenged both Whigs and Democrats during the early stages of the political upheaval. Nor did any subsequent realignment pose the question as to which party challenging the existing order would emerge as dominant. For a brief period, during 1854–55 and even in 1856, one might reasonably have wondered whether the national Americans or sectional Republicans would become the primary opposition to the national Democrats.

The capture of the presidency by a sectional party further distinguishes the realignment of the 1850s from the others. The limitations, as well as the remarkable aspects, of this Republican triumph merit attention. Although the Republicans had won a plurality of the popular vote and a majority of the electoral vote of the free states in their first campaign for the presidency, so strong did Democratic and Whig-American popular support remain in 1856 that Republican percentages fell short of 1852 Whig marks in five states and short of 1852 Whig-Free Soil marks in three more and the North as a whole. In 1860, of course, the Republican national ticket commanded *majority* support in all but three free states, so that no combination of opponents could have defeated it in those states and, with them, the electoral college.[9]

The Republicans' remarkable concentration of popular support—they received 98.6% of their votes in the free states *and 95.5% in states that they won*—enabled them to carry the presidency although they received only 2.1% of the total popular vote in the slave states and 39.8% nationwide. But the very concentration of popular support that maximized its impact in the electoral college placed the GOP at a disadvantage insofar as winning control of Congress was concerned. The Democratic party had, after all, been weakened in the North, not wiped out; the Republican party had virtually no support in the South, which accounted for 37.9% of House and 45.5% of Senate membership. It comes as no surprise, then, that the electoral realignment that swept Abraham Lincoln into the White House failed to carry his party into control of Congress. In this sense, the electoral realignment of the 1850s, unlike the realignments of the 1890s and 1930s, was incomplete.

The secession of slave states, entailing the resignation of their congressional delegations, *a direct consequence of Lincoln's election,* did give the Republicans control of the legislative branch of government, facilitating their subsequent capture of the federal judiciary as well, as justices died or resigned. The outbreak of the Civil War furthered the political realignment because the intensifying conflict necessitated executive and legislative actions of immediate and lasting importance to the nation. Wartime federal measures—emancipation and the enlistment of black troops; conscription; the establishment of national banks empowered to issue currency; the actual issuance of greenbacks; the imposition of a variety of taxes (including one on incomes); unprecedented federal spending and the incurring of budgetary deficits—went far beyond what one might have anticipated in peacetime in consequence of electoral realignment alone.[10]

Republican governmental activism carried over into the Reconstruction era, of course. During the wartime and postwar periods, clear-cut Republican control of Congress depended first on the absence of southern delegations (during the secession crisis and war), then on their exclusion (during the initial phase of Reconstruction), and finally on the transformation of southern politics achieved through the enfranchisement of freedmen and the temporary, partial disfranchisement of ex-Confederates, which gave rise to southern Republicanism (during the second phase of Reconstruction). With the collapse of Republican Reconstruction regimes in the South and the Democrats' recovery of strength in the North during 1873–76, the Republican phase of the third party system gave way to one of stalemate, which carried into the 1890s.[11]

The late nineteenth and early twentieth centuries figure significantly in Silbey's scheme of things because they witnessed both an electoral-political realignment, which ushered in a fourth party system, *and,* of more lasting significance, the end of the party era that had endured for over one-half century. I think that the interrelationships between the realignment and the demise of the party era will require close scrutiny—and likely partial separation. The forces to which the party era succumbed were varied; they operated before, during, and after the realignment of the 1890s, to which some were related and others were not; their influence on the political order of the twentieth century appears increasingly important in recent scholarship on the subject.

Realignment may be necessary to an understanding of this broad political transformation; it does not suffice to explain the "Very Large Sea Change" that Silbey discusses.[12] We are dealing, after all, not only with attacks on, and reduced roles for, political parties, plus reduced voter turnout and partisanship, but with the increased importance of interest groups and governmental regulation of aspects of the economy and society—of a political order very different from the party-based, voter-oriented system of the previous era.

A full explication of the postparty political order is important to Silbey's discussion of the New Deal realignment of the 1930s because this most recent (and final?) realignment occurred during a political era very different from the party era in which the political realignments of the 1850s and 1890s took place. Silbey's suggestion that residual political involvement within the electorate helped make the realignment possible indicates a potentially fruitful line of inquiry. Former Socialists, Progressives (class of '24, perhaps some from 1912), 1916 Wilson voters, and Farmer-Laborites may have been brought back into the electorate. Whether one stresses "mobilization" or "conversion" to explain the building of a majority New Deal Democratic coalition, persons who had voted irregularly if at all before the 1930s and young voters who came of age during the Great Depression and New Deal appear to have contributed significantly to increased turnout and turnout rates and to the now-dominant Democratic coalition.[13]

The New Deal electoral coalition was mobilized in part by a variety of organizations outside of the Democratic party, which, given its weakness in many localities during the Republican-dominated, postparty 1920s, would have been hard pressed to undertake this task alone. The Farmer-Labor, American Labor, and Liberal parties; the expanding bureaucracy of the welfare state; and a mass labor movement all played roles in the creation of a coalition that influenced government policy, as well as elections, for a generation beyond the New Deal itself.

Organized labor, especially, merits attention not only because it influenced politics in various ways but because it reveals the political importance of organizations outside of the political parties themselves during the postparty era and sheds light on the complexity of developments during the New Deal realignment. A range of circumstances contributed to the unionization of the nation's basic industries and the emergence of the Congress of Industrial Organizations (CIO) as a force in American politics.[14] Certainly the Depression—which bankrupted welfare capitalism, increased labor militancy, and, under particular circumstances, weakened management's resistance to unionization—played a role, as did the electoral triumphs of the Democrats in 1932 and 1934, which were followed, in 1933 and 1935, by enactment of the National Industrial Recovery Act and then the Wagner Labor Relations Act. Given that the Roosevelt administration did not press for the legislation of 1935, the swelling and shift leftward of the Democrats' congressional majority in the 1934 midterm elections assumed added significance in its enactment.

The emerging CIO contributed to Roosevelt's (and the Democrats') overwhelming victory in 1936, but soon thereafter, the militancy of organized labor and its enhanced role in the New Deal also contributed to divisions within the Democratic party, alienating southern congressmen in particular. By 1938–39, the innovative period of the New Deal appeared all but at an end. Roosevelt's 1937 plan to transform the Supreme Court had been thwarted after a fight that divided both Democrats and New Deal supporters; southern Democratic and Republican congressmen had begun to form a *de facto* coalition, at least with regard to labor legislation; the Republicans had staged a partial comeback in the midterm elections of 1938.[15]

Even as the New Deal tide ebbed among the public and within Congress, however, organized labor gained crucial ground when General Motors and United States Steel recognized CIO unions *even before* the *unreconstructed* Supreme Court upheld the constitutionality of the Wagner Labor Relations Act during 1937. The sharp economic downturn of 1937–38 hurt organized labor, as well as the Democrats, but with preparations for war (1940–41) and war itself (1941–45) went growing prosperity, and with it remarkable gains by industrial unions, supported by generally favorable rulings by the National Labor Relations Board and decisions by the federal courts. It may also be that the international crisis and American entry into the Second World War, as well as the increasingly widespread prosperity that accompanied them, contributed to Roosevelt's and the Democrats' victories during 1940–44, paving the way for continued Democratic success during the postwar, post-FDR, era. Developments during 1937–45, understandably viewed as the waning years of the New Deal, may nevertheless have been essential to the lasting success of the New Deal coalition and organized labor.[16]

Everett Carll Ladd's agenda for providing "a robust [historical] description" of "the [American] party system and its current evolution" strikes me as sound, especially in its recognition that the "enduring attributes" of that system are consequences of "persisting features of American society and its policy." Within "the boundaries set by these ideological and institutional constraints" successive partisan eras have differed from one another because successive social eras have likewise differed.[17] (One wonders, however, whether Ladd would agree with Silbey's emphasis on the essential continuity of a political era extending from the 1830s into the 1890s, a long span over which American society surely changed in fundamental ways under the impact of industrialization, urbanization, and immigration.)

I further accept Ladd's sketch of "major social change[s]" contributing to the emergence of the contemporary party system, a system "really not envisioned by the realignment perspective." Though "postindustrialism" figures prominently in Ladd's discussion of the social changes contributing to the emergence of the contemporary party system, it fortunately does not do so to the exclusion of factors not easily subsumed by the term.[18]

My primary concerns with Ladd's chapter relate to aspects of his discussion of V. O. Key "sneezing and political science catching a cold." Key did, of course, refer to two great "catastrophe[s]" (the American Civil War and the Great Depression) producing electoral realignments, this in an infrequently cited article on "The Future of the Democratic Party," published in 1952. I acknowledge that the New Deal's "burst of partisan change was alive in analysts' minds" at the time. Together, according to Ladd, Key's work and the recency of the New Deal—"the vividness of the specific instance"—contributed to political science's "preoccupation with realignment" when, "with more perspective, we can now see that the massive shifts in the party system and voting alignments in the 1930s were in fact *sui generis*. In many essential structural regards, nothing like the New Deal had ever occurred before—nor has it since."[19]

Unfortunately, Key did not return to the "catastrophe" of the American Civil War, or deal with the electoral realignment of the 1850s for that matter, in his subsequent analyses of election types. Indeed, his next article on the subject, "A Theory of Critical Elections," published *only three years* after "The Future of the Democratic Party," dealt with neither the 1850s–60s nor the 1930s, but with the presidental elections of 1896 and 1928, elections that, accepting at face value Key's sketchy discussion in his initial article, should not have qualified for study as realigning.[20] My reading of the literature in political science and history suggests to me that scholars who followed Key's leads were influenced by "Critical Elections," rather than "Future of the Democratic Party," because the later piece was more fully developed and was strongly buttressed by elementary analyses of election data.

In stressing—perhaps exaggerating—the importance of "The Future of the Democratic Party," Ladd credits Key with having introduced there the concept of "secular realignment." Key did deal with the growth of population groups that were to be politically activated by the Democrats during 1928–40, but his discussion actually focused on realignment by "mobilization," not "secular realignment." Key specifically contended that the Democrats won by capturing the loyalty of "persons who had not been enough concerned with public affairs to vote and of persons coming to voting age" and that the party likely "converted . . . few old-line Republicans." Key's later article on "secular realignment" explicated the significance of the infusion of new population elements into the electorate, of heightened political consciousness and increased political participation among such groups, and of generational replacement, essential elements in electoral realignment by "mobilization" rather than "conversion."[21]

While surely Key's seminal piece in the series of articles and essay that he published during the 1950s, "A Theory of Critical Elections" is not without its shortcomings. In it, though not in his classic books, Key treated changes in voting strength and electoral coalitions to the exclusion of other considerations. His reference to "more or less profound readjustments . . . in the relations of power within the community" to the contrary notwithstanding, Key's article dealt solely with voting shifts in "critical elections." Key did not even discuss the transfer of *party* control in the nation or in the states under analysis, let alone the policy and other political consequences of such a transfer. In fact, national party power did change hands in 1896, though not in 1928; the New England states under scrutiny shifted from one party column to the other in only three of eight instances (not that the outcome of presidential elections determines party control within states).[22]

On the positive side, Key's early analysis of the elections of 1896 and 1928 spurred historians' interest in "critical elections" and realignments, along with differences, as well as similarities, among them. After all, Key's "Theory of Critical Elections" did not confine itself to a recent political transformation still alive in the minds of scholars and the public. It not only extended the idea of critical elections into the late nineteenth century, it provided a comparative analysis of two such elections. In this sense, Key's work was less present-minded and richer in its implications than that of his contemporary, Samuel Lubell, whose *The Future of American Politics* also attracted scholarly attention.

If subsequent studies have increasingly questioned the criticality of the 1928 election, that is, its importance in the realignment sequence that resulted in an extended period of Democratic dominance in national elections and politics, that research has been largely stimulated by Key's original "Theory." Although the origins of the New Deal coalition have been traced to various sources and elections or series of elections, the election of 1928, which involved conflicts over religion and other cultural issues, is no longer viewed as having foreshadowed across the nation the controversies over public policy of the Great Depression and New Deal, nor the coalitions that formed then. In their contrasting responses to that depression, the Democratic and Republican parties affected their fortunes for years to come.[23]

Key's earlier "critical" election, that of 1896, has also undergone close examination over the years. To Key, the election involved large across-the-board shifts toward the Republicans in New England, which (along with the Middle Atlantic region) lived up to William Jennings Bryan's characterization of the Northeast as "The Enemy's Country." Key's view was developed in subsequent studies, especially the work of Walter Dean Burnham, who depicted the contest of 1896 as pitting the Metropole (the Northeast and Midwest) against the colonial South and West, especially the latter region, which experienced strong shifts toward Bryan.

Internal studies of the Northeast, my own included, did not differ markedly from Key's reading of the vote in New England. Paul Kleppner's original analysis of the Midwest viewed the election there as different from that in the Northeast: in a contest that shook traditional party loyalties, normally Democratic liturgical groups gave Bryan reduced support and normally Republican pietistic groups gave him increased support—two-way shifts that altered, though they did not transform, the competing parties' social bases. Kleppner's

most recent treatment of the election of 1896, which treats the Metropole as a
unit for analysis, modifies his earlier reading of the canvass.

Although not all questions regarding the election have been asked, let alone
answered, and ambiguities remain, it now appears that in the Metropole neither
major party gained significant support from the other's 1894 supporters. Democratic recruits from the Populists were outnumbered by Republican gains
among 1894 abstainers and new voters. (Disproportionate Democratic gains in
1900 among 1896 abstainers may also have meant a disproportionate Democratic loss among abstainers in 1896.) Some of the more dramatic shifts of
1896 were short-lived, but the Democrats came out of the realignment weaker
than they had entered it. "[T]he Democratic coalition shrank in size, and the
Republican electorate expanded, especially in the heavily populated Metropole, the shape (or social composition) of each party's support base changed
only marginally."[24] This summation does not differ widely from Key's necessarily brief characterization of the election of 1896.

Byron Shafer offers us more than a "Notion" in his richly textured analysis
of the contemporary electoral order, an order, he assures us, that did not follow
from and could not have been predicted by "the reality or the concept of realignment," or even dealignment. He describes the Democratic coalition (leaders, interest groups, and voters) that normally prevailed into the 1960s along
with the forces that disrupted the coalition (already marked by contradictions)
during that turbulent decade, especially its second half. The changing nature of
single-issue groups, the increasing importance of ideological activists *within*
(as well as outside of) party hierarchies, and the "demise of old-fashioned
party organizations," these and more are illuminated to reveal an electoral
order characterized by unprecedentedly "stable *split* partisan control of the
major institutions of national government."[25]

I wish first to raise one question, in the form of a single caveat. As Shafer
puts it at one point: "the presidency is about foreign policy and cultural values.
The House of Representatives is about social welfare and service provision."
Given that there is "a conservative majority in the nation" on issues of foreign
policy and cultural values and "a liberal majority . . . on issues of social welfare and service provision," it follows that the presidency is strongly
Republican and the House strongly Democratic. I would modify Shafer's formulation: Although Democrats liberal on economic, welfare, and social issues
thrive in the House environment, so do conservative Democrats, who retain
their seats, even as their party's liberal national tickets lose their districts,
thereby contributing to Democratic House majorities.[26]

The centrality of the 1965–72 period to the breakup of the Democratic presidential coalition and of conflicts over "foreign policy and cultural values" to
that debacle suggest the need for further study of a critical period which,
though it does not fit our realignment model, has shaped presidential politics

for two decades. One is struck, too, by elements of realignment present in that period, especially the deep divisions of the hitherto dominant Democrats, manifested in their bitterly divided national convention of 1968, in the capture of the party's nomination by George McGovern in 1972 and its effect on traditional Democratic constituencies, and in the third-party candidacy of George Wallace, which cost the Democrats disaffected supporters who were not (yet) voting Republican.

Mixed readings of the 1965–72 period and its aftermath obviously suggest the difficulties of squaring developments during the 1960–80s, so very different politically and socially from the nineteenth century or even from the more recent New Deal and post–New Deal periods, with a realignment model formed on the basis of studies of those earlier epochs. Less obviously, they serve to remind us (as I have argued at points) that from the beginning, generalizations regarding electoral-political realignment have run the risk of obscuring very real differences among the realignments themselves.

I am left vaguely uncomfortable about one aspect of Ladd's and Shafer's essays. Each seems not only to argue that realignment cannot be expected to transform the electoral order, but to imply that for various reasons, this order is likely unchangeable. Thus Ladd: "By no means realignment, these developments surely reflected whopping, consequential, *largely irreversible* change." And Shafer: ". . . this order is sufficiently institutionalized . . . that a single election with the desired characteristics is not likely to work permanent changes on its basic contours." (Silbey is more cautious. Although he rules out the likelihood of realignment under present circumstances, he shies away from discussion of the immutability of the current order.)[27]

I do not seek to raise realignment from the dead. Our panelists came to bury realignment, not to praise it. That Everett Ladd and Byron Shafer have contributed greatly to our understanding of the contemporary political order more than earns them our gratitude. Moreover, I certainly do not claim to possess insight into how, when, and under what circumstances our electoral order might give way to another. But Joel Silbey has drawn our attention to two profound systemic changes, both surely unforeseen—and who at the end of 1928 could have predicted the coming of a Democratic era, or at the end of 1964 the breakup of the Democratic presidential coalition? Put another way, if, as the three initial essays argue, critical realignment plays only a limited role in political change, then the inability of the present order to realign does not necessarily mean that the order cannot change. In short, in American politics, as in other affairs, we should not succumb to current talk of "the end of history as such."

Notes

1 Everett Carll Ladd, "Like Waiting for Godot: The Uselessness of *Realignment* for Understanding Change in Contemporary American Politics" (Paper presented at the annual meeting of the American Political Science Association, 1989, revised as chapter 2 of this volume), 25, 29.
2 Byron E. Shafer, "The Notion of an Electoral Order: The Structure of Electoral Politics at the Accession of George Bush" (Paper presented at the annual meeting of the American Political Science Association, 1989, revised as chapter 3 of this volume), 37.
3 Joel H. Silbey, "Beyond Realignment and Realignment Theory: American Political Eras, 1789–1989" (Paper presented at the annual meeting of the American Political Science Association, 1989, revised as chapter 1 of this volume), 4, 5 (emphasis mine).

    For a fine recent overview of studies relevant to the essays and commentaries, see Peter H. Argersinger and John W. Jeffries, "American Electoral History: Party Systems and Voting Behavior," in *Research in Micropolitics: Voting Behavior,* ed. Samuel Long, 2 vols. (Greenwich, Conn.: Jai Press, 1986), 1:33. Critiques of the realignment–party systems model are discussed on pp. 4–6.
4 Richard L. McCormick, "The Party Period and Public Policy: An Exploratory Hypothesis," *Journal of American History* 66 (September 1979): 279–98, anticipates aspects of Silbey's analysis.
5 Silbey, this volume, 9–13; Michael F. Holt, "The Election of 1840, Voter Mobilization, and the Emergence of the Second American Party System," in *A Master's Due: Essays in Honor of David Herbert Donald,* ed. William J. Cooper, Jr., Michael F. Holt, and John McCardell (Baton Rouge: Louisiana State University Press, 1985), 16–57 (quotation is from p. 17).
6 Holt, "The Election of 1840," 18, 56 (for quoted passages; emphasis mine). The disappointment of Whig recruits revealed itself in abstentions in off-year elections.
7 Ibid., 56–58; Jerome M. Clubb, William H. Flanigan, and Nancy Zingale. *Partisan Realignment: Voters, Parties, and Government in American History* (Beverly Hills, Calif.: Sage, 1980), 11–45, cited by Holt (p. 56, n. 37).

    Holt deals at far greater length with the Whigs' rise than with their decline. He refers once to the depression context of Whig voters' disillusionment, stating that "the congressional and gubernatorial results set forth in Table 1, for example, reveal not only a dramatic decline in Whig fortunes in 1842 and 1843, at least while the depression lasted . . ." (56). Holt's Table 1 (37) points to a marked, though incomplete, recovery of congressional seats and governorships during the subsequent economic recovery (October 1843–December 1844). That the Whigs recovered along with the economy, without having enacted their economic program, suggests the possibility that hard times and the end thereof merit closer attention in explaining fluctuations in Whig fortunes.
8 Silbey, this volume, 13: "That episode [the electoral realignment of the 1850s] had a powerful impact on American politics, leading to the demise of the Whig party, the emergence of the Republican party, and a shift in national political power.

But, its effect on the institutions and behavior of the political world was much more limited."

9 In 1856, Republican percentages did not match 1852 Whig percentages in New Jersey, Pennsylvania, Indiana, Illinois, and California, nor Whig-Free Soil percentages in New York, Ohio, and Iowa.

In 1860, the Republicans won with pluralities of the popular vote in California and Oregon; they trailed Douglas, but outpolled Breckinridge and Bell, to win four of seven electoral votes in New Jersey, where their opponents had fused electoral slates; they received majorities of the popular vote in all other northern states.

William E. Gienapp, *The Origins of the Republican Party, 1852–1856* (New York: Oxford University Press, 1987), combines diligent research in primary sources, a careful reading of secondary works, and the deft analysis of election and demographic data from nine northern states to provide us with the single most important study of the breakup of the second party system in the North and the emergence of the Republican party through the presidential election of 1856. Gienapp, "Who Voted for Lincoln?" in *Abraham Lincoln and the American Political Tradition,* ed. John L. Thomas (Amherst: University of Massachusetts Press, 1986), chap. 4, deals more briefly with the piecing together of the coalition that put the Republicans over the top in 1860. Gienapp sees the essential recruits coming disproportionately from the ranks of non-Catholic immigrants, young native-born Protestants, and Know-Nothings.

Walter Dean Burnham, *Critical Elections and the Mainsprings of American Politics* (New York: W. W. Norton, 1970), 6–7, generalizes that during critical alignments or elections "abnormally high intensity . . . typically spills over into the party nominating and platform-writing machinery," producing "major shifts in convention behavior from the integrative 'norm' " and "transformations in the internal loci of power in the major party most heavily affected by the pressures of realignment."

Certainly the Democratic national convention of 1860, meeting first in Charleston and then in Baltimore, lived up to Burnham's expectations. (It should be understood that one crucial disjuncture in the Democracy pitted a party-in-Congress, dominated by slave-state delegations, generally supported by the national administration, against a party-in-national convention, dominated by free-state delegations, which blocked the southerners' proposed platform plank endorsing federal protection of slavery in the territories.)

The Democratic national convention of 1896 also fit Burnham's description, but no national convention during the 1930s did—although the triumphant Democrats did repeal their venerable two-thirds rule at their celebratory convention of 1936, and there might be some significance attached to the Republicans' nomination of Wendell Willkie four years later. Once again, a generalization regarding the characteristics of realignment requires qualification.

10 Paul Kleppner, *Continuity and Change in Electoral Politics, 1893–1928* (Westport, Conn.: Greenwood Press, 1987), 245–246, 248 (n. 15), takes Clubb, Flanigan, and Zingale, *Partisan Realignment,* 263, to task for minimizing the importance of the electoral shifts of 1854–60 and emphasizing secession and its aftermath in the Republicans' achievement of the "unified control of government that results in political realignment." Kleppner is assuredly correct that "the 1860 returns were

themselves a proximate cause of secession" (248, n. 15); the targeted presentation in *Partisan Realignment* is, moreover, somewhat loose at points. Still, Clubb, Flanigan, and Zingale are correct in their basic point that voting shifts *per se* did not give the Republicans effective control of Congress.

11 Paul Kleppner. *The Third Electoral System, 1853–1892: Parties, Voters, and Polit-ical Cultures* (Chapel Hill: University of North Carolina Press, 1979), 26–32, 74–142, provides an important overview of the period from 1860 through 1876. As he makes clear, the Democratic upswing of 1873–76 was "reinstating," rather than "realigning"; it ushered in an "equilibrium" phase of the third electoral sys-tem, rather than a new electoral system. On government and Republican activism during and after the Civil War, see Morton Keller, *Affairs of State: Public Life in Late Nineteenth Century America* (Cambridge: Harvard University Press, 1977), chaps. 1–7.

12 Silbey, this volume, 13–15. To the important works cited by Silbey in this section of his chapter, I would add John F. Reynolds, *Testing Democracy: Electoral Behavior and Progressive Reform in New Jersey, 1880–1920* (Chapel Hill: University of North Carolina Press, 1988), which offers a subtle analysis of electoral politics and voting behavior in the Garden State.

13 See, e.g., Kristi Andersen, *The Creation of a Democratic Majority, 1928–1936* (Chicago: University of Chicago Press, 1979); and Walter Dean Burnham, "The Appearance and Disappearance of the American Voter," and "Shifting Patterns of Congressional Voting Participation," both in Burnham, ed., *The Current Crisis in American Politics* (New York: Oxford University Press, 1982), 121–65, 166–203.

14 My coverage of the labor movement during the New Deal realignment in this and the following paragraphs draws heavily on David Brody, *Workers in Industrial Amer-ica: Essays on the Twentieth-Century Struggle* (New York: Oxford University Press, 1980), 82–119, 138–46. The election of Democratic governors sympathetic to orga-nized labor in the hitherto Republican, key industrial states of Pennsylvania and Michigan, which revealed Democratic strength at the subnational level, also con-tributed to union successes therein *and elsewhere.*

15 Dewey W. Grantham, *The Life & Death of the Solid South: A Political History* (Lex-ington: University Press of Kentucky, 1988), chap. 5, treats "The South and the New Deal." Barbara Deckard Sinclair, "From Party Voting to Regional Fragmen-tation: The House of Representatives, 1933–1956," *American Politics Quarterly* 6 (April 1978): 130–33, indicates that the split between northern and southern Demo-crats first revealed itself in the Seventy-fifth Congress (1937–38) on issues relating to labor. Significantly, Democratic governors George H. Earle (Pennsylvania) and Frank Murphy (Michigan), both sympathetic to labor, were defeated for reelection in 1938. Each had served one term, Earle for four years, Murphy for two.

16 Early studies dealing with the relationships between the popularly elected admin-istrations and congresses, which take power during electoral-political realignments, and the Supreme Court, which presumably reflects the views held by earlier admin-istrations, senates, and political coalitions, only scratched the surface of a complex subject. To a certain extent, they were handicapped by questionable identifications of realignments and of the chronological limits of particular realignments and by an

inadequate appreciation of differences among successive realignments. See, e.g., Richard Funston, "The Supreme Court and Critical Elections," *American Political Science Review* 69 (September 1975): 795–811. For sound criticisms of Funston's article, and replies thereto, see Letters to the Editor, *American Political Science Review* 70 (September 1976): 930–32 (Paul Allen Beck), 932 (Richard Funston); *American Political Science Review* 70 (December 1976): 1215–18 (Bradley S. Canon and S. Sidney Ulmer), 1218–21 (Richard S. Funston).

Allan J. Lichtman, "Critical Election Theory and the Reality of American Presidential Politics, 1916–40," *American Historical Review* 82 (April 1976): 317–51, makes the point (p. 343) that pre-1940 public opinion polls revealed voter opposition to the New Deal and a third term for President Franklin Roosevelt, while a 1940 campaign poll indicated that but for the war in Europe, a majority of respondents would have opposed Roosevelt's election. Respondents did not face an actual choice in polling booths, of course, but their responses should not be discounted.

17 Ladd, this volume, 29.

18 Ibid., 30–34.

19 Ibid., 27. (Ladd's quoted words appear on p. 6.) Also V. O. Key, Jr., "The Future of the Democratic Party," *Virginia Quarterly Review* 28 (Spring 1952): 161–75. I rather suspect that Samuel Lubell, *The Future of American Politics* (New York: Harper & Row, 1951), also stimulated thinking with regard to electoral realignment, especially his discussion of immigrants and southern migrants and their mobilization by the Democrats during 1928–40. See, esp., chap. 3.

20 Indeed, in "The Future of the Democratic Party," 163, 165–66, Key stated only that "in the crucial election of 1896," the Republican coalition forged in the Civil War beat back the Bryanite challenge, aided by "the promise of the full dinner pail" to industrial workers. Key then referred briefly to the election of 1928 as initiating the activation of nonvoters as Democrats, i.e., "substantial numbers of Catholics, notably in Massachusetts and Rhode Island." He then stressed the róle of the New Deal in this regard. See, too, V. O. Key, Jr., "A Theory of Critical Elections," *Journal of Politics* 17 (February 1955): 3–18.

21 Compare Ladd, this volume, 26, with Key, "Future of the Democratic Party," 165–66 (quotation, 165). Also see V. O. Key, Jr., "Secular Realignment and the Party System," *Journal of Politics* 21 (May 1959): 198–210. Kristi Andersen has acknowledged her debt to Key's article on "secular realignment," which stimulated her thinking with regard to realignment by means of "electoral replacement" (or "mobilization"). One should not overlook V. O. Key, Jr., and Frank Munger, "Social Determinism and Electoral Decision: The Case of Indiana," in *American Voting Behavior,* ed. Eugene Burdick and Arthur J. Brodbeck (Glencoe, Ill.: Free Press, 1959), 281–99, 456–59.

22 Key, "A Theory of Critical Elections," 3–4. The first generation of scholars to follow Key's lead largely concerned itself with *electoral* realignments, concentrating on the formation of "new and durable [electoral] groupings" to the exclusion of other developments crucial to an understanding of *political* realignments in a broader sense, i.e., shifts in political power and policies and relationships between

such shifts and those in the electorate. Kleppner, *Continuity and Change,* chap. 1, offers a broad assessment of Key's work on realignment.

23 For important works and a critical analysis thereof, see Argersinger and Jeffries, "American Electoral History," 18–23.

24 Argersinger and Jeffries, "American Electoral History," 13–15. Compare Paul Kleppner, *The Cross of Culture: A Social Analysis of Midwestern Politics, 1850–1900* (New York: Free Press, 1970), chaps. 5–8, with Kleppner, *Continuity and Change,* chaps. 2–4 (quotation, 89). In *The Cross of Culture,* Kleppner incorrectly read Key to have specified that "the alignment of social groups before and after the fluctuation" had to differ (271). Key's definition did not necessarily involve any such shift in alignments, as his analysis of the critical election of 1896 made clear.

   In addition to works cited by Argersinger and Jeffries, see Reynolds, *Testing Democracy,* chap. 4; Dale Baum, "The Massachusetts Voter: Party Loyalty in the Gilded Age, 1872–1896," in *Massachusetts in the Golden Age: Selected Essays,* ed. Jack Tager and John W. Ifkovic (Amherst: University of Massachusetts Press, 1985), 37–66, esp. 56–60, 66; and James Wright, *The Progressive Years: Republican Reformers in New Hampshire, 1906–1916* (Hanover, N.H.: University Press of New England, 1987), chap. 2.

25 Shafer, this volume, 60 (emphasis his). Longterm Democratic dominance of the House of Representatives strikes me as worthy of a full-length study, for it antedates the post-1960s political order analyzed by Shafer. Indeed, it revealed itself impressively during the 1950s, an earlier period during which the Republicans dominated the presidency. Explanations of current Democratic advantages, real or imagined, e.g., districting, campaign costs and financing, incumbency and its perquisites, could be tested over time.

   I also think that we need a long-term analysis of the emergence of the West, the eleven Mountain and Pacific Coast states, as a GOP stronghold in national elections. Much has been written about the Republicans' breakthrough in the once solidly Democratic South, less about their western successes, successes that began with Dwight Eisenhower (1952, 1956) and Richard Nixon (1960), *not* Richard Nixon (1968, 1972) and Ronald Reagan (1980, 1984). In five presidential elections from 1932 through 1948, the Democrats carried these states 51-4. In nine of the ten most recent presidential elections—1952–60, 1968–88 (i.e., 1964 excepted)—Republican candidates won by 94-5. Even in defeat, Barry Goldwater revealed above-average strength in the region.

26 Shafer, this volume, 72. In one specific instance, Shafer likely attaches too much significance to belated ballot reform in Connecticut, i.e., to elimination of the party lever from voting machines, in explaining the defeat of Republican Senator Lowell Weicker in 1988. Conservatives' campaigns against Weicker and the pattern of the vote in the Nutmeg State suggest the primacy of ideology/values/associated policy preferences, *central to much of Shafer's analysis of contemporary politics,* in the outcome.

27 Ladd, this volume, 32 (emphasis mine); Shafer, this volume, 69 (emphasis his); Silbey, this volume, 17–18.

5 *Walter Dean Burnham*

Critical Realignment
Dead or Alive?

In the United States all elections are equal, but some are decidedly more equal than others. It has been clear to modern American historians for fifty years or more that likely candidates for the latter category of elections are found in the years 1800, 1828, 1860, 1896, and 1932. But it was for V. O. Key, Jr., to give modern analytic shape to the concept of "critical elections" in a seminal article published in 1955.[1] In doing so, he was to stimulate a gigantic outpouring of scholarly work by political scientists and historians over the next generation. Harold Bass's comprehensive bibliography, which concludes this volume, demonstrates just how vast this corpus of work has now become. Not a little of it discloses a persistent and remarkably regular pattern of cyclical change over time as a major, if not dominant, theme of American political history. The pattern is striking enough to include cyclical change and displacement in many empirical field areas, and there is notable diversity in explanatory schemes advanced to account for it.[2]

It is hardly surprising that many historians have found the realignment model attractive. It appears to divide up much of American political history into clearly demarcated "party-system eras," bounded by realigning upheavals from preceding and succeeding eras. This provides a framework for periodizing the subject, and periodization issues are of particularly central importance to historical methodology. Across time, a subinfinite number of events, personages, processes, and data pour forth for professional evaluation. A credible peri-

101

odization scheme is one essential tool for imposing some order on this otherwise unmanageable flow of information, even if at the inevitable cost of some
reductionism. It is associated with efforts at building descriptive and analytic
constructs through which some facts are asserted to have far greater ordering
importance than most others. Any periodization scheme is, among other things,
a schedule of priorities.[3] To the extent that a plausible causal story can be constructed around it, significant light can be shed on any given "system" of action included within its scope. Moreover, the characteristics of the periods involved can then be much more precisely compared and contrasted than would
otherwise be possible.

In the case of American politics, the apparent advantages of the "realignment synthesis" for historians have been well stated by Paul Kleppner.

> The realignment synthesis proved appealing because it provided a comprehensive
> framework for connecting elections, party coalitions, elite behaviors, and public policy,
> while offering a way to account for the static and dynamic qualities of the political
> system. This framework enabled political scientists and historians to organize masses of
> historical data, to interpret their rhythms over long periods of time, and to link these
> with policymaking. It freed historians of the onerous burdens of the "presidential syn-
> thesis" and the "great man" syndrome, encouraging them instead to unite their human-
> istic insight and attention to nuance with the social scientist's empirical rigor and con-
> cern with theory. . . . Finally, the absence of any equally comprehensive competitor
> cemented the popularity of the realignment synthesis as a framework for periodizing
> and understanding past U.S. politics.[4]

Note, however, the use throughout of the past tense. Kleppner's remarks are
presented in the context of an extensive discussion of the mounting disarray,
muddle, and disagreement over basic facts and their interpretation that have
developed in this area of research.

Some of this, as both Kleppner and Everett Carll Ladd pointed out, arises
from unresolved definitional problems: different scholars mean quite different
things when they use the term "realignment." The situation has reached the
point, Kleppner observes, that the easiest course is to "abandon the realignment framework entirely." This view obviously has wide support, as the very
existence of this volume attests. It is shared in one way or another by each of its
contributors but myself. Kleppner, however, rejects this "easy" solution in
favor of restatement/reevaluation. So do I, although along somewhat different
lines and for somewhat different reasons. After enough wrestling with persistent heteronomy in this field, weariness sets in and the temptation simply
to vote a motion of thanks to the chairperson and then adjourn becomes quite
strong. It will of course be resisted. It may be that a research program with
all the assets which Kleppner ascribed to it will turn out to be illusory or at
least "degenerating" rather than "progressive." I think not, but to explain why,
it will be necessary first to assess the arguments which Ladd, Byron Shafer,

and Joel Silbey make, and then to move on to more general considerations about theory/model construction concerning change in very complex systems of action.

Critique of Critical Criticism

These three essays converge on two primary assertions. The first is that, whatever utility realignment models may have had for the study of *past* American politics, they have systematically misled anyone attempting to use them to account for the *contemporary* state of affairs. The second argument is that they have no utility for studying the past either. Thirty-five years of error is, apparently, the final conclusion—misplaced effort on a truly gargantuan scale.

Ladd develops both sides in his critique, but places predominant stress on the deceptiveness of realignment models for dealing with the here and now. His is a wide-ranging criticism of those who have been "waiting for Godot" to turn up, election after election, ever since the late 1960s. He carefully and accurately describes many components of the large-scale political changes that have taken place over the past quarter-century, from voter behavior to elites and policymaking. Large as these changes have been, they do not analyze properly within the classic partisan-focused realignment model. A great many of the traditional criteria associated with critical realignment have obviously not been met. These, we recall, pointed to concentrated bursts of upheaval out of which arose an "electoral order" marked by control of all branches of government by the same party for considerable time thereafter, and with appropriate policy changes in tow. The present era shows the precise opposite. Instead of unified partisan control, we find pied electoral majorities—Republican at the executive level, Democratic at the legislative. Changes that have occurred in party-identification measures, while cumulatively substantial and pro-Republican, would be much better described in terms of secular trends rather than the jump-shift which a classic realignment model would predict (and which seems to have happened in the 1930s and, presumably, earlier). For purposes of moving along in this discussion, we can agree by stipulation to the facts presented in evidence: Ladd enjoys a deserved position of eminence among analysts of the American party/electoral system.

Shafer presents an elegantly crafted analysis of the "structure of politics at the accession of George Bush." (There may be more to the Namierite analogy than even he indicates. . . .) Shafer is carefully agnostic on the question of the utility of critical-realignment models for studying the past. But he does assert that it is quite possible to give a full analytic treatment to the workings of this "structure of politics" without in any way having to deal with realignment. That simply becomes irrelevant to the tasks at hand. We can again stipulate agreement as to the catena of facts presented in this fascinating essay; interpretation, as we shall see, is another matter. Implicit in Shafer's argument is the view that realignment issues should be left to historians to sort out. Political scientists concerned with the present and near-future of American politics should look elsewhere.

Silbey, a distinguished analyst of nineteenth-century American party/electoral politics, completes the assault by denying that the realignment framework has any particular utility for understanding the American past. He is joined in this by Ladd, for whom scholarship has become altogether too fixated on just two historic cases—the Civil War and the Great Depression/New Deal. He adduces an ideological explanation for this fixation, to which we shall return in due course. For his part, Silbey develops an alternative periodization scheme. In this scheme there are, broadly, three "political eras"—"prepartisan" up to 1838, "partisan" between 1838 and the early twentieth century, and a developing "postpartisan" era which has finally become consolidated in the past generation. (There is also, of course, a fourth "intermediate" stage, extending from just after 1900 through 1948).

Such an alternative periodization obviously commands respect. When Joel Silbey tells us that such crucial dimensions of American politics as political structure (party organization, mass mobilization, and characteristic patterns of voter response to electoral stimuli) are very different in the 1838–1900 period than anything before or after, we should believe him. Some such division of the time-bound pie is clearly indicated by the data, and of course it is the case that classic realignment theory has never directly recognized, much less confronted its implications (see Appendix). On the other hand, I, at least, have never argued that the punctuated-change pulses involved in critical realignments come even close to describing all significant dimensions of large-scale political change in United States history. In any event, any reasonably complete review of the electoral/party data for this period will surely confirm the general truth of what Silbey says about it. It will thus have to be accounted for (as will certain dimensions of secular realignment) in any more adequate model of transformation, assuming that one can be devised.

We turn first to a critical evaluation of Everett Ladd's chapter. In it several assertions are made either explicitly or by implication. Some of these are startling. It is asserted that overpreoccupation with critical realignment is an essentially ideological fruit of scholarly attachment to the policies and programs of the New Deal. Even more startling is the assertion, referenced by a quotation from Carmines and Stimson, that critical-realignment work has not been informed by any theory of American politics, which I suppose means that workers in this field have been no better than stamp collectors. A third assertion centers directly on the "strange case of the missing realignment" around 1968, which he, Allan Lichtman, and others regard as conclusive disproof of the model's predictive power.[5] Let us examine each of these in detail.

Fixation with Realignment

We begin with the observation that, Ladd to the contrary, realignment work has identified not only the Civil War and New Deal eras in that category, but the 1890s as well. And some would certainly continue to believe that something which profoundly changed the structure of American politics was going on in the "age of Jackson" as well. One can always make the case, granted sufficient evidence and theory, that it is justified to organize around megaevents that happen rarely (if recurrently). But they have not been quite as rare as Ladd says they have been.

Beyond that, one may certainly agree that excessive fixation on any topic is not to be encouraged. This sort of "pack" phenomenon can represent a real misallocation of scholarly resources, as, for example, with the spate of political science articles a few years back documenting for the nth time that incumbent-insulation effects in congressional elections were huge and growing. The sociology of research is likely to produce episodes of this sort, and the richer the apparent research payoff is estimated to be, the more likely that a kind of scholarly equivalent of "overtrading" in markets will occur. One does not need endless reiterations of the obvious, and no one can doubt that there has been some of this in critical-realignment research. On balance, however, the payoffs really have been large—perhaps large enough for us to be a little more tolerant of this commonly encountered aspect of scholarly research dynamics than Ladd is.

The accusation that leftist sociopolitical ideology drives the enterprise as a whole strikes me as nonsense, at least in the form in which it was expressed in this essay. Social ideology in fact affects many or most research settings and conceptual breakthroughs in the *natural* sciences, as historians of science have repeatedly demonstrated. Charles Darwin's conflation of natural selection with gradualist dogma is one of many classic cases in point.[6] And the geologist Richard H. Benson, in the context of dealing with these issues, cites a long-deceased predecessor who was quite precisely aware of this fact. "Clarence King, revered as a leader in the description of American geology in the early days, once said, 'Men are born either catastrophists or uniformitarians. You may divide the human race into imaginative people who believe in all sorts of impending crises . . . and others who anchor their very souls to the *status quo*.' "[7] Leaving aside the loaded adjective "imaginative," the American geologist King appears to have an independent discovery of the political axiom about liberals and conservatives laid down by Gilbert and Sullivan's *Iolanthe*. There is truth in it nevertheless, as there is in the tendency of scientists (including social scientists) to insist on the objective truth of one's own analyses, while attacking the opposition for its ideological fixations.

Perhaps I can sharpen the point by taking the stand myself and providing some autobiographical details. My first dawning awareness of sharply marked periodizations in American electoral history came from the work I did when very young indeed, on *Presidential Ballots, 1836–1892.*[8] At the time, having been well socialized politically, I had a Republican commitment which precluded any great enthusiasm for the New Deal. Subsequently, having become fascinated with constitutional history under one of the great masters of the era, Carl B. Swisher, I thought sufficiently highly of the subject to devote considerable attention to it in graduate school under two other masters, Robert G. McCloskey and Arthur B. Sutherland.[9] Quite well-defined periodizations of American constitutional history stood out all over the subjects and doctrinal areas I was studying. In particular, the era of judicial supremacy in American national politics (1890/95–1937) was, as most legal historians will agree, a singularly well-bounded period. It seemed perfectly clear then, as it does now, that there was a systemic connection between the outer bounds of this period and each of two critical realignments in the electoral order, those of the 1890s and the 1930s.

Whether or not some people are inherently predisposed to disruptive upheaval and others to glacially incremental change I leave to others to decide. The moral of the above story is simply that in the case of one person who has made some contribution to the genre, the constitutional-history segment of his professional formation was at least as significant a background input as the study of electoral data, and that the intellectual issues became increasingly exciting *as* intellectual issues. In retrospect, I would of course have to affirm that I am as affected by sociopolitical ideology as the next person, although in this particular case, the New Deal as such had precious little to do with any of it.

1968 and All That: Failure of the Predictive Model?

Later in this essay, I shall address this issue much more fully, since it turns on questions closely linked to my proposed reformulation of the critical-realignment framework. We may only note here that the first-generation critical-realignment model *assumed* rather than *analyzed* the dominance of political parties as connectors and channels of mass action in politics. In the middle of the vast political upheaval concentrated in the 1968–72 period, I went to some lengths to explain that this dominance was then problematic, that it was in the course of a disappearance, and that if those trends continued, critical realignment as then understood would probably become (or already be) extinct.[10] It was for this reason that I was of course not one of the company who "waited for Godot." Deficiencies which will not be discussed here left this insight floating; it should have been nailed down a long time ago, but it was not. Better late than never.

It goes without saying that people attempting to use a model whose basic premises are being systematically and cumulatively violated by changing empirical reality do so at their own peril. It was inevitable that those doing so in this field would look forward year after year to a revenant, and would look in vain. They would be faced with the equivalent of that famous Sherlockian puzzle in A. Conan Doyle's *The Adventure of Silver Blaze:*

> . . . I saw by the Inspector's face that his attention had been keenly aroused. . . .
> "Is there any point to which you wish to draw my attention?"
> "To the curious incident of the dog in the night-time."
> "The dog did nothing in the night-time."
> "That was the curious incident," remarked Sherlock Holmes.[11]

In the specific case before us, there in fact *was* a critical realignment in the 1968–72 period. One of its essential features lay in the very dissolution of the traditional partisan channels that had been implicitly incorporated as a non-problematic part of the classic realignment model. People therefore looked for it with the wrong tools and in the wrong places, and of course did not find what they were looking for. That very perceptive political commentator Sidney Blumenthal was perhaps the first to get the basic story right: "The realignment theory is useful today, but mostly as a counter-model. For it is a good guide to what is not happening. . . . The permanent campaign system is the "sixth great party system." It was established in the unheralded "critical election" of 1968. . . . The last time the old party system could deliver was in 1968, and the price was its demise."[12]

Nor need we cite only the brilliant insights of journalists. In the spring of 1990, John Aldrich and Richard G. Niemi produced an extensive analytic paper entitled "The Sixth American Party System: The 1960s Realignment and the Candidate-Centered Parties." This paper, while unpublished, will doubtless not remain so for very long. Its thesis is implied in its title: there *was* a critical-realignment upheaval centered around 1968 which moved the system through crisis and disruption from one relative equilibrium condition to another. This study will obviously be a significant contribution to the literature. The word is now getting out, as at long last it should. It seems that useful work in this genre continues to appear.

Critical Realignment Study as an "Atheoretical" Enterprise

If one thinks that one has in part been commiting theory all of one's life, what can be said when it is asserted that all such effort has been little or no better than mindless data-busting? V. O. Key, Jr., the godfather of the whole enterprise, was a very great political scientist. But neither he nor others have ever pretended that he was a systematic "great-ideas" thinker.[13] Few or no citations of Marx, Weber, or other grand theorists can be found in his work. In a sense, he sailed—rather like medieval navigators in the Mediterranean—from data point to data point, using his unparalleled capacity for intuitive integration to tell powerful stories about the shape and health of the American democratic system to which he was so passionately devoted. As for the mainstream of work in this area that has developed in the generation since his death, a very large part of it has indeed focused heavily on data retrieval and analysis with specific empirical questions in mind, often enough with little theoretical content. But—political philosophy and certain grand theories of "political development" apart—of what branch of political science can this complaint not be made?

There is little question that Everett Ladd is squarely on the mark when he insists that much too little effort has been made to spell out the propositional inventory of realignment, beginning even with a clear-cut definition of the subject matter. To this we shall turn in the next section of the chapter, where an attempt is made at providing one. I regret what must appear to others to be tedious egotism, but for my own part, I have never doubted—no matter how much the underspecification of models can be legitimately decried—that theory informs the whole enterprise. Patterns in data are discerned and measured over a lifetime of exposure to them. They reveal, among other things, the "remarkable regularity" in Aldrich and Niemi's term of important transformational processes. It can be shown by comparative analysis that the periodic recurrence of these processes sets the American political system historically and comparatively apart from all others in the universe. (Naturally, realigning as well as wholly revolutionary upheavals are often enough encountered elsewhere, but not the periodicity of their occurrence.)

It is obviously necessary to formulate some account for why these processes should exist at all, and what their ultimate (as well as their proximate) causes might be. This requires theorizing, and I had always assumed that there was considerable theoretical content in many of the more important formulations of the critical-realignment model. In the next section, I shall once again set out some of the propositions and arguments that possess theoretical import. If these constructs are to have empirical relevance—or any alternative constructs, for that matter—they must credibly explain the data. The history of science, once again, is replete with examples of the collision of data, especially inconvenient or anomalous data, with existing paradigms: a theme that dominates, but is by means limited to, Thomas R. Kuhn's famous treatment of "scientific revolutions."[14] One can deal with data by devaluing its significance, which I hope will not happen in Silbey's treatment of the Civil War realignment within his framework. Or one can altogether deny the objective reality of data configurations, no matter how exhaustively and by however many varieties of methods scholars have evaluated them. This happens depressingly often even in some of the natural sciences. Finally, one can accept both their reality and their importance in the larger scheme of things. In that case, one must have an explanation for it all; and unless the only criterion for theory is debate between Plato and Aristotle over the nature of the good, then theory of some sort must be employed that is more than "merely" descriptive in the shallow sense evidently imagined by Carmines and Stimson and endorsed by Ladd.

Varieties of Critical Realignment: An Amplified Statement

Punctuational Change

We begin with what may appear to be a digression: the recent emergence of models of punctuated change and punctuated equilibrium (perhaps what one might call modified catastrophe theory) in the study of the evolution of life forms on this planet—a natural science with a strong historical component.[15]

The long-dominant models in geology and evolutionary biology were laid down more than a century ago by Charles Stewart Lyell and Charles Darwin. These accounted for change in essentially linear and extremely gradualist terms; that is, they were uniformitarian models. Parts of uniformitarian doctrine, linked to parsimony of explanation and to rejection of supernatural miracles to account for events, retain enduring validity in ordering professional work. It is always better, wherever possible, to account for some phenomenon in terms of processes measurably at work in the here and now somewhere in the world. Lyell, the arch-uniformitarian, insisted that there could be no cases where this was not possible. Both he and Darwin set their faces like flint against both biblically linked theories of catastrophic change in earth history and against any cognate in science to the revolutionary change found in society and politics (and abhorred by middle-class Britons).[16] With billions of years to work with, one could slice change into the tiniest of incremental bits.

The anomalies in data eventually became so large as to swamp this extreme substantive-uniformitarian model. Even in Darwin's time, the fossil record seemed to show not infinite gradations of evolutionary modification, but the relatively sudden emergence of new species, often in something close to "final" developmental form. Moreover, there was the problem of mass extinction of life forms to consider. When 96% of all species rapidly disappear, as at the end of the Permian era, "survival of the fittest" through natural selection comes under some pressure as a *universal* explanation of what goes on. Darwin was quite aware of these, particularly of the first. His argument in rejoinder was an appeal to the existence of huge gaps in a tattered geological record. After a century and a half of vast further work, this appeal to missing data is no longer tenable. The mass extinctions have in fact been used from very early days to mark the boundaries of major epochs in earth history from the Cambrian (570 million years ago) to the present (Paleozoic-Mesozoic-Cenozoic). Recent work has made clear that catastrophic change involving processes clearly not at work anywhere in the world today has occurred, and its boundary points can be very tightly measured. There is now very strong evidence that these paroxysmal events involved collision between the earth and some extraterrestrial object, and even some evidence that major and minor episodes of mass extinction have occurred cyclically—perhaps every 30 million years or so—for a very long time.

It was in the context of apparently sudden speciation that the eminent paleontologists Niles Eldredge and Stephen Jay Gould developed a model of punctuated equilibrium in 1972.[17] The essential argument is that, as a result of a variety of causal factors some of which are still "poorly understood," as the phrase goes, the relevant systems have tendencies toward progressive destabilization until some "flipover" point of very rapid change is reached, and thereafter a new equilibrium phase is established. The authors of this model are not purporting to claim that their theory constitutes a *general* theory of change, still less that they are out to reject uniformitarianism root and branch. It deals with speciation issues only, within the larger network of issues in that field. But within that more limited domain, very important ranges of empirical evidence simply cannot credibly be explained in uniformitarian terms. Hence their proposed model. As in our case, this model grew out of intellectual confrontation with data highly refractory to traditional explanations. Despite that, and despite their view that only some ranges of change seem accountable in punctuational terms, these authors appear to believe that they have made some contribution to theory; and so they have.

Perhaps Gould and Eldredge have some imperialist ambition of one day subsuming all field change to their model. Or perhaps over decades to come—1972 is not so very long ago, and they are certainly in the first-generation stage of model development—a more completely integrative theoretical framework will be created by workers in this field. Be that as it may, it is worthy of note that leading scientists within the field believe that it is perfectly possible to do useful professional work within the bounds of a model of sudden change which has no pretense to universality. Finally, it is worth noting that, as Gould points out, such punctuational models are becoming increasingly frequent in the sciences as a whole. Perhaps, as he suggests, this is (as it were) sociologically permitted by the development of a contemporary *Zeitgeist* which is miles removed from the assumptions of nineteenth-century liberalism.

So far as our own field of inquiry is concerned, there are by now very abundant and well-documented ranges of evidence in our data record indicating the recurrent emergence of large-scale crisis-resolution episodes in American political history. These are "moments," or compressed event sequences, which differ not only in degree but to a considerable extent in kind from normal phenomena commonly found within chronological party systems. Some form of punctuational-change model seems necessary to deal with these phenomena.

Clearly, it is essential to the enterprise that a reasonably coherent and specified causal story be developed to account for what the data are telling us. It is equally clear that a number of things will be going on at discrete levels of the system, at discrete times, and in discrete contexts and places. It may eventually be possible to develop good stories for each—and across each—of these levels, but we can surely carry on thrivingly in the meantime. One is impressed with the considerable variety of possibilities in this regard, possibilities which in the present state of knowledge must be presumed to be nonexclusive. One can cite the recent development of three approaches to explanation in this field. One of them, stressed by Paul Abramson, Paul Allen Beck, and others, stresses generational replacement as a process which in time opens up the possibility for relatively massive reorganizations of party attachments during realignment crises.[18] There seem to be two very broad time-bound factors at work. Firstly, over time new polarizing issues develop that often cross-cut the normative and coalitional structure forged during the last realignment. Secondly, with the passage of enough time—and a modal value of 38 years from one realignment peak to the next is quite enough time—the overwhelming majority of the electorate can relive the impact of the previous trauma only at second hand.

It is evident that theories of political coalitions can also account for a good deal, along lines suggested some years ago by Lee Benson and William Riker.[19] Simply at the level of the important question of why established major-party elites so often fail to adapt incrementally to rising demand along a new cleavage axis, such perspectives can provide vital clues: the more complex the coalition and the narrower its overall majority, the greater the risk to its managers in incorporating *any* new claimants.

Finally, workers in the electoral field have been increasingly influenced by ideas derived from the burgeoning subfield of public (or rational) choice. Here, there may be real problems in sustaining the conventional affective-psychological view of such entities as party identification. It has been known for quite a few years that in a number of European contexts, including Britain, party ID "works" very differently from the propositions set forth by the Michigan survey-research model: voters frequently change their ID when they change their vote, that is, there is a strong instrumental element at work.[20] More recently, using panel data, Morris P. Fiorina has uncovered strong signs of instrumentally fueled identification change even in American situations.[21] Paul Kleppner has further stressed the significance of this kind of work in modifying and enriching the explanatory scheme for realignment. His view is that there are two types of party ID in the picture. For some voters, the Michigan paradigm explains things; for others, a neo-Downsian, rational-choice, instrumentalist framework seems operative.[22] I feel quite certain that all these and other formulations of causality at various levels of analysis will continue to enrich and solidify professional analysis of realignment sequences and "normal-state" politics as well.

The United States in a World Setting

If the higher reaches of critical-realignment theory do not purport to be a general theory of *all* change in American politics, they do in places deal with rather grandiose assertions about the underlying nature of the political system. The sources for such a theory might well be found in (and a propositional inventory developed from) the *comparative* peculiarities of American politics. Since Alexis de Tocqueville's pioneering and still *actuel* effort a century-and-a-half ago to the present, work has proceeded along these comparativist lines. People of the stature of Werner Sombart, Antonio Gramsci, Louis Hartz, David Potter, and Samuel Huntington, to name but a few workers in this field, have made significant contributions in almost every generation since de Tocqueville's time.[23]

One of the most striking features of this literature, produced by writers across a political spectrum from communist left to conservative right, is a remarkable degree of convergence on the *differentia specifica* of American political society. One can list just a few of these: a certain kind of "founding population," derived from certain specific locations within the European social matrix and detached therefrom at certain specific times; the dominance of liberal values, including very high levels of personal aspirations and a parallel weakness both of old-conservative traditions derived from the manorial mode of production and of socialism; an exceptionally high relative level of material affluence, enjoyed it seems from the beginning by a vastly larger share of the total (white) population than in even the most economically developed parts of the old European homeland; a considerable aversion to the state and the exercise of sovereign power over the citizenry; a constitutional regime which gives very full and concrete expression to that aversion; and much else besides. Indeed, such an inventory virtually compiles itself, and by this time we are dealing with oft-told tales in a great many cases.

Within some such set of parameters, stimuli affecting the organization and reorganization of American politics can be broadly subdivided into two categories: those which are endogenous to the system in relative isolation, and those which are external to the system of action itself. The first has been frequently discussed in critical-realignment literature, the second much less so. Analysis of endogenous processes must sooner or later touch upon the American constitution: the uppercase *C* document of 1787, and the lowercase (or Aristotelian) *c* that includes the structure of norms, behavior, and political culture which is reflected through and reinforces the power-centrifuge tendencies built into the large-*C* Constitution. Parties have been the only known counterweight to the power defaults embedded in it. Without them, we know, crisis of govern-ability becomes endemic and, often, acute.[24] On the other hand, parties them-selves are decisively shaped and limited in their collective-representation, power-integration functions by both C and c. The existence of two institu-tionally decentralized parties in an imperial-sized nation marked by utmost subnational economic and cultural diversity mandates that their elites must organize and sustain effective brokerage among a plethora of interests and claimants. Only thus can they win elections. But this inevitably implies that the network of interests in the established political game are profoundly resistant to emergent demand.[25]

This demand arises from the crowds of losers who are produced by the coun-try's stormily rapid socioeconomic development. The ultimate forces at work to produce both major critical realignments and more minor "midlife crises" are embedded in the relationship between the world's most dynamically evolv-ing socioeconomic system and a political system so prone to stasis that Samuel Huntington could credibly describe it as a "Tudor polity." Put in crude terms, the socioeconomic "base" has a persistent dynamic tendency to slide out over time from an inertia-prone political "superstructure." This produces growing destabilization and growing stresses on popular support for the existing regime order. There are many indicators of this—from decay in party differentiation on congressional roll calls, to turnout depression, to the extraordinarily diag-nostic significance attached both to the timing and content of significant third parties—to name but a few. The stage is then set for a triggering event (or event sequence) which produces a punctuational-change explosion, a "flipover" lead-ing in due course to a new and stable regime order. It is obvious that such an account is general in the extreme and that much work on details is required—and much has by now been performed—to make the story concrete at specific times and places. But something of this sort lies at the base of this remarkably recurrent pattern of stability-stasis-growing destabilization-flipover-restabilization.

External stimuli involve above all else the economic and especially geo-political contexts within which the United States operates as an actor on the world stage. Major changes in these parameters have been of the utmost importance in shaping the opportunity structures for various organizations and reorganizations of the domestic political structure. The great "partisan era" of American politics discussed by Silbey flourished in the long period between the Napoleonic and German wars in which we uniquely enjoyed free national security. By contrast, national security preoccupations were not only present but acute both in the "pre-partisan" era of American political development and in the post-1945 world of superpower rivalry under the shadow of atomic terror.

It strikes me as by no means coincidental that the very existence of the so-called first party system was determined to a very large degree, along with the peculiar dynamics of its evolution, by overwhelming concerns for national identity and indeed national survival as an ex-colony in an ideologically fueled world war between Great Britain and France. In the period before 1829, there was little enough to distinguish Jeffersonian from Federalist domestic public policy. This accounts in large part, incidentally, for the remarkable success which the Federalist "great Chief Justice," John Marshall, had in shaping the foundations of American constitutional law for nearly thirty years after his party had been swept from national power. The key issues of this period centered on the economic development of this infant "empire," on dealing with the national security effects on this semiperiphery of world war in the European metropole, and above all on freeing the country from the psychology as well as the political economics of a "colonial situation" that persisted long after formal political independence.

Nineteenth-century historians quite precisely captured the essence of the latter set of issues in their description of the War of 1812 as "the second war of American independence," which in fact it was. Nor was it coincidence that the final end of the world conflict was promptly followed by the rapid eclipse of Federalism and even "party spirit" more generally.[26] During the interval, from 1801 to 1816, the balance of political forces in the infant republic followed, virtually month by month, the impact of the world crisis and Jeffersonian responses to it. Data viewed in that light suggest considerable reason to suppose that, had the 1802 Peace of Amiens provided a definitive settlement between Great Britain and Napoleonic France, the so-called first party system would have evaporated at least a decade before it did. For on the front of purely domestic politics prior to the transportation revolution and to the democratic revolution in popular mentality, there were simply not enough other consensual perceptions to hold this system together.

The post-1940 disappearance of free national security has been lavishly documented as a major part of the revolution in world politics that shifted the United States from isolation to the role of one of two imperial superpowers. Its significance for the evolution of characteristic structures, processes, and behaviors in American domestic politics is, however, still underdeveloped and poorly integrated in that literature. There is considerable evidence extending all the way through the 1988 presidential campaign that this international "threat system" has played a major role in dissociating presidential from other-level voting coalitions.[27] In particular, the disruption of the Cold War liberal consensus in the fires of the Vietnam War led straightway to the development of a prime Republican asset in presidential campaigns, a widespread public perception of Democratic candidates (and President Carter) as being "soft" in dealing with this threat system. Its centrality over the past decades has made a signal contribution to the completion of twentieth-century trends toward "liberating" the presidency from constraints imposed by other political actors in the now-defunct partisan era of American political development. The East European revolution of 1989 and Mikhail Gorbachev's proclamation of the end of the Cold War may signify that 1988 will have been the last of the Cold War elections in this long sequence. If so, and if the significance of the external threat system has been as profound as suggested here in shaping American politics, a severe decline in its salience may well open hitherto-unsuspected opportunity structures in the articulation of our domestic politics. The end of the Cold War bodes little good for Republican presidential coalition-makers, though whether Democrats can take advantage of that fact (assuming that it is a fact) is quite another question.

Defining the Larger Phenomenon

Let us begin by making a categorical statement in response to the analyses of other contributors, especially Everett Ladd's. Classic critical realignments, those that have been exhaustively analyzed in the first-generation literature since 1955, all occurred during the "partisan era"—which in my view ended not in 1948, but in 1968. If the only manifestation of systemwide punctuational change reflected in the historic record is this partisan-channeled, "classic" critical realignment, then the critique must be accepted as entirely valid. I have already suggested reasons for doubting this which appear to be weighty and which appear to include ongoing work by others affirming, for example, that the 1968–72 crisis can be regarded as being a critical realignment. But the only way more or less effectively to deal with this challenge is to decouple the partisan element from the underlying phenomenon and see what happens. Let us argue, then, that punctuational change is a permanent, embedded characteristic of American politics over time, *however* that politics is specifically organized. Classic critical realignment would thus constitute one of a number of possible modes through which this characteristic achieves expression. In doing so, let us begin by counterposing an alternative to Professor Ladd's definition.

Definition: Critical realignments are moments of intense, comprehensive, and periodically recurring systemic change in American politics. These moments will be more or less protracted depending on the level of development in institutional structure which exists at the time of their occurrence. Periodically recurring, critical realignments are phenomena unique to the American political system, though they have nonrecurrent cognates elsewhere, including their "first cousins," revolutions. They have existed in one form or another throughout American political history from the American Revolution to the present. They occur when and only when:

(a) politically decisive minorities of the politically relevant population of any given time stop doing what they have traditionally been doing in politics (including participation or nonparticipation); rather suddenly begin doing something very different; and thereafter, for many years, keep on doing it;

(b) there are exceptionally important and enduring consequences for the organization of the political system, including at least the following:

    (i) The way in which the political system as a whole is articulated;

    (ii) The identity and circulation of dominant national elites and the identity of prime extragovernmental beneficiaries of their policies;

    (iii) The shape and content of dominant sets of public policy agendas and outputs, and of the dominant sets of political ideas justifying and integrating them;

    (iv) The identity, size, scope, and effective constitutional role of each branch of the federal government, the national and state governments, and the "politically relevant population," as well as of dominant and subordinate coalitions within it.

Now this definition is admittedly cumbersome. But it has at least the virtue of moving attention away from the "partisan synthesis" that implicitly governed the first generation of critical-realignment research. The definition implies the possible existence not only of our Type A partisan-focused realignment, but of a Type B—non-partisan-channeled—realignment as well.

It is evident that a number of thorny problems could be expected in identifying, much less getting agreement on, a Type B version of punctuational change—though I think there are still far fewer of them in correctly identifying the realignment of the late 1960s than in dealing with very early periods of American political history. For one thing, many aspects of the phenomenon would inevitably look more diffuse in the absence of the defining power which partisan channeling provides. The transition period would probably be more protracted, and there would necessarily be more ambiguity in identifying "cutting-point peaks" of transition than in Type A situations. Indeed, both for the most recent era but especially for the earlier pre-1838 world, electorally focused analysis would need to be more thoroughly supplemented by other relevant methodologies (e.g., weighing and counting events, perhaps greater focus on policy and elite personnel). Nevertheless, table 5.1 is a preliminary and impressionistic effort to treat all of American political history in these terms.

Realignments, Midlife Crises, and Regime Orders:
The "Prepartisan Era" as Case in Point

Let us try, without being excessively repetitive, to evaluate the earliest phase of national political history in these terms, highlighting certain features in the telling of a story which may seem outrageous to some. Viewed holistically, the

Table 5.1. Punctuated Change and American Political History: One Suggested Pattern

Era	Approximate Dating	System or Electoral Order	Realignment Band	Peak	"Midlife Crisis"
Colonial/ neocolonial order	1770–1818	1 18th-century system (1st party system, 1793–1816)	1775–83	1780	1799/1800
Democratized politics (1): Rural Republic	1816–ca. 1900/04	2 Democratizing (Jacksonian or 2d system)	1820–30 (state) 1824–32 (national)	1818 1828	1838[a]
		3 Civil War system	1854–60	1856	1875
Democratized politics (2): Industrial Order	ca.1900/04; early 1960s	4 System of 1896	1893–96	1894	1912/13[a]
		5 New Deal system (electoral order)	1928–38	1932	1948/52[a]
Postindustrial/ postparty politics	ca. 1967/68– present	6 Permanent campaign as electoral order; interregnum state as regime order	1964–74	1970	(1990?)

[a]Times identified by Joel Silbey as associated with major "sea changes" from one broad era to the next, except for ca. 1912, which I think the appropriate maximum impact point of that particular "sea change." For comparison, see Silbey's table 1.1, this volume, p. 17.

most significant upheavals in this period surely were the American Revolution at its beginning and the upwardly cascading democratizing revolution of the 1815–30 period at its end. Political struggles centered first around independence, then around the shape and form of the national state, and finally around issues connected with national identity in a highly charged international context, including large elements of continuing American dependence. As Ronald Formisano and others have pointed out, American politics in this early period is best understood as a form of late eighteenth-century, Greater British politics, in which participation—even though growing steeply around 1800—was balanced by deferential cultural-political norms.[28] As Formisano has also pointed out, much politics in this period turned around mainstream politicians' search for a "Revolutionary Center" political mode.[29] This search led to decisive success for the Jeffersonians at the national level in the pivotal election and regime change of 1800–1801. Massachusetts was different in that Federalism remained not only robust but dominant for another quarter-century. But here, too, the dominant party produced gubernatorial candidates, as a rule, whose style was plain-republican rather than aristocratic and whose substance was centrist rather than ideologically extreme. When it did not, as in 1810–11 or 1824, it lost elections.

At the national level, it has long been obvious from the earliest qualitatively based literature to the present day that the election of 1800–1801 is in many respects a turning point. In terms of elite identity and circulation there is no doubt. Federalist *identifiers* were systematically proscribed by Jeffersonians wherever they gained power: they were regarded as essentially unsafe on national republican identity questions. But *policy* is something else again. After Alexander Hamilton was safely dead, Secretary of the Treasury Albert Gallatin (1801–14) went out of his way to sing his praises. The First Bank of the United States failed to be rechartered in 1811 on the tie-breaking negative vote cast by Vice President Clinton.

As soon as the war was over, in 1816, the charter of the Second Bank of the United States was enacted into law by an overwhelmingly Jeffersonian Congress. And again, there are the great "nationalist" decisions made by the Supreme Court between 1816 and 1824 to consider. Of the seven justices sitting at that time, only John Marshall and Bushrod Washington had been appointed by Federalist presidents; the other five had been appointed by Jefferson or Madison. Marshall's Federalist views prevailed in all of these cases, and in the pivotal bank case *McCulloch v. Maryland,* 4 Wheat. 316 (1819), among others, the decision was unanimous. Surely in this sense at least, "We are all Republicans, we are all Federalists," as Jefferson said in his first inaugural address; or if not quite "all," then at least the Revolutionary Center could be so described.

Considering all this, a good case could be made for the view that the 1800–1801 pivot is best described as being not a realignment but *a midlife crisis in an ongoing and still robust regime order.* We should now devote some attention to these events which, during the whole partisan Type A sequence, have occurred almost exactly midway between one critical realignment boundary and the next. The regime orders created out of the vortex of realignment have frequently been described as stable, but they are not quite as stable as earlier formulations indicated. As full-scale realignments ultimately arise from the persistent relationships between dynamic socioeconomic development and a static political order, so these midlife crises appear to proceed from the same root causes. It may well be that only the continued working out of agendas and oppositions linked to the last realignment and the still incomplete generational succession in the electorate prevent these midcourse stress episodes from becoming more nearly equivalents of critical realignment.

Without unduly protracting this discussion, there are abundant signs in the data pointing to the cyclical recurrence of these subrealigning moments. The relevant crisis during the Civil War electoral era occurred in the 1874–78 period—a "midpoint" of ca. 1875 would not be out of place. Two leading features of this were, first, the end of Reconstruction and the emergence of a solidly Democratic South and, second, major economic depression beginning in 1873. Associated with the latter were unprecedented labor unrest peaking in

1877 and the rapid emergence and disappearance of one of the really large-scale, third-party protest movements, the Greenback/National party, which won 12.9% of the vote in the 1878 congressional election. As happens after midlife stress events, "normalcy" was rapidly restored, in this case with the 1880 election. But things were not the same after as before: the Republican majority controlling all branches of government from 1860 to 1874 vanished, and a unique period of fully mobilized and intensely competitive politics, with usual Democratic majorities in the House, lasted for the next twenty years. The Civil War system as a whole was clearly very much of a piece from the 1850s to the 1890s; but it is also clearly demarked into two phases, A and B, with the midlife crisis dividing them. (see table 5.1.)

The midcourse upheaval in the lifetime of the "System of 1896" which followed was the most spectacular and protracted of such events, including, as it did, not only the eruption of an antiestablishment third party (the Socialists, capturing 6% of the 1912 presidential and congressional vote), but rupture within the hegemonic Republican party itself. Space does not allow even a brief exposition of the forces and factors involved in Progressivism and in the temporary ascendancy of the Democrats under Woodrow Wilson.[30] We note again the eventual restoration of "normalcy," the fact that the system as a whole is a coherent entity—that any "within" differences uncovered in the 1896–1932 period pale into insignificance when compared with the "between" differences between any part of it and the electoral/regime orders that preceded and followed it. And we note that it is very clearly divisible into Phases A and B, in this case with a notably extended interregnum.

It is also not difficult to evaluate the period centering on 1948–52 as the cognate moment of midlife crisis in the history of the New Deal electoral order. The 1948 Democratic convention's adoption of a civil rights plank not only triggered a Dixiecratic bolt which secured more than 5% of the electoral vote that year, but paved the way for Eisenhower's breakthrough into the formerly solid South four years later. This breakthrough, unlike Hoover's temporary achievement in 1928, proved to be the beginning of this region's long march into the Republican column. In the Mountain States as well, 1952 marks a cutting point of durable realignment toward the presidential Republican party. The 1952 campaign itself prefigures in an early, still-primitive way the dominant modes of organizing an electoral market through media that characterize the electoral order of today: the completion of the transcontinental coaxial television cable in 1951 is a really important date in the evolution of American electoral politics. Yet in the end, "normalcy," in part defined by the Michigan survey-research center group as the "reinstating election" of 1960, appeared to many to have been restored in its due course.

Presumably the most significant differentiation between critical realignments and midcourse subrealigning crises lies in the balance between elements of continuity and change, with this balance tilting much more toward continuity in the latter cases than in the former. I have suggested the real possibility that 1800–1801 can be profitably viewed as a midcourse transition rather than a full-fledged realignment. It goes without saying that more detailed work would need to be done, and both "continuity" and "change" much more sharply and operationally defined than is possible here. But the potential exists, I believe, for doing it profitably.

What of the possibility, therefore, that the 1838 transition which looms so large in Silbey's explanatory scheme is best viewed instead, at the punctuational-change level, as yet another midcourse crisis like those occurring somewhere around 1875, 1913, and 1951? There is no doubt that something very substantial happened to the political and electoral systems after the initiator of the Jacksonian revolution had left the White House. Of course, we can hardly speak of a fully completed "second party system" until the opposition had been consolidated under the Whig banner and the Anti-Masons had disappeared, between 1834 and 1839; nor of a fully, nationally competitive system until two-party politics spread to the South in the wake of the Nullification crisis, an event developing no earlier than 1834–38. Moreover, as is well known to specialists, congressional/state turnouts of 1838–39 and the presidential turnout in the 1840 election—the latter just over 80% of the potential electorate—surged forward at the end of that momentous decade. (It is less well known that such turnout rates could not be sustained thereafter, and did not truly become normal until the realignment of the 1850s replaced the second party system with another.)

On the other hand, consider the elements of continuity before and after the transitional moment of 1838. At the elite level, of course, there was profound continuity among Democratic chieftains before and after, as there tended to be from "friends of Adams" to National Republicans to Whigs, in the non-southern states at least. The policy agendas and conflicts between the Jacksonians' negative liberalism and their opposition's positive liberalism extended in a coherent, persistent fashion all the way from Jackson's vetoes of the Maysville Road Bill in 1830 and of the rechartering of the Second Bank of the United States in 1832. During the sole moment in the entire era when the Whigs gained control of both houses of Congress and, as they thought, the presidency, they moved to implement the positive-liberal program, including a charter for a third Bank of the United States. Their failure at John Tyler's hands meant of course that the Jacksonian schedule of priorities remained in charge. Yet all of this does nothing to detract from the point that the issues which helped to focus a democratizing political system immediately after 1828 continued to dominate national politics until the end—increasingly cross-cut and vitiated, to be sure, by rising slavery-related and nativist pressures.

The period extending from just after 1815 to 1838–40 is significantly different from all others. For this was a kind of "alignment-realignment," which is dominated by a protracted building of the structures, processes, and popular norms associated with classic, nineteenth-century, partisan-dominated politics. There are a variety of well-known reasons why the process took so long. It began where it had to, at the state and local level, and quite promptly after the decoupling of the United States from geopolitical conflicts. The period 1815–21 was one of noteworthy democratizing pressures, leading to change in state constitutions and electoral laws, especially in the Northeast. It is also noteworthy how early one can detect democratizing pressures on issues specific to presidential selection, and the extent to which they could not be given adequate institutional expression until material conditions—the transportation-communication revolution in particular—had made it physically possible to construct a nationwide electoral market. Not only was the 1816 Congressional Caucus which nominated James Monroe to succeed James Madison sharply divided over candidate choice, it was also the target of unprecedented attack. One mass meeting was held in Baltimore to denounce the caucus in unmeasured terms as an imposition by a narrow, self-serving elite, and as a device by which Virginia retained a hold over the presidential chair which its declining importance in the Union no longer warranted. One of the participants in this mass meeting was a Federalist who was to become a key Jacksonian Democrat, Roger B. Taney.[31]

The fact that Monroe sought reelection in 1820 may well have deferred the final showdown over the Congressional Caucus which duly materialized in 1824, when it promptly collapsed. In that same year, a political meeting of Lancaster County (Pa.) Republicans decried caucus nominations, pointed to a national nominating convention of delegates from the several states as its desirable replacement, but then concluded that such a convention could not be assembled because transportation media were too primitive to allow it to meet.[32] Both 1824 and 1828 were transitional years, with the major candidates chosen by recommendations from state legislatures and sometimes other, less official bodies. At length, the innovation of a national nominating convention was launched by the Anti-Masons in 1831, followed next year by the Democrats. The Whigs, who had notorious difficulties getting their act together, finally followed in 1839.

In many key respects, the presidential election of 1824 was the last of the primordial sequence that began perhaps in 1796. It was of course a four-man "factional" race among Jeffersonian-Republican notables, in which party was wholly absent. Throughout this entire early period, substantial numbers of presidential electors—between about 40% and 60% of them, depending on the election—were chosen not by voters but by state legislatures acting in their "federal" capacity. In 1824, six states, including crucially important New York, still chose electors in this way. By 1828, except for tiny Delaware and obdurate South Carolina, popular-vote choice was the universal norm, and by

1836 this choice was reflected in the selection of at-large tickets elected by plurality—the system we have had ever since.

It is a pity that reporting of national popular votes for president extends back only to 1824, itself far from completely nationalized. For there is a great deal of known electoral data for the earlier period, and far more that still lies buried in various archival sources. I present one segment of these poorly known data, turnout estimates for presidential and other elections in presidential years, as well as those for off-year elections in a period extending from 1788 to 1845 (see table 5.2).

There are several points that stand out clearly from this array. One notes initially that a very large increase in voting from the preceding base occurs first with the off-year election of 1798–99 and then in the presidential election years of 1800–1801. Particularly in the nonsouthern states, a plateau was achieved which persisted until the early 1830s, leaving turnouts even without full-fledged party anchors at levels characteristically higher than they are at the present time. The second point to note is that, even when the polls lay open to would-be presidential voters, turnouts for that office were always lower (and except for 1800 and 1812, *much* lower) than for nonpresidential offices. This persisted straight through 1824, where the gap was more than 25% in the nonsouthern states, and instantaneously disappeared in the 1828 election. The pattern of greater turnout for president than for other offices in presidential years, the normal pattern from 1840 to the present, stands forth in 1828, if not in 1832 and 1836.

The third and final feature of this array which should attract our attention is that the mobilization rates suddenly achieved in the non-South in 1828 were very substantial and were to be sustained over the next two elections, with turnout in 1832 being not much lower than it was to be in 1852. The South bespeaks a quite different story, to be sure, for there was practically no opposition to Jackson in this region in either 1828 or 1832. There is no doubt that southern integration into a competitive political universe was a leading feature differentiating "1838" (actually, 1834–36) from politics earlier in the second party system. But one needs to evaluate this fact along with others. In the entire century and a half from 1800 to 1952, the South can be said to have enjoyed competitive party politics scarcely one-fifth of the time (1834–60, 1868–76). And it is noteworthy that the abrupt disappearance of this competition with the end of Reconstruction, while it notably modified the Civil War system's balance, did not bring that system to an end.

The underlying theme is that a crucial threshold of national democratization was in fact crossed no later than 1828. This in no way diminishes the existence of many further pulses of democratization somewhat later, though it suggests that they have a somewhat lesser analytic significance. The leads and lags in this upward-mobilizing, nationalizing process were of course very substantial,

Table 5.2. Turnout by Region and Office Category, 1788/89–1844/45 (percentage)

	Presidential Years						Non-South
	Non-South		South		USA		Presidential
Year	Presidential	Other	Presidential	Other	Presidential	Other	minus Other
1788/89	11.0	21.7	13.5	24.6	11.4	21.9	-10.7
1792/93	2.6	26.9	NA	NA	2.6	26.9	-24.3
1796/97	21.0	25.8	NA	NA	21.0	25.8	-4.8
1800/01	40.1	47.0	28.5	40.1	32.0	46.6	-6.9
1804/05	29.6	51.0	12.2	57.2	26.0	51.3	-20.4
1808/09	44.4	59.8	18.3	61.2	38.0	59.8	-15.4
1812/13	48.3	52.6	18.4	46.6	42.7	52.2	-4.3
1816/17	27.4	52.3	8.4	70.1	20.9	53.5	-24.9
1820/21	12.1	48.1	3.9	69.2	9.9	48.2	-36.0
1824/25	26.6	52.1	27.4	51.1	26.9	52.0	-25.5
1828/29	61.7	58.7	42.6	63.9	57.3	59.5	+3.0
1832/33	64.2	64.6	30.1	69.2	56.7	65.3	-0.4
1836/37	58.5	60.1	49.2	61.7	56.5	60.4	-1.6
1840/41	81.6	78.7	75.4	69.1	80.3	76.6	+2.9
1844/45	80.5	77.6	74.2	68.0	79.2	75.6	+2.9

	Off Years			Dropoff, Presidential Years to Off Years		
Year	Non-South	South	USA	Non-South	South	USA
1790/91	21.1	NA	21.1	2.8	NA	2.8
1794/95	25.5	NA	25.5	5.2	NA	5.2
1798/99	33.4	35.6	34.6	-29.5	NA	-29.5
1802/03	43.7	57.2	44.2	7.0	-42.6	5.2
1806/07	47.7	37.9	47.3	6.5	33.7	7.8
1810/11	48.6	49.0	48.6	17.3	19.9	18.7
1814/15	50.1	75.7	51.5	4.8	-62.4	1.3
1818/19	41.4	77.7	44.5	20.8	-10.8	16.8
1822/23	46.4	56.2	47.2	3.5	18.8	2.1
1826/27	46.0	76.3	50.7	11.7	-49.3	2.5
1830/31	53.7	72.3	57.5	8.5	-13.1	11.8
1834/35	63.3	61.7	63.0	2.0	-10.8	3.5
1838/39	69.5	62.5	67.9	-15.6	-1.3	-12.4
1842/43	63.7	64.6	63.9	19.1	6.5	16.6

Notes: Election data are fragmentary before the mid-1820s, especially in the southern states. "Other" offices are chiefly gubernatorial at the nearest (adjacent) election, but are also sometimes congressional results and (much more rarely) state-legislative returns.

For purposes of composition, presidential year–off year dropoff is measured throughout on the basis of presidential year turnouts for "other" offices.

Minus signs indicate "negative dropoff" (turnout *growth* from presidential year to succeeding off year). A relatively normal condition in the South until 1842/43, this occurs just twice for the non-South and the United States as a whole (1798/99, with primary mobilization to the Jefferson-era "platform," and 1838/39, reflecting final consolidation).

as was only to be expected under the specific material and political constraints that were operative in the earlier phases of the democratizing revolution. From the perspective of institutional change, far the most decisive was the development of the presidency as a tribunician office. This fundamentally and, regardless of subsequent vicissitudes, permanently changed the balance of power among the institutions of national government. Yet another manifestation of realignment is visible in the outbreak of political conflict over the Supreme Court's role and decisions, and John Marshall's loss of control of its decisions no later than *Craig v. Missouri,* 4 Pet. 410 (1830).

Georgia's successful nullification of Marshall's decision upholding the rights of the Cherokee Indian Nation, *Worcester v. Georgia,* 6 Pet. 515 (1832), was enthusiastically supported by the president. And one may note that somewhat earlier, a concerted effort was launched (in 1827) to "curb the Court" through congressional action. A leader in this effort was a prominent member of the Jacksonian party, Senator Richard M. Johnson of Kentucky, later vice president under Martin Van Buren.[33] There are reasons why there is a natural periodization of Supreme Court history associated with the transition from the Marshall Court to its successor, the Taney Court. One of the most important indicators of critical realignment is the eruption of political controversy centering on the Supreme Court, as happened in the crises of the 1860s, 1890s, 1930s, and 1960s. By this criterion too, the period 1827–35 would qualify as another leading example of realignment.

Let us recapitulate. A case can perhaps barely be made for dating significant indicative change as early as 1816 at the grassroots level. The coordination and mobilization of this impulse at higher and higher levels of aggregation required time, the development of adequate physical infrastructure, and the emergence of issues and oppositions whose first expression was personalized support for individual notables of the period, the chief of whom was of course Andrew Jackson. Later, this charisma was to be routinized with the passing of the torch and completion of the political organization functionally needed to meet the requirements of a stable democratized regime order. An earlier phase of this process, highly diffuse and institutionally unfocused, was quite rapidly replaced between 1825 and 1828 by clarity, electorally speaking, as well as along many other dimensions.

What we are thus looking at, in this view, is a Type B critical-realignment sequence, centering on 1828 at the national level and somewhat earlier below it. Under these circumstances, it is a bootless enterprise to attempt beyond a certain point to define some precise moment when "the" decisive breakthrough was achieved. But if we concentrate on regime orders as intelligible units of analysis, we may well find that, important as "1838 and all that" were for subsequent developments at certain levels of analysis, they are best comprehended structurally as manifestations of midcourse stress in an ongoing and robust regime order.

Postpartisan Politics: The Present Order

Let us now turn more briefly to the other end of the historical continuum, the present era. Its origins are located in the vast general crisis of the late 1960s, though as always one can find considerable premonitory evidence somewhat earlier. It arose on the ruins of a New Deal order, which it has not completely supplanted. As always, transition to it was linked to important institutional change, here chiefly the reorganization of the rules of presidential nomination in ways congruent to (and reinforcing) a full transition to the postpartisan, permanent-campaign mode of organizing the electoral market.

Probably the most important, single, structural feature of this new order is divided government as a normal condition, interacting with parties that are much more sharply defined inside the Beltway than as agents of mass mobilization outside. From the Civil War to the present day, there had been only one period—1875–97, the "50-50" mobilizing deadlock that marked Phase B of the Civil War party system—in which divided government was commonplace, though it was not as commonplace then as in today's radically different circumstances. Otherwise, such divisions had either been a temporary "sport" (as after the 1946 election) or had been associated with staggered-term leads and lags involved in major White House turnovers (1910, 1918, and 1930 are good examples). The shape of things to come was discernible, here as elsewhere, in the concurrent reelection of President Eisenhower with (narrow) Democratic majorities in Congress.

The pattern changes—permanently, it would seem—with the advent of Richard Nixon in 1969. From then through 1993—continuing Democratic control of at least the House of Representatives after the 1990 election can be assumed with about .999 probability—there will have been a 24-year period in which divided control prevailed in 20 of these years. Reelection of President Bush in 1992, not an improbable event at the moment of writing, would very likely extend this pied-outcome pattern to an era of 28 years' length, 24 of which would have been years of divided partisan control.

This is quite enough to assert that a distinctive norm has been established. This is particularly so when one can also see the same pattern evolving and deepening year by year at the level of state government. By 1988, the proportion of nonsouthern Americans living under state governments with split partisan control had climbed to just over four-fifths. This is by far an all-time record in a data file extending back 150 years. There is some evidence that it has developed so impressively because politically decisive minorities of voters, trusting neither gang, are purposively splitting their tickets.[34]

What difference does divided government make? Probably quite a lot. For one thing, the Reagan Revolution remained incomplete because, among other things, levels of domestic programmatic expenditures inherited from the inter-

est-group–liberal state it replaced could not be cut to anything like the specifications sought by the Right. Too many congressional Democrats stood in the
way. The monument to this is the sustained, year-after-year, budget deficit
along with a tripling of the national debt within a single decade. More generally, under these conditions and with often rather sharp conflicts over politico-
economic objectives, the pattern of opposition is more clearly defined than ever
in institutional terms.

But deadlock is also punctuated, as it necessarily must be, by collusion.
Searches are undertaken for "transpolitical" solutions to complex problems,
as in the bipartisan commission which resolved social-security funding problems in 1984. The recipe in such cases is for formal treaties to be negotiated
between the Republican administration and Democratic congressional leadership by which they march on a united front against all opposition. In this way,
an insider's policy solution is confected that makes it impossible for either
party (or institution) to gain political advantage over the other. Both sides have
assets, both sides seek to avoid blame. Congressional Democrats profit in
many ways from being key players in an established and obviously stable
regime order. And there is little incentive for them to gain credible blame for
being partisan obstructionists; the King's government must somehow be carried on. Along the way, noncongressional Democrats are probably the chief
losers in the game. "Coalition government" erodes the salience of the Democratic party itself in public opinion; in considerable part, it strips the opposition of its main stock in trade, the very fact of its being an opposition.

Second, divided government which oscillates between deadlock and coalition is incompetent government. Since at least the 1930s, Democrats have been
the pro-state party and Republicans the anti-state party. This reflects an enduring link between the party and core interests in the society and economy which
support it. The leaders of the regime order that became fully consolidated after
1980 work in a multitude of ways to persuade the citizenry that government can
do little or nothing to deal with those many domestic issues and problems
which the private market is congenitally incapable of addressing. So long as no
overwhelming, sudden, and general insufficiency engulfs the economic system, its political cognate becomes more stable over time. Anti-state norms are
reinforced by various practical experience with a government whose task
capacity has been massively eroded over the years. Prophecies become in truth
self-fulfilling, with more than a little help from politicians. Pathologies like the
spectacular savings-and-loan disaster only reinforce anti-state and anti-politi-
cian views among the public. And when, as in this very expensive failure for
which only ordinary Americans can expect to pay, Democrats as well as Republicans, Congress as well as the Executive are implicated, the public response to
all of them and to the government whose levers they control will be that all
without exception are the problem, and none the solution to any problem.

More should not be said here; Ladd and Shafer between them give us valuable accounts of the current regime order and its electoral underpinnings. I think it will be increasingly obvious as time goes on that this order was not constructed in 1980, but in and just before 1972, and that it grew out of a truly monumental upheaval which in my view was a Type B realignment. The crisis was not resolved for a number of specific contingent reasons with the elevation of Richard Nixon and the consolidation of the permanent campaign. Instead, it persisted across more than a decade and was associated with that historically unique phenomenon, four repudiated presidencies in a row. Out of this vacuum came Ronald Reagan's opportunity. Success in his own terms was substantial. Conservative revitalization seemed for a long season to work. We need only add that there are reasons related to the nature of Type B realignments and the settings in which they operate which should lead us not to be surprised to find that there can be substantial lags from structural change to subsequent policy and elite transformations.

Speculations on the future of this divided-government, permanent-campaign regime need not detain us long here. It is an impressively stable system, many of whose parts work to reinforce each other. On the other hand, as it is in crucial respects a postpartisan order, it suffers from endemic problems of governability and of democratic accountability and popular support. So long as the need for a state is as dimly perceived and vividly denied as at present, there is no apparent reason why it should not persist indefinitely into the future, no matter how baroque its steering incompetencies and failures become, and no matter how far turnout in elections drops while the "confidence gap" rises.[35]

To assume all this in the longer term, however, would be tantamount to claiming that a fundamental driving mechanism which throughout the whole of American history has recalibrated a stasis-prone political system to the needs of a dynamically changing socioeconomic order has itself become extinct. In our field, this would be "the end of history" with a vengeance. More probably, we can reasonably anticipate another season of basic, realigning, punctuated-equilibrium change, following our amplified discussion here, some time within the next two decades. For in all probability, at some point between now and then, contingencies will develop demanding a reenergized governmental system. And that, the politics of collision and coalition, the politics of the permanent campaign, is intrinsically incapable of providing.

Concluding Observations

At the end of the day, the question of whether critical-realignment research programs will prove "degenerating" or still "progressive," in Imre Lakatos' phrase, will be decided not here but by the relevant research community at large.[36] As always, the criteria involved will be strictly empirical. When a given conceptual model which purports to give a schedule of priorities for ordering data ceases to have professional utility, researchers will stop using it and start using something else (if something else is available). It will then eventually disappear from view, except perhaps as a footnote to disciplinary history. If, on the other hand, its ordering utility has not been exhausted or a clearly superior model developed, this will be empirically revealed in the continuing willingness of researchers to use it, and especially to contribute to its further development. I am more confident than ever that the flow of current work, down to the most recent possible moment, confirms that the latter, not the former, is the case.

Along the way, a certain sense of perspective is sometimes needed: it is literally true that Rome was not built in a day. The so-called realignment synthesis took place within our living memory, over a period not longer than 35 years. This is a short time in the history of science. We deal essentially with first-generation work, and the history of development in scientific concepts is replete with cases in which the first-generation pioneers got important parts of the story wrong. One first-rate modern example of this is the disciplinary history of the plate-tectonic revolution in earth sciences, which has also occurred within our own professional lifetimes.[37] The founding father of this revolution was the German meteorologist Alfred Wegener (1880–1930), who as long ago as 1912 proposed a clearly defined scientific theory of continental drift. The universal view among geologists before 1912, and of the large majority for the next fifty years, was "stabilist": the continents had always been geographically where they are now. The heretic Wegener was duly relegated to footnotes discussing crackpots and exploded scientific theories.

Why? A primary reason for Wegener's fate in his own lifetime was that he could produce no convincing driving mechanism for continental movements. The forces he adduced were shown either not to be measurable or were far too weak to produce the desired results. Continents, as it proved, indeed did not plow through oceanic crust as he had argued. Instead, they are rafted along as a result of sea-floor spreading that propels plates containing *both* continents *and* ocean basins. But discovery of the latter view of the earth, confirming Wegener's core insight, could not be achieved until it became technologically possible to probe the ocean floor, and when it was discovered that rock magnetism contained vital clues as to the processes and timings of change on the ocean floor. This breakthrough could not occur before the years 1959–66. But when it did, the causal story that emerged was so overwhelmingly convincing that professional conversion to the mobilist view of earth history was nearly total and nearly instantaneous. In the process, continental drift as a concept became superseded by (or subsumed under) plate tectonics.

The point of this tale—there are many others—is that the first generation had somehow come up with a conceptualization which, while wrong and undeveloped in many cases, was brilliant enough, and seemed, if it could be brought to adequate standards in sorting out some very troublesome data, likely never to be entirely forgotten. It needed the input of subsequent generations to arrive at some resolution, and to achieve a far better approximation to truth than any hitherto known. In the field of realignment research as well, first-generation work has not, I believe, exhausted all the possibilities. The impasses so richly described and critiqued here very commonly arise in the early history of conceptual formulations. Sometimes they are never resolved. Here I think in time they will be. Proclamations of the death of critical realignment, as of Mark Twain while he was still alive, are thus considerably exaggerated.

Appendix

This essay is hardly the place for elaborate quantitative demonstrations of arguing-points. At the same time, it might perhaps clarify some of the verbal discussion in this essay to present the outline of one such quantitative analysis, using just one particular technique. Readers are referred to tables 5.A1 and 5.A2.

Back in 1954, V. O. Key, Jr., published a short review of elementary statistical technique—*very* elementary by today's standards—entitled *A Primer of Statistics for Political Scientists.*[38] One of the exercises he employed to demonstrate the uses of regression-correlation technique took as its base the Democratic percentages of the two-party presidential vote in 1944 and 1948 for each of New Hampshire's ten counties. Falling as these elections did in the stable phase of the New Deal order, the fits were very close: the correlation coefficient for this bivariate array was + .979, and its square (the amount of variance in the 1948 segment explained by the 1944 pattern) was .959. In other words, more than 95% of the 1948 variance was explicable in terms of the 1944 distribution: the present then was very much like the past on this dimension.[39]

This is one of a variety of useful techniques for exploring the impact of certain kinds of critical realignments where there is considerable internal redistribution of voting patterns among the units in a given state (or other jurisdiction). If the stable-state norm can be said to show a variance explained of, say, at least 80%, it is quite possible to find situations where this plummets to close to zero and rebounds afterward to new and very high values—after the punctuational-change flipover has been succeeded by a new steady-system state. But it is also useful as a more general marker for evaluating the relative degree to which party labels manage to order outcomes across a number of offices during the same election. Since one can in fact run series of this sort back to 1828, evaluation of the r^2s permits identification of some change which is blazingly salient,

Table 5.A1. One Measure of Partisan Salience: Coefficients of Determination (r^2s) between State-Level Major-Party Percentages of the Total Vote for Major Offices, in Presidential Years, 1828–1988

Year	Federal-Federal			Federal-State			Means		Total
	Pres-HR	Pres-USS	USS-HR	Pres-Gov	Gov-USS	Gov-HR	Fed-Fed	Fed-State	
1828	.876			.900		.687	.876	.794	.821
1832	.465			.833		.318	.465	.576	.539
1836	.756			.802		.632	.756	.717	.730
1840	.870			.967		.984	.870	.976	.940
1844	.817			.936		.874	.817	.905	.876
1848	.347			.586		.841	.347	.714	.591
1852	.580			.810		.640	.580	.725	.677
1856	.959			.936		.935	.959	.935	.943
1860	.911			.985		.987	.911	.986	.961
1864	.900			.980		.869	.900	.925	.916
1868	.982			.965		.990	.982	.978	.979
1872	.793			.786		.950	.793	.868	.843
1876	.973			.947		.978	.973	.963	.966
1880	.932			.971		.919	.932	.945	.941
1884	.856			.883		.944	.856	.914	.894
1888	.975			.969		.982	.975	.975	.975
1892	.947			.862		.913	.947	.888	.907
1896	.920			.963		.977	.920	.970	.953
1900	.969			.849		.904	.969	.877	.907
1904	.816			.420		.448	.816	.434	.561
1908	.820			.448		.425	.820	.437	.564
1912	.600			.775		.608	.600	.691	.661
1916	.564	.608	.587	.336	.341	.538	.586	.405	.496
1920	.539	.440	.323	.142	.308	.276	.434	.242	.338
1924	.372	.136	.143	.451	.013	.365	.217	.276	.247
1928	.239	.150	.412	.286	.430	.303	.267	.340	.303
1932	.329	.045	.693	.503	.065	.201	.356	.256	.306
1936	.460	.156	.262	.653	.022	.107	.293	.261	.277
1940	.738	.489	.447	.232	.514	.262	.558	.336	.447
1944	.653	.614	.889	.562	.812	.683	.719	.686	.702
1948	.561	.483	.478	.464	.438	.599	.507	.500	.504
1952	.734	.665	.663	.641	.464	.606	.687	.570	.629
1956	.688	.379	.529	.173	.267	.382	.532	.274	.403
1960	.497	.284	.343	.166	.324	.213	.375	.234	.305
1964	.361	.525	.290	.099	.444	.067	.392	.203	.298
1968	.368	.113	.051	.005	.102	.011	.177	.039	.108
1972	.137	.027	.051	.255	.109	.063	.072	.142	.107
1976	.212	.129	.080	.057	.353	.220	.140	.210	.175
1980	.061	.250	.021	.005	.115	.186	.111	.102	.106
1984	.277	.114	.229	.021	.052	.111	.207	.061	.134
1988	.179	.060	.091	.070	.244	.007	.110	.107	.108

Table 5.A1. Notes:

(1) As experts well know, elections before the twentieth century—especially before the Civil War—were often held at quite diverse dates. Indeed, it is not until the 1880 election that all regular U.S. House elections were held in the same year, and a few states held effective elections in some month other than November. The rule here has been to include those cases of "September–November" or "October–November" elections down through 1900, and omit them thereafter. Larger time spreads than that are excluded throughout. If in an off-year in this period a state held a gubernatorial and House election, say, on the same April day in 1843, it is of course included in that array.

(2) All major-office races held within those time bounds and having both Democratic and National Republican/Whig/Republican candidates are included. Obviously, we have aggregated congressional votes up to the statewide level as the base for that office, and it will happen that these totals will reflect the presence of one or more uncontested district elections. Where the uncontested race is for a single at-large seat, it is omitted. Otherwise, such distortions—extremely rare in the nonsouthern states before the early twentieth century, then increasingly common down through 1930, rare again for a generation thereafter, and becoming quite common again in the 1970s and 1980s—could be said to be part of the issues we are describing with this technique.

(3) As indicated in the text, the geographical coverage of data points is at the statewide level, and is confined to the nonsouthern states not seceding in 1860–61. The partisan-percentable basis is for the Democratic share of the total vote through 1860 and the Republican share of the total vote thereafter. On two occasions, "bolters" are added to "regulars": northern and southern Democrats in 1860, and Republican and Progressive candidates in 1912 and 1914.

(4) The coefficients of determination (r^2s) are of course based on a unique regression equation for each pair in each election. All of this information, including numbers of cases and standard errors of estimate, has been omitted for the sake of simplicity of presentation. Two more detailed points are worth mentioning: the direction of the slope and any dynamic change in the N of cases.

(a) Following Key's little New Hampshire example, there would a priori be every reason to assume that the regression slopes would always be positive, very strongly (as in the nineteenth century) or more weakly (as in the twentieth). In other words, we would expect that as the Republican share of the vote for one office increases, it will also increase for the other. This assumption, however, has been frequently violated since 1960, as follows: table 5.A1: *1964:* Pres-Gov, Gov-USS, Gov-USHR; *1968:* Pres-Gov, Gov-USS; *1972:* Pres-Gov, Gov-USS, Gov-USHR; *1980:* Gov-USS; table 5.A2: *1966:* Gov-USHR; *1970:* Gov-USS; *1974:* USS-USHR; *1978:* Gov-USHR. Whether the disappearance of these anomalies after 1980 means anything of dynamic moment remains to be seen.

(b) Numbers generally grow over time with the number of states and offices that are included. After 1914, they remain stable, with one chief exception. The number of gubernatorial races in the non-South that are held in presidential election years has steeply declined from 28 in 1932 and 24 in 1952 to no more than 11 in the 1980s—the chief downward inflection here occurs (as one might expect?) between 1968 and 1976. In his study, *American State Politics* (New York: Knopf, 1956), V. O. Key, Jr., pointed with some alarm to this development as further decoupling state politics from national ("insulating state politics from national tides"). Like so many other things that gave Key worry toward the end of his life, this dynamic change has produced far *more* extreme decoupling than was the case when he wrote.

Table 5.A2. Another Measure of Partisan Salience: Coefficients of Determination (r²s) between State-Level Major-Party Percentages of the Total Vote for Major Offices, in Off Years, 1830/31–1986

Year	Federal-Federal USS-HR	Federal-State Gov-USS	Federal-State Gov-HR	Means Federal-State	Total
1830/31			.512	.512	.512
1834/35			.980	.980	.980
1838/39			.651	.651	.651
1842/43			.856	.856	.856
1846/47			.868	.868	.868
1850/51			.776	.776	.776
1854/55			.972	.972	.972
1858/59			.966	.966	.966
1862/63			.962	.962	.962
1866/67			.983	.983	.983
1870/71			.940	.940	.940
1874			.857	.857	.857
1878			.860	.860	.860
1882			.762	.762	.762
1886			.692	.692	.692
1890			.881	.881	.881
1894			.913	.913	.913
1898			.859	.859	.859
1902			.839	.839	.839
1906			.241	.241	.241
1910			.589	.589	.589
1914	.478	.545	.338	.442	.454
1918	.417	.298	.183	.241	.299
1922	.343	.711	.502	.607	.519
1926	.336	.318	.574	.446	.409
1930	.542	.154	.168	.161	.288
1934	.729	.545	.632	.589	.635
1938	.757	.663	.550	.607	.657
1942	.413	.869	.645	.757	.642
1946	.533	.647	.581	.613	.587
1950	.706	.662	.554	.608	.641
1954	.471	.395	.546	.471	.471
1958	.270	.121	.194	.158	.195
1962	.425	.078	.353	.215	.285
1966	.077	.000	.149	.075	.075
1970	.084	.008	.069	.026	.054
1974	.013	.025	.099	.089	.046
1978	.067	.105	.000	.053	.057
1982	.007	.090	.158	.124	.085
1986	.225	.076	.073	.074	.124

See notes to table 5.A1.

and other change which is worth at least a mention. Obviously, the descriptive argument is that the closer r² approaches 1.0, the closer the fit among electoral coalitions arrayed across major federal and state offices. The closer it is to zero, the poorer this fit in terms of party, and the more one can assume that "unexplained" factors play growingly important roles—presumably, for example, large growth in ticket splitting and the emergence of candidate-dominated elections.

The relationships are defined at the state level. They involve measurements of the partisan percentages of the total vote, Democratic before 1860 and Republican from then on. Only the nonsouthern states are analyzed, where relevant data exists. The former Confederate states are excluded because their uniquely deviant political history produces too much background noise in an indicator which is highly sensitive to extreme values in its distributions. To avoid possible contamination by any "presidential synthesis," relationships are included between partisan percentages for governor and U.S. House, governor and U.S. Senate (from 1914 on), and U.S. House and Senate (again, from 1914 on). Moreover, off-year elections are included (see table 5.A2) as well as presidential year elections (table 5.A1). It should be stressed, finally, that this array is indicative as only one measure of tightness of coalitional fit at a very high level of aggregation. It can of course say nothing directly about individual-level behavior, nor is it a convenient way of projecting the "real" volume of ticket splitting in an electorate, since gross movement is always considerably more than net.

The data are highly suggestive nevertheless, and on a number of dimensions. There is, of course, a huge difference between these relationships during the "lost Atlantis" of the partisan nineteenth century and those of the departisanized twentieth.[40] The argument that there was indeed a "party period" that has since lapsed receives yet one more confirmation. At the same time, it may be worth more than a passing note that this era has a notably lower partisan "fit" before 1854–56 than from then until the early years of the next century. This is not merely a question of waiting for "consolidation" to crystallize around 1838. A noteworthy feature of the so-called second party system was what has been called its "fragility"; no sooner had it been consolidated than it began to rot under the pressure of antislaveryism and nativism. One may add that this is reflected in turnout (systemic capacity to mobilize) as well as in terms of progressively lower partisan-fit r²s across offices. In this regard, 1838–40 represented a high water mark not to be achieved again until critical realignment and the destruction of this system brought forth the immense mobilizations of 1856–1858–1860.

These factors not only suggest the energizing effect of the critical realignment of those years, but suggest at least a slight modification of any possible argument that post-1838 electoral politics is uniformly all of a partisan-mobi-

lized piece. Among other things, the 69% turnout rate in the 1852 election
(only slightly lower than in 1848) represented the lowest level of mass mobilization achieved between 1836 and 1904; one must wait until 1928 to find a
poorer state-level fit between president and U.S. House than the depth reached
in 1848. By contrast, the period 1856–1900 looks very much more like a unified "era." Even the temporary, presidentially linked decline in 1872 can be
straightforwardly explained by the curious dynamics of defeat that led the
Democrats to embrace the Liberal Republican nominee, Horace Greeley. Perhaps the only other matter of some moment is the sign of decay in the goodness
of fit between governor and U.S. House in off-year elections, at least between
its all-time high stand of 1866 and 1886. These elections, not linked to the
presidential-election galvanizer, show a pattern which at least some versions of
realignment-based analysis would predict.

The move from this integrated system to its opposite, by this metric at least,
can be rather precisely pinpointed as occurring in 1904–6 as far as federal-state
decoupling is concerned, and in 1912 at the federal level (president-House).
The breakaway movement downward is abrupt and very large, with subsequent
declines tending to produce a nadir which corresponds with the Normalcy Era
of the 1920s. The pattern thereafter is extremely complex: where there is a sat-
isfying jump-increase in this measure of coalitional cohesion in the 1934 off-
year election, it takes far longer for similar increases to be registered in many of
the presidential-year election pairs. Partly, this reflects specific peculiarities of
politics in the 1930s, e.g., the existence of significant third-party distorting
effects in Minnesota and Wisconsin. But there is a more general heteroclite
pattern of outcomes, concentrated as one might expect in the "colonial" prairie
and mountain states. As numerous analysts of state and regional politics have
pointed out, the full integration of parties and coalitions in many of these states
with the national alignment structure was a long drawn-out process not completed until the mid-to-late 1940s.[41]

Nevertheless, the pattern shows a broad reversal toward higher levels of partisan coalitional integration, with the federal-level peak pretty clearly defined
as falling between 1940 and 1956 and declining thereafter. It strikes me that
there is far too much movement in this direction for analysis to remain comfort-
able with the idea that, say, everything from 1904 on is part of a uniform "postpartisan" era. Even if the r^2s at their New Deal system peak never return to
nineteenth-century levels, they stand out far above the previous depths, or the
abyssal plains of later decades.

It has been intimated before in this chapter that significant trends toward the
development of the "real" postpartisan era became clearly visible as early as
the later 1950s. The decay occurred in stages, with certain kinds of indicators
(swing ratios between partisan percentages of votes and seats in House elections, along with the ones used here, are two good cases) being much more

sensitive than others to this development. There is clearly a two-step downshift pattern visible in these arrays in both tables: the first in the late 1950s, the second falling between 1966 and 1968 (or, so far as president–U.S. House relationships are concerned, between 1968 and 1972). The eyeball tells us as much, and the application of breakpoint search routines produces gratifyingly high levels of *t*. There is a directional flow here, but—with different breakpoint moments and magnitudes—there are also very clear signs of jump-shift. In all likelihood, this particular array could not convincingly demonstrate that 1968–72 was the "moment" in which a "Type B" critical realignment occurred, bringing us eventually the Reagan-Bush regime order and the total dominance of the "permanent campaign" in the entrepreneurial organization of the American electoral market. But, taken in conjunction with the other measures of events and categoric entities particularly needed in dealing with Type B realignments, the array's shape—and its lack of any convincing post-1966/72 directional pattern—is certainly consistent with that hypothesis. It is one more piece of evidence, but many others must also exist—and tell a tale which at least does not clearly contradict a given causal story that purports to order all of them.

Viewing the last five or six elections in each series, it would be difficult to imagine a clearer demonstration of "postpartisanship": indeed, some of the federal-state relationships between 1964 and 1980 are actually *negative* (as the Republican share of the vote for Office X goes up, it actually goes *down* for Office Y, sometimes (G-USS 64 and P-G 72) with rather respectable r²s. We have almost the mathematical inverse of the situation that dominated the 1856–1900 period. In any event, as the 1988 line reveals, this is part of the "structure of politics at the accession of George Bush." On this dimension at least, there has been a similar structure extending back to, but not before, the 1966–72 period, especially on the important dimension of relationships between outcomes for federal offices.

The point of this exercise was to render a little more concrete a discussion attempting to affirm a series of propositions about critical realignment. The array does suggest that there is something historically unique and unprecedented about the current electoral era in which we now live, at least in the setting of the mass partisanship that began to crystallize in the late 1820s. The current regime/electoral order is thus perhaps even *more* interesting than Shafer's account conveys, and the comparisons with past orders perhaps even more telling. But there was a wall of general crisis standing between now and then, and this too must be analyzed and put into some coherent conceptual perspective. I have attempted here to sketch the outline of one.

Notes

1 V. O. Key, Jr., "A Theory of Critical Elections," *Journal of Politics* 17 (February 1955): 3–18.

2 One may note, for example, work by the sociologist J. Zvi Namenwirth on cycles of value change in American political history, the underlying data base being American party platforms from 1844 onward, and the method being content analysis based on the Yale-Lasswell propositional dictionary: "The Wheels of Time and the Interdependence of Value Change in America," in J. Zvi Namenwirth and Robert P. Weber, *Dynamics of Culture* (Boston: Allen & Unwin, 1987), 57–88.

3 Cf. Helge Kragh, *An Introduction to the Historiography of Science* (New York: Cambridge University Press, 1987), 75–78.

4 Paul Kleppner, *Continuity and Change in Electoral Politics, 1893–1928* (Westport, Conn.: Greenwood Press, 1987). This work also has a relevant and important appendix, "Realignment Theory After Key," 240–49.

5 Cf. Allan J. Lichtman, "Critical Election Theory and the Reality of American Presidential Politics, 1916–1940," *American Historical Review* 81 (April 1976): 317–50; and idem, "The End of Realignment Theory? Toward a New Research Program for American Political History," *Historical Methods* 15 (Fall 1982): 170–88.

6 An unnecessary burden against which his arch-champion Thomas Henry Huxley warned him. See Stephen Jay Gould, "Toward the Vindication of Punctuational Change," in *Catastrophes and Earth History: The New Uniformitarianism*, ed. W. A. Berggren and John A. Van Couvering (Princeton: Princeton University Press, 1983), 21–22.

7 Richard H. Benson, "Perfection, Continuity, and Common Sense in Historical Geology," in ibid., 36.

8 Walter Dean Burnham, *Presidential Ballots, 1836–1892* (Baltimore: Johns Hopkins University Press, 1955). This study was stimulated by reading and reflecting on Edgar Eugene Robinson's pioneering work, *The Presidential Vote, 1896–1932* (Stanford: Stanford University Press, 1934). Eighteen thirty-six is the first presidential election in which substantially complete county-level returns are available for all states having a popular vote—a collateral supporting indicator for Silbey's emphasis on important change long after Andrew Jackson had become president. The end of my study and both the beginning and the end of Robinson's coincide with inflection points in critical realignment. Contemplation of and reflection on these data over a sustained period made something of the sort dimly obvious to me even then.

9 A first-rate and brilliantly compressed account of the main currents of Supreme Court history remains Robert G. McCloskey, *The American Supreme Court* (Chicago: University of Chicago Press, 1960).

10 Cf. one of a number of comments to like effect in Walter Dean Burnham, *Critical Elections and the Mainsprings of American Politics* (New York: W. W. Norton, 1970): ". . . the party system may have already moved beyond the possiblity of critical realignment because of the dissolution of party-related identification and voting choice at the mass base. Such a development would in itself mark one of the

great turning points in the history of American politics. Political parties have had a profoundly significant constituent function in our political system. This function has been most characteristically realized through critical realignments with durable consequences. The disappearance of these parties as the primary channel through which mass opinion is articulated would necessarily imply, therefore, a most profound and irreversible transformation in the American constitution itself" (173).

11 A. Conan Doyle, *The Complete Sherlock Holmes* (Garden City, N.Y.: Garden City Publishing, 1938), 397.

12 Sidney Blumenthal, *The Permanent Campaign,* rev. ed. (New York: Scribners, 1982), 305.

13 Cf. Walter Dean Burnham, "V. O. Key, Jr., and the Study of Political Parties," in *V. O. Key, Jr. and the Study of American Politics,* ed. Milton C. Cummings (Washington: American Political Science Association, 1988), 3–23.

14 Thomas R. Kuhn, *The Structure of Scientific Revolutions,* 2d ed. (Chicago: University of Chicago Press, 1970).

15 Cf. Gould, "Vindication of Punctuational Change," and sources cited. Gould's most recent book, *Wonderful Life: The Burgess Shale and the Nature of History* (New York: W. W. Norton, 1989) extends this discussion in places, and has much else to say which should prove stimulating for historians of human affairs as well as historians of life forms.

16 Cf. Gould, "Vindication of Punctuational Change," esp. 27–31. His is not an eccentric view of the subject. It should be stressed somewhere that even if quite great scholars are committing ideology all over the place, this by no means implies that one research idea or paradigm is no more scientifically valuable than another. One assumes that in the long run at least, a major reason for the existence of scientific standards and of research communities using them is to winnow out the wheat from the chaff.

17 Niles Eldredge and Stephen Jay Gould, "Punctuated Equilibria: An Alternative to Phyletic Gradualism," in *Models in Paleobiology,* ed. T. M. J. Schopf (San Francisco: Freeman, Cooper, 1972), 82–115.

18 Cf., e.g., Paul R. Abramson, "Generational Change in American Electoral Behavior," *American Political Science Review* 68 (March 1974): 93–105; idem, "Generational Change and the Decline of Party Identification in America: 1952–1974," *American Political Science Review* 70 (June 1976); 469–78; Paul Allen Beck, "A Socialization Theory of Partisan Realignment," in Richard D. Niemi et al., *The Politics of Future Citizens* (San Francisco: Jossey-Bass, 1974), pp. 199–219.

19 Lee Benson, *The Concept of Jacksonian Democracy: New York as a Test Case* (Princeton: Princeton University Press, 1961). His discussion of the structural and cultural foundations of American voting behavior implicitly compiles a catalogue of reasons why highly complex brokerage games should be developed and maintained as long as possible by entrepreneur-politicians seeking to win elections. Cf. the still growing professional influence of William H. Riker, arising from work such as his *The Theory of Political Coalitions* (New Haven: Yale University Press, 1962).

20 Cf. David Butler and Donald Stokes, *Political Change in Britain: Forces Shaping Electoral Choice* (London: Macmillan, 1969), 23–43.

21 Morris P. Fiorina, *Retrospective Voting in American National Elections* (New Haven: Yale University Press, 1981).

22 Kleppner, *Continuity and Change*, 11–15.

23 Among the more recent: Louis Hartz, *The Liberal Tradition in America* (New York: Harcourt, Brace, 1955); Louis Hartz et al., *The Founding of New Societies* (New York: Harcourt, Brace, 1964); David Potter, *People of Plenty: Economic Abundance and the American Character* (Chicago: University of Chicago Press, 1954); Samuel P. Huntington, *Political Order in Changing Societies* (New Haven: Yale University Press, 1968), esp. chap. 2, "Political Modernization: America Versus Europe," 93–139.

24 This is virtually axiomatic, and can be traced back to the beginning. Cf. James Sterling Young, *The Washington Community, 1800–1828* (New York: Columbia University Press, 1966), and Eric L. McKitrick, "Party Politics and the Union and Confederate War Efforts," in *The American Party Systems: Stages of Political Development,* ed. William N. Chambers and Walter Dean Burnham, 2d ed. (New York: Oxford University Press, 1975), 117–51.

25 A still lively and penetrating discussion of this issue is Theodore J. Lowi, "Toward Functionalism in Political Science: The Case of Innovation in Party Systems," *American Political Science Review* 57 (September 1963): 570–83.

26 An important account remains Shaw Livermore, *The Twilight of Federalism: The Disintegration of the Federalist Party, 1815–1830* (Princeton: Princeton University Press, 1962).

27 Cf. Samuel Popkin et al., "Comment: What Have You Done For Me Lately? Toward an Investment Theory of Voting," *American Political Science Review* 70 (September 1976): 779–805.

28 Ronald P. Formisano, "Deferential-Participant Politics: The Early Republic's Political Culture, 1789–1840," *American Political Science Review* 68 (June 1974): 473–87. His assessment of the peculiar "first party system" strikes me as just about right: idem, "Federalists and Republicans: Parties, Yes—System, No," in Paul Kleppner et al., *The Evolution of American Electoral Systems* (Westport, Conn.: Greenwood Press, 1981), 33–76.

29 Ronald P. Formisano, *The Transformation of Political Culture: Massachusetts Parties, 1790s–1840s* (New York: Oxford University Press, 1983), 57–106.

30 Granted the dynamism of socioeconomic development and the tensions between government and society in the United States, the stability of the between-realignment electoral eras is always more or less relative. There was a particularly powerful dynamic thrust to the "System of 1896," following the decisive defeat of colonial interests by the Metropole. Once that question was decided, however, major "modernization" conflicts broke out within the Metropole itself. To some considerable extent, the Progressive impulse is linked to the rationalization-modernization processes discussed at the governmental level by Stephen Skowronek's important study, *Building a New American State: The Expansion of National Administrative Capacity, 1877–1920* (New York: Cambridge University Press, 1982). See also Samuel P. Hays, "Political Parties and the Community-Society Continuum," in Chambers and Burnham, *The American Party Systems,* 152–81.

31 See Edward Stanwood, *A History of the Presidency* (Boston: Houghton Mifflin, 1906), 110.

32 Ibid., 130.

33 A brief account of this episode is given in Alfred H. Kelly and Winifred Harbison, *The American Constitution, Its Origins and Development* (New York: W. W. Norton, 1955), 298–99.

34 Morris P. Fiorina, "An Era of Divided Government" (Harvard University Center for American Political Studies, Occasional Paper 89-6, December 1989), esp. 22–33.

35 Seymour Martin Lipset and William Schneider, *The Confidence Gap* (New York: Free Press, 1983). Like so many other important indicators, measures of public trust and confidence in the performance of key American institutions—particularly political institutions—began their breakaway descent in the general crisis of the late 1960s. This continued across the 1970s, and then was partially (but only partially) reversed after the advent of Ronald Reagan in 1981. Both the timing and magnitude of these shifts, and the relative durabilitiy of the subsequent opinion configuration, look very much like "flipover" into a new systemic equilibrium.

36 Imre Lakatos, *The Methodology of Scientific Research Programmes* (Cambridge: Cambridge University Press, 1978), esp. 1–5, 47–52ff.

37 Two fine and accessible accounts of the subject are H. E. LeGrand, *Drifting Continents and Shifting Theories* (Cambridge: Cambridge University Press, 1988), and the relevant portions of a work which provides fascinating insight throughout: A. Hallam, *Great Geological Controversies* (Oxford: Oxford University Press, 1983).

38 V. O. Key, Jr., *A Primer of Statistics for Political Scientists* (New York: Crowell, 1954).

39 Ibid., 120–23.

40 The comment about this method's sensitivity to extreme values should be taken seriously, and the technique is limited thereby. It would be very rash to assume that because, by using it, we get a 1988 presidential-Senate r^2 of .060, individual-level voting coalitions have become entirely dichotomous. To the contrary, a large majority of individuals continue to vote for the same party's candidates for both offices, according to CPS survey-research data. But this majority is considerably less than it used to be, and the aggregate state-level regression measures used here reflect this in an "extreme" way. Here, precisely, is a case in which politically decisive minorities of the politically relevant population since 1952 have stopped doing what they were doing, started doing something else, and then kept on doing it.

41 A good account of one aspect of these regional deviations, the Minnesota Farmer-Labor Party, is Richard M. Valelly, *State-Level Radicalism* (Chicago: University of Chicago Press, 1989).

Harold F. Bass, Jr.

Background to Debate
A Reader's Guide and Bibliography

Realignment: A Reader's Guide

A map facilitates a journey, in this case through the voluminous scholarly literature on realignment, one spanning the disciplines of history and political science. To that end, this reader's guide organizes the literature under three overlapping headings, pointing readers to noteworthy and representative examples of each: foundations, applications, and controversies.

Foundations

By general agreement, a relative handful of classic works provide the foundations for realignment scholarship. V. O. Key, Jr., introduced the concept to the scholarly community in "A Theory of Critical Elections," *Journal of Politics* 17 (February 1955): 3–18. He extended it in "Secular Realignment and the Party System," *Journal of Politics* 21 (May 1959): 198–210.

The team of Angus Campbell, Philip E. Converse, Warren E. Miller, and Donald E. Stokes, at the University of Michigan's Survey Research Center, made several important contributions in their considerations of partisan identification and electoral behavior. *Elections and the Political Order* (New York: John Wiley and Sons, 1966) assembles these valuable early efforts.

Walter Dean Burnham made realignment central to his interpretation of the American political process in *Critical Elections and the Mainsprings of American Politics* (New York: W. W. Norton, 1970). James L. Sundquist concluded the "founding era" with *Dynamics of the Party System: Alignment and Re-*

141

alignment of Political Parties in the United States (Washington, D.C.: Brookings Institution, 1973; rev. ed., 1983).

Upon this bedrock, scholarship on realignment has proliferated far and wide. For three follow-up expressions of conceptual development, in typically diverse forms, see Walter Dean Burnham, Jerome M. Clubb, and William H. Flanigan, "Partisan Realignment: A Systemic Perspective," in *The History of American Electoral Behavior,* ed. Joel H. Silbey, Allen G. Bogue, and William H. Flanigan (Princeton: Princeton University Press, 1978), 45–77; Jerome M. Clubb, William H. Flanigan, and Nancy H. Zingale, *Partisan Realignment: Voters, Parties, and Government in American History* (Beverly Hills, Calif.: Sage, 1980); and Bruce A. Campbell and Richard J. Trilling, eds., *Realignment in American Politics: Towards a Theory* (Austin: University of Texas Press, 1979).

Applications

Specific applications of the realignment perspective address institutions, territories, groups, issues, eras, and individual elections. In the institutional context, studies were initially centered on the political party, especially on party in the electorate; they now embrace the other elements of party as well, that is, organization and government. Studies of party organization that utilize realignment perspectives include James L. Gibson, "The Role of Party Organizations in the Mountain West, 1960–1980," in *The Politics of Realignment: Party Change in the Mountain West,* ed. Peter Galderisi et al. (Boulder, Colo.: Westview Press, 1987): 197–219; and Dorothy Davidson Nesbit, "Changing Partisanship Among Southern Party Activists," *Journal of Politics* 50 (May 1988): 322–34.

Linking elections with public policy, realignment perspectives have looked beyond the presidency to the other institutions of American national government: Congress, the bureaucracy, and the Supreme Court. For a general statement, see Benjamin Ginsberg, "Elections and Public Policy," *American Political Science Review* 70 (March 1976): 41–49. David W. Brady sets the standard for those using the concept to consider Congress. See his *Critical Elections and Congressional Policy Making* (Stanford: Stanford University Press, 1988). Also consult Barbara D. Sinclair, "Party Realignment and the Transformation of the National Agenda: The House of Representatives, 1925–1938," *American Political Science Review* 71 (September 1977): 940–53.

Martin Shefter assesses the influence of realignments on the bureaucracy in "Party, Bureaucracy, and Political Change in the United States," in *Political Parties: Development and Decay,* ed. Louis Maisel and Joseph Cooper (Beverly Hills, Calif.: Sage, 1978), 211–65. David Adamany blazed the trail for applications of the realignment perspective to studies of the Supreme Court in "Law and Society: Legitimacy, Realigning Elections, and the Supreme Court," *Wisconsin Law Review* (September 1973): 790–846. William Lasser makes realignment the analytical centerpiece of his general study, *The Limits of Judicial Power: The Supreme Court in American Politics* (Chapel Hill: University of North Carolina Press, 1988).

Numerous realignment studies have examined particular regions within the United States, with the South receiving the most substantial consideration. For an early effort, see Philip E. Converse, "A Major Political Realignment in the South?" in *Change in the Contemporary South,* ed. Allan P. Sindler (Durham, N.C.: Duke University Press, 1963), 195–222. Subsequent contributions include Raymond E. Wolfinger and Robert B. Arsenau, "Partisan Change in the South, 1952–1972," in *Political Parties: Development and Decay,* ed. Louis Maisel and Joseph Cooper (Beverly Hills, Calif.: Sage, 1978), 179–210; and John R. Petrocik, "Realignment: New Party Coalitions and the Nationalization of the South," *Journal of Politics* 49 (May 1987): 347–75. For thorough treatment of another region, see the aforementioned Galderisi et al., *Politics of Realignment.*

At the state level, work under the realignment banner takes in the pioneering contribution of Duncan Macrae, Jr., and James Meldrum, "Critical Elections in Illinois: 1888–1958," *American Political Science Review* 54 (September 1960): 669–83. More recently, James Dyer, Arnold Vedlitz, and David B. Hill present "New Voters, Switchers, and Political Party Realignment in Texas," *Western Political Quarterly* 41 (Spring 1988): 155–67. Maureen Moakley is editing a volume, *Party Realignment in the American States* (Columbus: Ohio State University Press, forthcoming) that will consider the evidence for realignment in fifteen states.

Moving the level of analysis further down, from state to city, David J. Alvarez and Edmund J. True present "Critical Elections and Partisan Realignment: An Urban Test Case," *Polity* 5 (Summer 1973): 563–76. The suburbs receive attention more generally in Fred I. Greenstein and Raymond E. Wolfinger, "The Suburbs and Shifting Party Loyalties," *Public Opinion Quarterly* 22 (Winter 1958): 473–82.

The realignment perspective has by now been applied to many political settings outside the United States. Russell J. Dalton, Scott C. Flanagan, and Paul Allen Beck, eds., provide a useful compilation of country studies in *Electoral Change in Advanced Industrial Democracies: Realignment or Dealignment?* (Princeton: Princeton University Press, 1984). For comparisons between the United States and other systems, see Ronald Inglehart and Avram Hochstein, "Alignment and Dealignment of the Electorate in France and the United States," *Comparative Political Studies* 5 (October 1972): 343–72; and Ivor Crewe, "Prospects for Party Realignment: An Anglo-American Comparison," *Comparative Politics* 12 (July 1980): 379–400.

An alternative approach in the realignment literature examines the partisan shifts of specific groups whose members constitute the party coalitions. See the recurring reflections of Robert Axelrod, initially presented in "Where the Votes Come From: An Analysis of Electoral Coalitions, 1952–1978," *American Political Science Review* 66 (March 1972): 11–20. Also see Robert S. Erikson, Thomas D. Lancaster, and David W. Romero, "Group Components of the Presidential Vote, 1952–1984," *Journal of Politics* 51 (May 1989): 337–46.

For examples of considerations of particular groups, see Rita W. Gordon, "The Change in the Political Alignment of Chicago's Negroes during the New Deal," *Journal of American History* 56 (December 1969): 584–603; and Alan M. Fisher, "Realignment of the Jewish Vote," *Political Science Quarterly* 94 (Spring 1979): 97–116. For class-based analyses, look at Norval D. Glenn, "Class and Party Support in the United States: Recent Trends," *Public Opinion Quarterly* 36 (Spring 1972): 31–47; and Richard Oestreicher, "Urban Working Class Political Behavior and Theories of American Electoral Politics, 1870–1940," *Journal of American History* 74 (March 1988): 1257–86.

The role of issues in effecting realignments has been a major concern, as with James E. Piereson, "Issue Alignment and the American Party System, 1956–1976," *American Politics Quarterly* 6 (July 1978): 275–308; and Edward Carmines and James A. Stimson, *Issue Evolution: Race and the Transformation of American Politics* (Princeton: Princeton University Press, 1989).

Realignment is perhaps most often considered chronologically, with reference to realigning elections or periods and their party systems. William Nisbet Chambers and Walter Dean Burnham, eds., *The American Party Systems: Stages of Political Development,* 2d ed. (New York: Oxford University Press, 1975), and Paul Kleppner et al., *The Evolution of American Electoral Systems* (Westport, Conn.: Greenwood Press, 1981), provide outstanding collections on both the overall approach and distinct party systems. For an excellent survey of this stream of scholarship, examine the review article by Peter H. Argersinger and John W. Jeffries, "American Electoral History: Party Systems and Voting Behavior," *Research in Micropolitics* 1 (1986): 1–33.

Michael F. Holt, *The Political Crisis of the 1850s* (New York: John Wiley and Sons, 1978), treats the upheaval of that decade. William E. Gienapp, *The Origins of the Republican Party, 1852–1856* (New York: Oxford University Press, 1987), deals with the emergence of a new party. Ray M. Shortridge, "The Voter Realignment in the Midwest in the 1850s," *American Politics Quarterly* 4 (April 1976): 193–202, offers a regional focus. Paul Kleppner, *The Third Electoral System, 1853–1892* (Chapel Hill: University of North Carolina Press, 1979), ably addresses the new party system created.

Considerations of events leading up to the election of 1896 and its repercussions in diverse locales and levels include Paul Kleppner, "The Political Realignment of the 1890s: A Behavioral Interpretation," in *Voters, Parties, and Elections,* ed., Joel H. Silbey and Samuel T. McSeveney (Lexington, Mass.:

Xerox, 1972), 184–95; Richard Jensen, *The Winning of the Midwest: Social and Political Conflict, 1888–1896* (Chicago: University of Chicago Press, 1971); Samuel T. McSeveney, *The Politics of Depression: Voting Behavior in the Northeast, 1893–1896* (New York: Oxford University Press, 1972); and Sally S. Zanjani, "A Theory of Critical Alignment: The Nevada Example, 1892–1908," *Pacific Historical Review* 49 (May 1979): 259–80.

The emergence of the New Deal realignment receives attention from Kristi Anderson, *Creation of a Democratic Majority, 1928–1936* (Chicago: University Press, 1979). John Petrocik assesses its aftermath in *Party Coalitions: Realignments and the Decline of the New Deal Party System* (Chicago: University of Chicago Press, 1981).

Within the party systems framework, scholars have concentrated on specific elections, critical and otherwise. The 1928 presidential election, as the predecessor to the contest which really generated the realignment framework, attracts extraordinary attention. See Ruth V. Silva, *Rum, Religion, and Votes: 1928 Reconsidered* (University Park: University of Pennsylvania Press, 1962); Jerome M. Clubb and Howard W. Allen, "The Cities and the Election of 1928: Partisan Realignment?" *American Historical Review* 74 (April 1969): 1205–20; and Allen J. Lichtman, *Prejudice and the Old Politics: The Presidential Election of 1928* (Chapel Hill: University of North Carolina Press, 1979).

For the past quarter-century, however, *every* presidential election has elicited assessments of its realigning potential. The 1980 election may be especially noteworthy in this regard among recent contests. See Walter Dean Burnham, "The 1980 Earthquake: Realignment, Reaction, or What?" in *The Hidden Election,* ed. Thomas Ferguson and Joel Rogers (New York: Pantheon, 1981), 98–140; William Schneider, "The November 4 Vote for President: What Does It Mean?" in *The American Elections of 1980,* ed. Austin Ranney (Washington, D.C.: American Enterprise Institute, 1981), 212–62; and Nelson W. Polsby, "Party Realignment in the 1980 Election," *Yale Review* 72 (August 1982): 41–54.

Controversies

Several scholars have attacked the realignment perspective, in whole or in part. For two general critiques anticipating the challenges presented in this volume, see Allen J. Lichtman, "The End of Realignment Theory? Toward a New Research Program for American Political History," *Historical Methods* 15 (Fall 1982): 170–88; and Richard L. McCormick, "The Realignment Synthesis in American History," *Journal of Interdisciplinary History* 13 (Summer 1982): 85–105.

More specific debates have occurred over the nature, extent, and timing of realignments. For a provocative interpretation challenging the "critical" character of the election of 1896, see Allen J. Lichtman, "Political Realignment and 'Ethnocultural' Voting in Late Nineteenth Century America," *Journal of Social History* 16 (Spring 1983): 55–82. Also see John L. Shover, "Was 1928 a Critical Election in California?" *Pacific Northwest Quarterly* 58 (October 1967): 196–204. Bernard Sternsher capably summarizes scholarship on the New Deal party system and its attendant controversies in two articles: "The Emergence of the New Deal Party System: A Problem in Historical Analysis of Voter Behavior," *Journal of Interdisciplinary History* 6 (October 1975): 127–49; and "The New Deal Party System: A Reappraisal," *Journal of Interdisciplinary History* 15 (Summer 1984): 52–81.

Realignment issues also arise as historians argue over whether partisan changes in the past are better explained in socioeconomic class terms or ethnocultural ones. See James E. Wright, "The Ethnocultural Model of Voting: A Behavioral and Historical Critique," *American Behavioral Scientist* 16 (May 1973): 653–74; Richard L. McCormick, "Ethno-cultural Interpretations of Nineteenth Century American Voting Behavior," *Political Science Quarterly* 89 (June 1974): 351–77; and Allan G. Bogue, Jerome M. Clubb, and William H. Flanigan, "The New Political History," *American Behavioral Scientist* 21 (November–December 1977): 201–20.

An abiding controversy asks whether conversion of disenchanted partisans or mobilization of new voters better accounts for realignments. See Kristi Anderson, "Generation, Partisan Shift, and Realignment: A Glance Back at the New Deal," in Norman H. Nie, Sidney Verba, and John R. Petrocik, *The Changing American Voter* (Cambridge: Harvard University Press, 1976), 74–95; Robert S. Erickson and Kent L. Tedin, "The 1928–1936 Partisan Realignment: The Case for the Conversion Hypothesis," *American Political Science Review* 75 (December 1981): 951–62; and James E. Campbell, "Sources of the New Deal Realignment: The Contributions of Conversion and Mobilization to Partisan Change," *Western Political Quarterly* 38 (September 1985): 357–76. For a discussion of this debate in the context of another realignment, see John Wanat and Karen Burke, "Estimating the Degree of Mobilization and Conversion in the 1890s: An Inquiry into the Nature of Electoral Change," *American Political Science Review* 76 (June 1982): 360–70.

For many scholars, declining partisanship in the electorate undermines the foundations on which the concept of realignment rests, sparking suggestions that dealignment, rather than realignment, is forthcoming. For examples of this perspective, see Edward G. Carmines, "Unrealized Partisanship: A Theory of Dealignment," *Journal of Politics* 49 (May 1987): 376–400; Everett Carll Ladd, "The Brittle Mandate: Electoral Dealignment and the 1980 Election," *Political Science Quarterly* 86 (Spring 1981): 1–25; Paul Allen Beck, "Partisan Dealignment in the Postwar South," *American Political Science Review* 77 (June 1977): 477–96; and Ivor Crewe, Bo Särlvick, and James Alt,

"Partisan Dealignment in Britain," *British Journal of Political Science* 7 (April 1977): 129–90.

As these controversies continue, comments and rejoinders fill the journals. Realignment studies thus proceed amid continuing ferment. Readers must now consider whether this volume fans or douses the flames.

Bibliography

Abney, Glenn. "Partisan Realignment in a One-Party System: The Case of Mississippi." *Journal of Politics* 31 (November 1969): 1102–6.

Abramson, Paul R. "Developing Party Identification: A Further Examination of Life-Cycle, Generational, and Period Effects." *American Journal of Political Science* 23 (February 1979): 78–96.

Abramson, Paul R. "Generational Change and the Decline of Party Identification in America: 1952–1974." *American Political Science Review* 70 (June 1976): 469–78.

Abramson, Paul R. "Generational Change in American Electoral Behavior." *American Political Science Review* 68 (March 1974): 93–105.

Abramson, Paul R. *Generational Change in American Politics*. Lexington, Mass.: D. C. Heath, 1975.

Abramson, Paul R. "Generational Replacement and Partisan Dealignment in Britain and the United States." *British Journal of Political Science* 8 (October 1978): 505–9.

Abramson, Paul R. "Generational Replacement, Ethnic Change, and Partisan Support in Israel." *Journal of Politics* 51 (August 1989): 545–74.

Abramson, Paul R. "Generations and Political Change in the United States." *Research in Political Sociology* 4 (1989): 235–80.

Abramson, Paul R. "Measuring the Southern Contribution to the Democratic Coalition." *American Political Science Review* 81 (June 1987): 567–70.

Abramson, Paul R., John J. Aldrich, and David W. Rohde. *Change and Continuity in the 1980 Elections*. Washington, D.C.: CQ Press, 1982.

Abramson, Paul R. *Change and Continuity in the 1984 Elections*. Washington, D.C.: CQ Press, 1986.

Adamany, David. "Law and Society: Legitimacy, Realigning Elections, and the Supreme Court." *Wisconsin Law Review* (September 1973): 790–846.

Adamany, David. "The Supreme Court's Role in Critical Elections." In *Realignment in American Politics: Toward a Theory,* ed. Bruce A. Campbell and Richard J. Trilling, 229–59. Austin: University of Texas Press, 1980.

Aiesi, Margaret, and Walter A. Rosenbaum. "Not Quite Like Yankees: The Diffusion of Partisan Competition in Two Southern Cities." In *Party Politics in the South,* ed. Robert P. Steed, Lawrence W. Moreland, and Tod A. Baker, 152–74. New York: Praeger, 1980.

Aitkin, Donald. *Stability and Change in Australian Politics*. New York: St. Martin's, 1977.

Alexander, Thomas B. *Sectional Stress and Party Strength: A Study of Roll-Call Voting*

Patterns in the United States House of Representatives, 1836–1860. Nashville, Tenn.: Vanderbilt University Press, 1967.

Alford, Robert R. *Party and Society: The Anglo-American Democracies.* Chicago: Rand McNally, 1963.

Allardt, Eric, and Stein Rokkan, eds. *Mass Politics: Studies in Political Sociology.* New York: Free Press, 1970.

Allen, Howard W., and Erik W. Austin. "From the Populist Era to the New Deal: A Study of Partisan Realignment in Washington State, 1889–1950." *Social Science History* 3 (Winter 1979): 115–43.

Allsop, Dee, and Herbert Weisberg. "Measuring Change in Party Identification in an Election Campaign." *American Journal of Political Science* 32 (November 1988): 996–1017.

Allswang, John M. *A House for All Peoples: Ethnic Politics in Chicago, 1890–1936.* Lexington: University of Kentucky Press, 1971.

Allswang, John M. *The New Deal and American Politics: A Study in Political Change.* New York: John Wiley and Sons, 1978.

Alt, James E. "Dealignment and the Dynamics of Partisanship in Britain." In *Electoral Change in Advanced Industrial Democracies,* ed. Russell J. Dalton, Scott C. Flanagan, and Paul Allen Beck, 298–329. Princeton: Princeton University Press, 1984.

Alvarez, David J., and Edmund J. True. "Critical Elections and Partisan Realignment: An Urban Test Case." *Polity* 5 (Summer 1973): 563–76.

Anderson, Kristi. *Creation of a Democratic Majority, 1928–1936.* Chicago: University of Chicago Press, 1979.

Anderson, Kristi. "Generation, Partisan Shift, and Realignment: A Glance Back at the New Deal." In *The Changing American Voter,* Norman H. Nie, Sidney Verba, and John R. Petrocik, 74–95. Cambridge: Harvard University Press, 1976.

Argersinger, Peter H., and John W. Jeffries. "American Electoral History: Party Systems and Voting Behavior." *Research in Micropolitics: Voting Behavior,* ed. Samuel Long, 2 vols. (Greenwich, Conn.: Jai Press, 1986), 1:1–33.

Axelrod, Robert. "Communication." *American Political Science Review* 68 (June 1974): 717–20.

Axelrod, Robert. "Communication." *American Political Science Review* 72 (June 1978): 622–24.

Axelrod, Robert. "Communication." *American Political Science Review* 72 (December 1978): 1010–11.

Axelrod, Robert. "Communication." *American Political Science Review* 76 (June 1982): 393–96.

Axelrod, Robert. "Presidential Election Coalitions in 1984: A Research Note." *American Political Science Review* 80 (March 1986): 281–84.

Axelrod, Robert. "Where the Votes Come From: An Analysis of Electoral Coalitions, 1952–1968." *American Political Science Review* 66 (March 1972): 11–20.

Baker, Kendall L. "Generational Differences in the Role of Party Identification in German Political Behavior." *American Journal of Political Science* 22 (February 1978): 106–29.

Barber, James David. *The Pulse of Politics: Electing Presidents in the Media Age.* New York: W. W. Norton, 1980.

Barilleaux, Charles J. "A Dynamic Model of Partisan Competition in the American States." *American Journal of Political Science* 30 (November 1986): 822–40.

Barnes, Samuel H. "Secular Trends and Partisan Realignment in Italy." In *Electoral Change in Advanced Industrial Democracies,* ed. Russell J. Dalton, Scott C. Flanagan, and Paul Allen Beck, 205–30. Princeton: Princeton University Press, 1984.

Bartley, Numan V. "Voters and Party Systems: A Review of Recent Literature." *The History Teacher* 8 (May 1975): 452–69.

Bartley, Numan V., and Hugh D. Graham. *Southern Politics and the Second Reconstruction.* Baltimore: Johns Hopkins University Press, 1985.

Bass, Jack, and Walter DeVries. *The Transformation of Southern Politics: Social Change and Political Consequence since 1945.* New York: Basic Books, 1976.

Baum, Dale. *The Civil War Party System: The Case of Massachusetts, 1848–1876.* Chapel Hill: University of North Carolina Press, 1984.

Baum, Dale. "The 'Irish Vote' and Party Politics in Massachusetts, 1860–1876." *Civil War History* 26 (June 1980): 117–41.

Baum, Dale. "Know-Nothingism and the Republican Majority in Massachusetts: The Political Realignment of the 1850s." *Journal of American History* 64 (March 1978): 959–86.

Baum, Dale, and Dale T. Knobel. "Anatomy of a Realignment: New York Presidential Politics, 1848–1860." *New York History* 65 (January 1984): 61–81.

Beck, Paul Allen. "Communication—Critical Elections and the Supreme Court: Putting the Cart after the Horse." *American Political Science Review* 70 (September 1976): 930–32.

Beck, Paul Allen. "The Dealignment Era in America." In *Electoral Change in Advanced Industrial Democracies,* ed. Russell J. Dalton, Scott C. Flanagan, and Paul Allen Beck, 240–66. Princeton: Princeton University Press, 1984.

Beck, Paul Allen. "The Electoral Cycle and Patterns of American Politics." *British Journal of Political Science* 9 (April 1979): 129–56.

Beck, Paul Allen. "Incomplete Realignment: The Reagan Legacy for Parties and Elections." In *The Reagan Legacy: Promise and Performance,* ed. Charles O. Jones, 145–71. Chatham, N.J.: Chatham House, 1989.

Beck, Paul Allen. "Partisan Dealignment in the Postwar South." *American Political Science Review* 71 (June 1977): 477–96.

Beck, Paul Allen. "Realignment Begins: The Republican Surge in Florida." *American Politics Quarterly* 10 (October 1982): 421–38.

Beck, Paul Allen. "A Socialization Theory of Partisan Realignment." In *The Politics of Future Citizens,* ed. Richard D. Niemi and Associates, 199–219. San Francisco: Josey-Bass, 1974.

Benedict, Robert C. "Policy Change and Regional Realignment." In *The Politics of Realignment: Party Change in the Mountain West,* ed. Peter F. Galderisi, Michael S. Lyons, Randy T. Simmons, and John G. Francis, 129–47. Boulder, Colo.: Westview Press, 1987.

Bennett, W. Lance, and William Haltrum. "Issues, Voter Choice, and Critical Elections." *Social Science History* 4 (Fall 1980): 379–418.

Benson, Edward G., and Paul Perry. "Analysis of Democratic-Republican Strength by Population Groups." *Public Opinion Quarterly* 4 (September 1940): 464-73.

Benson, Edward G., and Evelyn Wicoff. "Voters Pick Their Party." *Public Opinion Quarterly* 8 (Summer 1944): 165–87.

Benson, Lee. *The Concept of Jacksonian Democracy: New York as a Test Case.* Princeton: Princeton University Press, 1961.

Benson, Lee, Joel H. Silbey, and Phyllis F. Field. "Toward a Theory of Stability and Change in American Voting Patterns: New York State, 1792–1970, as a Test Case." In *The History of American Electoral Behavior,* ed. Joel H. Silbey, Allan G. Bogue, and William H. Flanigan, 78–105. Princeton: Princeton University Press, 1978.

Black, Errol. "Political Realignment in Canada?" *Monthly Review* 39 (November 1987): 33–39.

Black, Merle, and George Rabinowitz. "American Electoral Change: 1952–1972 (With a Note on 1976)." In *The Party Symbol: Readings on Political Parties,* ed. William Crotty, 226–56. San Francisco: Freeman, 1980.

Blake, Donald E. "1896 and All That: Critical Elections in Canada." *Canadian Journal of Political Science* 12 (June 1979): 259–79.

Blunt, Barrie Edwin Miller. "The Goldwater Candidacy and Liberalism in the House of Representatives." *Presidential Studies Quarterly* 15 (Winter 1985): 119–27.

Bogue, Allan G. *Clio and the Bitch Goddess: Quantification in American Political History.* Beverly Hills, Calif.: Sage, 1983.

Bogue, Allan G., Jerome M. Clubb, and William H. Flanigan. "The New Political History." *American Behavioral Scientist* 21 (November–December 1977): 201–20.

Borre, Ole. "Critical Electoral Change in Scandinavia." In *Electoral Change in Advanced Industrial Democracies,* ed. Russell J. Dalton, Scott C. Flanagan, and Paul Allen Beck, 330–64. Princeton: Princeton University Press, 1984.

Bower, Robert T. "Opinion Research and Historical Interpretation of Elections." *Public Opinion Quarterly* 12 (Fall 1948): 455–64.

Boyd, Richard W. "Popular Control of Public Policy: A Normal Vote Analysis of the 1968 Election." *American Political Science Review* 66 (June 1972): 429–49.

Boylan, James R. *The New Deal Coalition and the Election of 1946.* New York: Garland Press, 1981.

Brady, David W. *Critical Elections and Congressional Policy Making.* Stanford: Stanford University Press, 1988.

Brady, David W. "Critical Elections, Congressional Parties, and Clusters of Policy Change." *British Journal of Political Science* 8 (January 1978): 79–99.

Brady, David W. "Elections, Congress, and Public Policy Changes." In *Realignment in American Politics: Toward a Theory,* ed. Bruce A. Campbell and Richard J. Trilling, 176–201. Austin: University of Texas Press, 1980.

Brady, David W. "A Reevaluation of Realignments in American Politics: Evidence from the House of Representatives." *American Political Science Review* 79 (March 1985): 28–49.

Brady, David W., and Phillip Althoff. "Party Voting in the U.S. House of Representatives, 1890–1910: Evidence from the House of Representatives." *Journal of Politics* 36 (August 1974): 753–75.

Brady, David W., Charles S. Bullock III, and Louis Maisel. "Realigning Elections: A Comparative Application." Paper presented at the annual meeting of the International Political Science Association, Paris, 1985.

Brady, David, Joseph Cooper, and Patricia A. Hurley. "The Decline of Party in the U.S. House of Representatives, 1887–1968." *Legislative Studies Quarterly* 4 (August 1979): 381–407.

Brady, David, and Patricia A. Hurley. "The Prospects for Contemporary Partisan Realignment." *PS* 18 (Winter 1985): 63–68.

Brady, David W., and Naomi B. Lynn. "Switched Seat Congressional Districts: Their Effect on Party Voting and Public Policy." *American Journal of Political Science* 17 (August 1973): 528–43.

Brady, David W., and Joseph Stewart, Jr. "Congressional Party Realignment and the Transformation of Public Policy in Three Realignment Eras." *American Journal of Political Science* 26 (May 1982): 333–60.

Brady, David W. "When Elections Really Matter: Realignments and Changes in Public Policy." In *Do Elections Matter?* ed. Benjamin Ginsberg and Alan Stone, 19–34. Armonk, N.Y.: Sharpe, 1986.

Brown, Courtney. "Mass Dynamics of U.S. Presidential Competitions." *American Political Science Review* 82 (December 1988): 1153–82.

Brye, David L. *Wisconsin Voting Patterns in the Twentieth Century, 1900 to 1950.* New York: Garland Press, 1979.

Bullock, Charles S., III. "Regional Realignment from an Officeholding Perspective." *Journal of Politics* 50 (August 1988): 553–74.

Burner, David. *The Politics of Provincialism: The Democratic Party in Transition, 1918–1932.* New York: Alfred A. Knopf, 1968.

Burnham, Walter Dean. "The 1976 Election: Has the Crisis Been Adjourned?" In *American Politics and Public Policy,* ed. Walter Dean Burnham and Martha Wagner Weinberg, 1–25. Cambridge: MIT Press, 1978.

Burnham, Walter Dean. "The 1980 Earthquake: Realignment, Reaction, or What?" In *The Hidden Election,* ed. Thomas Ferguson and Joel Rogers, 98–140. New York: Pantheon, 1981.

Burnham, Walter Dean. "American Politics in the 1970s: Beyond Party." In *The American Party Systems: Stages of Political Development,* ed. William Nisbet Chambers and Walter Dean Burnham, 2d ed., 308–57. New York: Oxford University Press, 1975.

Burnham, Walter Dean. "American Politics in the 1980s." *Dissent* (Spring 1980): 149–62.

Burnham, Walter Dean. "American Voting Behavior and the 1964 Election." *Midwest Journal of Political Science* 12 (February 1968): 1–40.

Burnham, Walter Dean. "The Changing Shape of the American Political Universe." *American Political Science Review* 59 (March 1965): 7–28.

Burnham, Walter Dean. *Critical Elections and the Mainsprings of American Politics.* New York: W. W. Norton, 1970.

Burnham, Walter Dean. *The Current Crisis in American Politics.* New York: Oxford University Press, 1982.

Burnham, Walter Dean. "Election 1968: The Abortive Landslide." *Trans-Action* (December 1968): 18–24.

Burnham, Walter Dean. "The End of American Party Politics." *Trans-Action* (December 1969): 12–22.

Burnham, Walter Dean. "Insulation and Responsiveness in Congressional Elections." *Political Science Quarterly* 90 (Fall 1975): 411–35.

Burnham, Walter Dean. "Party Systems and the Political Process." In *The American Party Systems: Stages of Political Development,* ed. William Nisbet Chambers and Walter Dean Burnham, 2d ed., 277–307. New York: Oxford University Press, 1975.

Burnham, Walter Dean. "Periodization Schemes and 'Party Systems': The 'System of 1896,' as a Case in Point." *Social Science History* 10 (Fall 1986): 263–314.

Burnham, Walter Dean. "The Politics of Crisis." *Journal of Interdisciplinary History* 8 (Spring 1978): 747–63.

Burnham, Walter Dean. "The Reagan Heritage." In *The Election of 1988: Reports and Interpretations,* ed. Gerald M. Pomper, 1–32. Chatham, N.J.: Chatham House, 1989.

Burnham, Walter Dean. "Rejoinder to 'Comments' by Philip Converse and Jerrold Rusk." *American Political Science Review* 68 (September 1974): 1050–57.

Burnham, Walter Dean. "Revitalization and Decay: Looking Toward the Third Century of American Electoral Politics." *Journal of Politics* 37 (August 1976): 146–72.

Burnham, Walter Dean. "The System of 1896: An Analysis." In *The Evolution of American Electoral Systems,* ed. Paul Kleppner et al., 147–202. Westport, Conn.: Greenwood Press, 1981.

Burnham, Walter Dean. "Theory and Voting Research: Some Reflections on Converse's 'Change in the American Electorate.'" *American Political Science Review* 68 (September 1974): 1002–23.

Burnham, Walter Dean. "The United States: The Politics of Heterogeneity." In *Electoral Behavior: A Comparative Handbook,* ed. Richard Rose, 653–725. New York: Free Press, 1974.

Burnham, Walter Dean. "V. O. Key, Jr., and the Study of Political Parties." in *V. O. Key, Jr. and the Study of American Politics,* ed. Milton C. Cummings, 3–23. Washington, D.C.: American Political Science Association, 1983.

Burnham, Walter D., Jerome M. Clubb, and William H. Flanigan. "Partisan Realignment: A Systemic Perspective." In *The History of American Electoral Behavior,* ed. Joel H. Silbey, Allan G. Bogue, and William H. Flanigan, 45–77. Princeton: Princeton University Press, 1978.

Butler, David, and Donald Stokes. *Political Change in Britain: Forces Shaping Electoral Choice.* New York: St. Martin's, 1969.

Cain, Bruce E. "Dynamic and Static Components of Political Support in Britain." *American Journal of Political Science* 22 (November 1978): 849–66.

Campbell, Angus. "A Classification of the Presidential Elections." In *Elections and the Political Order,* Angus Campbell, Philip E. Converse, Warren E. Miller, and Donald E. Stokes, 63–77. New York: John Wiley and Sons, 1966.

Campbell, Angus. "Interpreting the Presidential Victory." In *The National Election of 1964,* ed. Milton C. Cummings, Jr., 256–81. Washington, D.C.: Brookings Institution, 1966.

Campbell, Angus. "Surge and Decline: A Study of Electoral Change." In *Elections and the Political Order,* Angus Campbell, Philip E. Converse, Warren E. Miller, and Donald E. Stokes, 40–62. New York: John Wiley and Sons, 1966.

Campbell, Angus, Philip E. Converse, Warren E. Miller, and Donald E. Stokes. *The American Voter.* New York: John Wiley and Sons, 1960.

Campbell, Angus, Philip E. Converse, Warren E. Miller, and Donald E. Stokes. *Elections and the Political Order.* New York: John Wiley and Sons, 1966.

Campbell, Bruce A. "Change in the Southern Electorate." *American Journal of Political Science* 21 (February 1977): 37–64.

Campbell, Bruce A. "Patterns of Change in the Partisan Loyalties of Native Southerners: 1952–1972." *Journal of Politics* 39 (August 1977): 730–61.

Campbell, Bruce A. "Realignment, Party Decomposition, and Issue Voting." In *Realignment in American Politics: Toward a Theory,* ed. Bruce A. Campbell and Richard J. Trilling, 82–109. Austin: University of Texas Press, 1980.

Campbell, Bruce A., and Richard J. Trilling, eds. *Realignment in American Politics: Toward a Theory.* Austin: University of Texas Press, 1979.

Campbell, James E. "Sources of the New Deal Realignment: The Contributions of Conversion and Mobilization to Partisan Change." *Western Political Quarterly* 38 (September 1985): 357–76.

Campbell, James E. "Voter Mobilization and the New Deal Realignment: A Rejoinder." *Western Political Quarterly* 39 (December 1986): 733–35.

Canon, Bradley C., and S. Sidney Ulmer. "Communication—The Supreme Court and Critical Elections: A Dissent." *American Political Science Review* 70 (December 1976): 1215–18.

Canon, David T., and David J. Sousa. "Realigning Elections and Political Career Structures in the U.S. Congress." Paper presented at the annual meeting of the American Political Science Association, Chicago, 1987.

Carmines, Edward G., John McIver, and James A. Stimson. "Unrealized Partisanship: A Theory of Dealignment." *Journal of Politics* 49 (May 1987): 376–400.

Carmines, Edward G., Steve Renten, and James A. Stimson. "Events and Alignments: The Party Image Link." In *Controversies in Voting Behavior,* ed. Richard Niemi and Herbert Weisberg, 2d ed., 545–60. Washington, D.C.: CQ Press, 1984.

Carmines, Edward G., and Harold W. Stanley. "Ideological Realignment in the Contemporary South: Where Have All the Conservatives Gone?" In *The Disappearing South? Studies in Regional Change and Continuity,* ed. Robert P. Steed, Lawrence W. Moreland, and Tod A. Baker, 21–33. Tuscaloosa: University of Alabama Press, 1990.

Carmines, Edward G., and James A. Stimson. "The Dynamics of Issue Evolution: The United States." In *Electoral Change in Advanced Industrial Democracies,* ed. Russell J. Dalton, Scott C. Flanagan, and Paul Allen Beck, 134–58. Princeton: Princeton University Press, 1984.

Carmines, Edward G. "Issue Evolution, Population Replacement, and Normal Partisan Change." *American Political Science Review* 75 (March 1981): 107–18.

Carmines, Edward G., and James A. Stimson. *Issue Evolution: Race and the Transformation of American Politics*. Princeton: Princeton University Press, 1989.

Carmines, Edward G. "On the Structure and Sequence of Issue Evolution." *American Political Science Review* 80 (September 1986): 901–20.

Carmines, Edward G. "The Racial Reorientation of American Politics." In *The Electorate Reconsidered*, ed. John C. Pierce and John L. Sullivan, 199–218. Beverly Hills, Calif.: Sage, 1980.

Cassel, Carol A. "Cohort Analysis of Party Identification among Southern Whites, 1952–1972." *Public Opinion Quarterly* 41 (Spring 1988): 28–33.

Castle, David S. "Goldwater's Presidential Candidacy and Political Realignment." *Presidential Studies Quarterly* 20 (Winter 1990): 103–10.

Cavanagh, Thomas E., and James L. Sundquist. "The New Two-Party System." In *The New Directions in American Politics,* ed. John E. Chubb and Paul E. Peterson, 33–68. Washington, D.C.: Brookings Institution, 1985.

Chambers, William Nisbet. "Party Development and the American Mainstream." In *The American Party Systems: Stages of Political Development,* ed. William Nisbet Chambers and Walter Dean Burnham, 2d ed., 3–32. New York: Oxford University Press, 1975.

Chambers, William Nisbet, and Walter Dean Burnham, eds. *The American Party Systems: Stages of Political Development.* 2d ed. New York: Oxford University Press, 1975.

Champagne, Richard. "Civil Rights Policy and the Tranformation of the New Deal Party System." Paper presented at the annual meeting of the American Political Science Association, Washington, D.C., 1986.

Champagne, Richard. "Conditions for Realignment in the U.S. Senate: Or What Makes a Steamroller Start?" *Legislative Studies Quarterly* 8 (May 1983): 231–49.

Chubb, John E. "Systems Analysis and Partisan Realignment." *Social Science History* 2 (Winter 1978): 144–71.

Claggett, William. "Partisan Acquisition, Policy Relevant Parties, and Realignments." *Western Political Quarterly* 42 (June 1989): 225–44.

Claggett, William. "Partisan Acquisition Versus Partisan Intensity: Life Cycle, Generation, and Period Effects." *American Journal of Political Science* 25 (May 1981): 193–214.

Claggett, William, William Flanigan, and Nancy Zingale. "Nationalization of the American Electorate." *American Political Science Review* 78 (March 1984): 77–91.

Clarke, Harold D. "The Parti Québécois and Sources of Partisan Realignment in Contemporary Quebec." *Journal of Politics* 45 (February 1983): 64–85.

Clarke, Harold D., and Marianne C. Stewart. "Dealignment and Degree of Partisan Change in Britain, 1974–83." *Journal of Politics* 46 (August 1984): 689–718.

Clarke, Harold D. "Partisan Inconsistency and Partisan Change in Federal Systems: The Case of Canada." *American Journal of Political Science* 31 (May 1987): 383–407.

Clubb, Jerome M. "Partisan Realignment Revisited." Paper presented at the annual meeting of the American Political Science Association, Atlanta, 1989.

Clubb, Jerome M. "Party Coalitions in the Early Twentieth Century." In *Emerging*

Coalitions in American Politics, ed. Seymour M. Lipset, 61–79. San Francisco: Institute for Contemporary Studies, 1978.

Clubb, Jerome M., and Howard W. Allen. "The Cities and the Election of 1928: Partisan Realignment?" *American Historical Review* 74 (April 1969): 1205–20.

Clubb, Jerome M., and Howard W. Allen, eds. *Electoral Change and Stability in American History.* New York: Free Press, 1971.

Clubb, Jerome M., William H. Flanigan, and Nancy H. Zingale. *Analyzing Electoral History: A Guide to the Study of American Voting Behavior.* Beverly Hills, Calif.: Sage, 1981.

Clubb, Jerome M., William H. Flanigan, and Nancy H. Zingale. *Partisan Realignment: Voters, Parties, and Government in American History.* Beverly Hills, Calif.: Sage, 1980.

Clubb, Jerome M., and Santa A. Traugott. "Partisan Cleavage and Cohesion in the House of Representatives, 1861–1974." *Journal of Interdisciplinary History* 7 (Winter 1977): 375-401.

Clymer, Adam, and Kathleen Frankovic. "The Realities of Realignment." *Public Opinion* 4 (June–July 1981): 42–47.

Converse, Philip E. "Change in the American Electorate." In *The Human Meaning of Social Change,* ed. Angus Campbell and Philip E. Converse, 263–337. New York: Russell Sage, 1972.

Converse, Philip E. "Comment on Burnham's 'Theory and Voting Research.'" *The American Political Science Review* 68 (September 1974): 1024–27.

Converse, Philip E. "The Concept of a Normal Vote." In *Elections and the Political Order,* Angus Campbell, Philip E. Converse, Warren E. Miller, and Donald E. Stokes, 9–39. New York: John Wiley and Sons, 1966.

Converse, Philip E. *The Dynamics of Party Support.* Beverly Hills, Calif.: Sage, 1976.

Converse, Philip E. "Information Flow and the Stability of Partisan Attitudes." *Public Opinion Quarterly* 26 (Winter 1962): 578–99.

Converse, Philip E. "A Major Political Realignment in the South?" In *Change in the Contemporary South,* ed. Allan P. Sindler, 195–222. Durham, N.C.: Duke University Press, 1963.

Converse, Philip E. "Of Time and Partisan Stability." *Comparative Political Studies* 2 (July 1969): 139–71.

Converse, Philip E. "On the Possibility of a Major Political Realignment in the South." In *Elections and the Political Order,* Angus Campbell, Philip E. Converse, Warren E. Miller, and Donald E. Stokes, 212–42. New York: John Wiley and Sons, 1966.

Converse, Philip E. "Recent Evidence on the Stability of Party Identification: The New Michigan Election Study Panel." In *Realignment in American Politics: Toward a Theory,* ed. Bruce A. Campbell and Richard J. Trilling, 132–53. Austin: University of Texas Press, 1980.

Converse, Philip E., Angus Campbell, Warren E. Miller, and Donald E. Stokes. "Stability and Change in 1960: A Reinstating Election." *American Political Science Review* 55 (June 1961): 269–80.

Converse, Philip E., Aage R. Clausen, and Warren E. Miller. "Electoral Myth and Reality: The 1964 Election." *American Political Science Review* 59 (June 1965): 321–36.

Converse, Philip E., and Gregory B. Markus. " 'Plus Ça Change?' The New CPS Election Study Panel." *American Political Science Review* 73 (March 1979): 32–48.

Converse, Philip E., Warren E. Miller, Jerrold G. Rusk, and Arthur C. Wolfe. "Continuity and Change in American Politics: Parties and Issues in the 1968 Election." *American Political Science Review* 63 (December 1969): 1083–1105.

Cooper, Joseph, David W. Brady, and Patricia A. Hurley. "The Electoral Basis of Party Voting: Patterns and Trends from the U.S. House of Representatives, 1887–1969." In *The Impact of the Electoral Process,* ed. Louis Maisel and Joseph Cooper, 133–65. Beverly Hills, Calif.: Sage, 1977.

Crewe, Ivor. "Prospects for Party Realignment: An Anglo-American Comparison." *Comparative Politics* 12 (July 1980): 379–400.

Crewe, Ivor, Bo Särlvick, and James Alt. "Partisan Dealignment in Britain, 1964–1974." *British Journal of Political Science* 7 (April 1977): 129–90.

Crewe, Ivor. "Reply." *British Journal of Political Science* 8 (October 1978): 509–10.

Crewe, Ivor, and David Denver, eds. *Electoral Change in Western Democracies: Patterns and Sources of Electoral Volatility.* New York: St. Martin's, 1985.

Crittendon, John. "Aging and Party Affiliation." *Public Opinion Quarterly* 26 (Winter 1962): 648–57.

Cutler, Neal E. "Generation, Maturation, and Party Affiliation: A Cohort Analysis." *Public Opinion Quarterly* 33 (Winter 1969): 583–88.

Daalder, Hans, and Peter Mair, eds. *West European Party Systems: Continuity and Change.* Beverly Hills, Calif.: Sage, 1983.

Dalton, Russell J. "The West German Party System between Two Ages." In *Electoral Change in Advanced Industrial Democracies,* ed. Russell J. Dalton, Scott C. Flanagan, and Paul Allen Beck, 104–33. Princeton: Princeton University Press, 1984.

Dalton, Russell J., Scott Flanagan, and Paul Allen Beck, eds. *Electoral Change in Advanced Industrial Democracies: Realignment or Dealignment?* Princeton: Princeton University Press, 1984.

David, Paul T., "The Changing Party Pattern." *Antioch Review* 16 (Fall 1956): 333–50.

David, Paul T. *Party Strength in the United States: 1872–1970.* Charlottesville: University Press of Virginia, 1972.

David, Paul T. "Party Strength in the United States: Changes in 1972." *Journal of Politics* 36 (August 1974): 785–96.

David, Paul T. "Party Strength in the United States: Changes in 1974." *Journal of Politics* 38 (May 1976): 416–25.

David, Paul T. "Party Strength in the United States: Changes in 1976." *Journal of Politics* 40 (August 1978): 771–80.

David, Paul T. "Party Strength in the United States: Some Corrections." *Journal of Politics* 37 (May 1975): 641–42.

Declerq, Eugene R., Thomas L. Hurley, and Norman R. Luttbeg. "Voting in American Presidential Elections, 1956–1972." *American Politics Quarterly* 3 (July 1975): 222–46.

Devine, Joel A., and Timothy M. Stearns. "Class, Party, and Electoral Mobilization: A Reappraisal of the British Experience." *Social Science Quarterly* 66 (March 1985): 90–104.

DeVries, Walter, and V. Lance Tarrance. *The Ticket Splitter: A New Force in American Politics.* Grand Rapids, Mich.: Wm. B. Eerdmans, 1972.

Dobson, Douglas, and Duane A. Meeter. "Alternative Markov Models for Describing Change in Party Identification." *American Journal of Political Science* 18 (August 1974): 487–500.

Dobson, Douglas, and Douglas St. Angelo. "Party Identification and the Floating Vote: Some Dynamics." *American Political Science Review* 69 (June 1975): 481–90.

Douglas, Paul H. *Why a Political Realignment?* New York: League for Independent Political Action, 1930.

Dreyer, Edward. "Change and Stability in Party Identificaton." *Journal of Politics* 35 (August 1973): 712–22.

Dunleavy, Patrick. "The Political Implications of Sectoral Cleavages and the Growth of State Employment, Part II: Cleavage Structures and Political Alignment." *Political Studies* 28 (December 1980): 527–49.

Dunleavy, Patrick. "Urban Bases of Political Alignment: Social Class, Domestic Property Ownership, and State Interference in Consumption Processes." *British Journal of Political Science* 9 (October 1979): 409–43.

Dutton, Frederick G. *Changing Sources of Power.* New York: McGraw-Hill, 1971.

Dyer, James, Arnold Vedlitz, and David B. Hill. "New Voters, Switchers, and Political Party Realignment in Texas." *Western Political Quarterly* 41 (Spring 1988): 155–67.

Eldersveld, Samuel J. "The Influence of Metropolitan Party Pluralities in Presidential Elections Since 1920." *American Political Science Review* 43 (December 1949): 1189–1206.

Epstein, Laurily K. "1984—A Realigning Election." *Election Politics* 2 (Winter 1984–85): 2–4.

Epstein, Laurily K. "The Changing Structure of Party Identification." *PS* 18 (Winter 1985): 48–52.

Erbring, Lutz, Norman Nie, and Edward Hamburg. "The Dynamics of Political Realignment: Mobilization, Recruitment, and Conversion." Paper presented at the annual meeting of the American Political Science Association, Washington, D.C., 1986.

Erikson, Robert S., Thomas D. Lancaster, and David W. Romero. "Group Components of the Presidential Vote, 1952–1984." *Journal of Politics* 51 (May 1989): 337–46.

Erikson, Robert S., and Kent L. Tedin. "The 1928–1936 Partisan Realignment: The Case for the Conversion Hypothesis." *American Political Science Review* 75 (December 1981): 951–62.

Erikson, Robert S. "Voter Conversion and the New Deal Realignment: A Response to Campbell." *Western Political Quarterly* 39 (December 1986): 729–32.

Eulau, Heinz. "Perceptions of Class and Party in Voting Behavior: 1952." *American Political Science Review* 49 (June 1955): 364–84.

Farah, Barbara G., and Helmut Norpoth. "Trends in Partisan Realignment, 1976–1986." Paper presented at the annual meeting of the American Political Association, Washington, D.C., 1986.

Ferguson, Thomas, and Joel Rogers. *Right Turn: The Decline of the Democrats and the Future of American Politics.* New York: Hill & Wang, 1986.

Finch, Gerald B. "Physical Change and Partisan Change: The Emergence of the New

American Electorate." In *The Future of American Politics*, ed. Louis Maisel and Paul M. Sacks, 13–62. Beverly Hills, Calif.: Sage, 1975.

Fiorina, Morris P. *Retrospective Voting in American National Elections*. New Haven: Yale University Press, 1981.

Fiorina, Morris P., David W. Rohde, and Peter Wissel. "Historical Change in House Turnover." In *Congress in Change: Evolution and Reform*, ed. Norman Ornstein, 24–57. New York: Praeger, 1975.

Fisher, Alan M. "Realignment of the Jewish Vote." *Political Science Quarterly* 94 (Spring 1979): 97–116.

Flanagan, Scott C. "Electoral Change in Japan: A Study of Secular Realignment." In *Electoral Change in Advanced Industrial Democracies*, ed. Russell J. Dalton, Scott C. Flanagan, and Paul Allen Beck, 159–294. Princeton: Princeton University Press, 1984.

Flanigan, William H., and Nancy H. Zingale. "The Measurement of Political Change." *Political Methodology* 1 (Summer 1974): 49–82.

Flanigan, William H. *Political Behavior of the American Electorate*. 6th ed. Boston: Allyn and Bacon, 1987.

Flinn, Thomas. "Continuity and Change in Ohio Politics." *Journal of Politics* 24 (August 1962): 521–44.

Folsom, Burton W. "Tinkerers, Tipplers, and Traitors: Ethnicity and Democratic Reform in Nebraska during the Progressive Era." *Pacific Historical Review* 50 (February 1981): 53–75.

Formisano, Ronald P. *The Birth of Mass Political Parties: Michigan, 1827–1861*. Princeton: Princeton University Press, 1971.

Formisano, Ronald P. "Deferential-Participant Politics: The Early Republic's Political Culture." *American Political Science Review* 68 (June 1974): 473–87.

Formisano, Ronald P. "Federalists and Republicans: Parties, Yes—System, No." In *The Evolution of American Electoral Systems*, ed. Paul Kleppner et al., 33–76. Westport Conn.: Greenwood Press, 1981.

Formisano, Ronald P. *The Transformation of Political Culture: Massachusetts Parties, 1790s–1840s*. New York: Oxford University Press, 1983.

Francis, John G. "The Political Landscape of the Mountain West." In *The Politics of Realignment: Party Change in the Mountain West*, ed. Peter F. Galderisi, et al., 19–32. Boulder, Colo.: Westview Press, 1987.

Franklin, Charles H. "Party Identification and Party Realignment." Paper presented at the annual meeting of the American Political Science Association, Washington, D.C., 1986.

Franklin, Charles H., and John E. Jackson. "The Dynamics of Party Identification." *American Political Science Review* 77 (December 1983): 957–73.

Frankovic, Kathleen A. "Sex and Politics—New Alignments, Old Issues." *PS* 15 (Summer 1982): 439–48.

Fraser, Steve, and Gary Gerstle, eds. *The Rise and Fall of the New Deal Order, 1930–1980*. Princeton: Princeton University Press, 1989.

Frendreis, John P. "Migration as a Source of Changing Party Strength." *Social Science Quarterly* 70 (March 1989): 211–20.

Funston, Richard. "Communication." *American Political Science Review* 70 (September 1976): 932.

Funston, Richard. "Communication: Reply to Canon and Ulmer." *American Political Science Review* 70 (December 1976): 1218–21.

Funston, Richard. "The Supreme Court and Critical Elections." *American Political Science Review* 69 (September 1975): 795–811.

Galderisi, Peter F., and Michael S. Lyons. "Realignment: Past and Present." In *The Politics of Realignment: Party Change in the Mountain West,* ed. Peter F. Galderisi et al., 1–17. Boulder, Colo.: Westview Press, 1987.

Galderisi, Peter F., Michael S. Lyons, Randy T. Simmons, and John G. Francis, eds. *The Politics of Realignment: Party Change in the Mountain West.* Boulder, Colo.: Westview Press, 1987.

Gallagher, Michael. "Societal Change and Party Adaptation in the Republic of Ireland." *European Journal of Political Research* 9 (September 1981): 269–86.

Gamm, Gerald H. *The Making of the New Deal Democrats: Voting Behavior and Realignment in Boston, 1920–1940.* Chicago: University of Chicago Press, 1989.

Garvey, Gerald. "The Theory of Party Equilibrium." *American Political Science Review* 60 (March 1966): 29–38.

Gates, John B. "The American Supreme Court and Electoral Realignment." *Social Science History* 8 (Summer 1984): 267–90.

Gates, John B. "Partisan Realignment, Unconstitutional State Policies, and the U.S. Supreme Court, 1837–1964." *American Journal of Political Science* 31 (May 1987): 259–80.

Gatlin, Douglas S. "Party Identification, Status, and Race in the South: 1952–1972." *Public Opinion Quarterly* 39 (Spring 1975): 39–51.

Gibson, James L. "The Role of Party Organization in the Mountain West: 1960–1980." In *The Politics of Realignment: Party Change in the Mountain West,* ed. Peter F. Galderisi et al., 197–219. Boulder, Colo.: Westview Press, 1987.

Gienapp, William E. "Nativism and the Creation of a Republican Majority in the North Before the Civil War." *Journal of American History* 72 (December 1985): 529–59.

Gienapp, William E. *The Origins of the Republican Party, 1852–1856.* New York: Oxford University Press, 1987.

Gienapp, William E. "Who Voted for Lincoln?" In *Abraham Lincoln and the American Political Tradition,* ed. John L. Thomas, 50–96. Amherst: University of Massachusetts Press, 1986.

Gilbert, Charles E. "National Political Alignments and the Politics of Large Cities." *Political Science Quarterly* 79 (March 1964): 25–51.

Ginsberg, Benjamin. "Communication." *American Political Science Review* 71 (March 1977): 280–81.

Ginsberg, Benjamin. "Critical Elections and the Substance of Party Conflict: 1844–1968." *Midwest Journal of Political Science* 16 (November 1972): 603–25.

Ginsberg, Benjamin. "Elections and Public Policy." *American Political Science Review* 70 (March 1976): 41–49.

Ginsberg, Benjamin, and Martin Shefter. "A Critical Realignment? The New Politics, the Reconstituted Right, and the 1984 Election." In *The Elections of 1984,* ed. Michael Nelson, 1–25. Washington, D.C.: CQ Press, 1985.

Ginsberg, Benjamin, and Martin Shefter, *Politics by Other Means: The Declining Importance of Elections in America.* New York: Basic Books, 1990.

Glenn, Norval D. "Class and Party Support in the United States: Recent and Emerging Trends." *Public Opinion Quarterly* 37 (Spring 1973): 1–20.

Glenn, Norval D., and Ted Hefner. "Further Evidence on Aging and Party Identification." *Public Opinion Quarterly* 36 (Spring 1972): 31–47.

Gordon, Rita W. "The Change in the Political Alignment of Chicago's Negroes during the New Deal." *Journal of American History* 56 (December 1969): 584–603.

Gosnell, Harold F., and William G. Colman. "Political Trends in Industrial America: Pennsylvania as an Example." *Public Opinion Quarterly* 4 (September 1940): 473–86.

Greely, Andrew M. *Building Coalitions: American Politics in the 1970s.* New York: Franklin Watts, 1974.

Greenstein, Fred I., and Raymond E. Wolfinger. "The Suburbs and Shifting Party Loyalties." *Public Opinion Quarterly* 22 (Winter 1958): 473–82.

Hadley, Charles D. "Dual Partisan Identification in the South." *Journal of Politics* 47 (February 1985): 254–68.

Hadley, Charles D., and Susan E. Howell. "Partisan Conversion in the Northeast: An Analysis of Split-Ticket Voting, 1952–1976." *American Politics Quarterly* 8 (January 1980): 129–34.

Hadley, Charles D. "The Southern Split-Ticket Voter, 1952–1974: Republican Conversion or Democratic Decline." In *Party Politics in the South,* ed. Robert P. Steed, Lawrence W. Moreland, and Tod A. Baker, 127–51. New York: Praeger, 1980.

Hamilton, Richard F. *Class and Politics in the United States.* New York: John Wiley and Sons, 1972.

Hammarberg, Melvyn. *The Indiana Voter: The Historical Dynamics of Party Allegiance During the 1870s.* Chicago: University of Chicago Press, 1977.

Hammond, John L. "Minor Parties and Electoral Realignments." *American Politics Quarterly* 4 (January 1976): 63–85.

Hansen, Steven. *The Making of the Third Party System: Voters and Parties in Illinois, 1850–1876.* Ann Arbor: University of Michigan Press, 1980.

Hansen, Susan B. "Partisan Realignment and Tax Policy, 1789–1976." In *Realignment in American Politics: Toward a Theory,* ed. Bruce A. Campbell and Richard J. Trilling, 288–323. Austin: University of Texas Press, 1980.

Harris, Louis. *Is There a Republican Majority?* New York: Harper, 1954.

Havard, William C., ed. *The Changing Politics of the South.* Baton Rouge: Louisiana State University Press, 1972.

Hays, Samuel P. "Political Parties and the Community-Society Continuum." In *The American Party Systems: Stages of Political Development,* ed. William Nisbet Chambers and Walter Dean Burnham, 2d ed., 152–81. New York: Oxford University Press, 1975.

Hays, Samuel P. "Politics and Society: Beyond the Political Party." In *The Evolution of*

American Electoral Systems, ed. Paul Kleppner et al., 243–67. Westport, Conn.: Greenwood Press, 1981.

Heard, Alexander. *A Two-Party South?* Chapel Hill: University of North Carolina Press, 1952.

Hibbs, Douglas H., Jr. "Dynamics of Political Support for American Presidents among Occupational and Partisan Groups." *American Journal of Political Science* 26 (May 1982): 312–32.

Holcombe, Arthur N. "The Changing Outlook for a Realignment of Parties." *Public Opinion Quarterly* 10 (Winter 1946): 455–69.

Holt, Michael F. *Forging a Majority: The Formation of the Republican Party in Pittsburgh, 1848–1860.* New Haven: Yale University Press, 1969.

Holt, Michael F. *The Political Crisis of the 1850s.* New York: John Wiley and Sons, 1978.

Howell, Susan E. "The Behavioral Component of Changing Partisanship." *American Politics Quarterly* 8 (July 1980): 279–302.

Huckfelt, Robert, and Carol Weitzel Kohfield. *Race and the Decline of Class in American Politics.* Urbana: University of Illinois Press, 1989.

Humes, Brian D., and Evelyn C. Fink. "Risky Business: Electoral Realignments and Institutional Change in Congress." Paper presented at the annual meeting of the Southern Political Science Association, Memphis, 1989.

Hunt, Albert R. "National Politics and the 1982 Campaign." In *The American Elections of 1982,* ed. Thomas E. Mann and Norman J. Ornstein, 1–43. Washington, D.C.: American Enterprise Institute, 1983.

Hurley, Patricia A. "Partisan Representation and the Failure of Realignment in the 1980s." *American Journal of Political Science* 33 (February 1989): 240–61.

Hutter, James L. "The 1988 Presidential Election: Maintaining, Deviating, or Realigning?" Paper presented at the annual meeting of the Southwestern Political Science Association, Fort Worth, 1990.

Inglehart, Ronald. "The Changing Structure of Political Cleavages in Western Society." In *Electoral Change in Advanced Industrial Democracies,* ed. Russell J. Dalton, Scott C. Flanagan, and Paul Allen Beck, 25–69. Princeton: Princeton University Press, 1984.

Inglehart, Ronald. *Culture Shift in Advanced Industrial Society.* Princeton: Princeton University Press, 1990.

Inglehart, Ronald. *The Silent Revolution: Changing Values and Political Styles among Western Publics.* Princeton: Princeton University Press, 1977.

Inglehart, Ronald, and Avram Hochstein. "Alignment and Dealignment of the Electorate in France and the United States." *Comparative Political Studies* 5 (October 1972): 343–72.

Inglehart, Ronald, and Jacques-René Rabier. "Political Realignment in Advanced Industrial Society: From Class-Based Politics to Quality-of-Life Politics." *Government and Opposition* 21 (Autumn 1986): 456–79.

Irvine, William P., and H. Gold. "Do Frozen Cleavages Ever Go Stale? The Bases of the Canadian and Australian Party Systems." *British Journal of Political Science* 10 (April 1980): 187–218.

162   *Harold F. Bass, Jr.*

Irwin, Galen, and Karl Dittrich. "And the Walls Came Tumbling Down: Party Dealignment in America." In *Electoral Change in Advanced Industrial Democracies,* ed. Russell J. Dalton, Scott C. Flanagan, and Paul Allen Beck, 267–97. Princeton: Princeton University Press, 1984.
"Is It RReally RRealignment?" Symposium. *Public Opinion* 7 (December 1984–January 1985): 2–19.
Jackman, Robert W. "Political Parties, Voting, and National Integration: The Canadian Case." *Comparative Political Studies* 4 (1972): 512–36.
Jackson, John E. "Issues and Party Alignment." In *The Future of Political Parties,* ed. Louis S. Maisel and Paul M. Sacks, 101–23. Beverly Hills, Calif.: Sage, 1975.
Jacobson, Gary C. "The Etiology of Congressional Realignment in the Mountain West." In *The Politics of Realignment: Party Change in the Mountain West,* ed. Peter F. Galderisi et al., 149–73. Boulder, Colo.: Westview Press, 1987.
Jahnige, Thomas P. "Critical Elections and Social Change: Toward a Dynamic Explanation of National Party Competition in the United States." *Polity* 3 (Summer 1971): 465–500.
Jennings, M. Kent, and Gregory B. Markus. "Partisan Orientation Over the Long Haul: Results from the Three-Wave Political Socialization Panel Study." *American Political Science Review* 78 (December 1984): 1000–1018.
Jennings, M. Kent, and Richard Niemi. "Continuity and Change in Political Orientations: A Longitudinal Study of Two Generations." *American Political Science Review* 69 (December 1975): 1316–35.
Jennings, M. Kent, and Richard Niemi. *Generation and Politics.* Princeton: Princeton University Press, 1981.
Jennings, M. Kent, and Richard Niemi. "The Persistence of Political Orientations: An Over-Time Analysis of Two Generations." *British Journal of Political Science* 8 (July 1978): 333–63.
Jensen, Richard. "The Last Party System: Decay of Consensus: 1932–1980." In *The Evolution of American Electoral Systems,* ed. Paul Kleppner et al., 203–41. Westport, Conn.: Greenwood Press, 1981.
Jensen, Richard. "Party Coalitions and the Search for Modern Values." In *Emerging Coalitions in American Politics,* ed. Seymour M. Lipset, 11–40. San Francisco: Institute for Contemporary Studies, 1978.
Jensen, Richard. *The Winning of the Midwest: Social and Political Conflict, 1888–1896.* Chicago: University of Chicago Press, 1971.
Kawato, Sadafuni. "Nationalization and Partisan Realignment in Congressional Elections." *American Political Science Review* 81 (December 1987): 1235–50.
Kelley, Stanley, Jr. *Interpreting Elections.* Princeton: Princeton University Press, 1983.
Kellstedt, Lyman A. "Religion and Partisan Realignment." Paper presented at the annual meeting of the Midwest Political Science Association, Chicago, 1989.
Kemp, David. "Social Change and the Future of Political Parties: The Australian Case." In *The Future of Political Parties,* ed. Louis Maisel and Paul M. Sacks, 124–164. Beverly Hills, Calif.: Sage, 1975.
Kenski, Henry C. "Campaigns and Elections in the Mountain States, 1984." In *The*

Politics of Realignment: Party Change in the Mountain West, ed. Peter F. Galderisi et al., 175–95. Boulder, Colo.: Westview Press, 1987.

Kessel, John H. *The Goldwater Coalition: Republican Strategies in 1964.* Indianapolis, Bobbs-Merrill, 1968.

Kessel, John H., John A. Clark, John M. Bruce, and William G. Jacoby. "I'd Rather Switch than Fight: Lifelong Democrats and Converts to Republicanism among Campaign Activists." Paper presented at the annual meeting of the American Political Science Association, Atlanta, 1989.

Key, V. O., Jr. "The Future of the Democratic Party." *Virginia Quarterly Review* 28 (April 1952): 161–75.

Key, V. O., Jr. "Secular Realignment and the Party System." *Journal of Politics* 21 (May 1959): 198–210.

Key, V. O., Jr. "A Theory of Critical Elections." *Journal of Politics* 17 (February 1955): 3–18.

Key, V. O., Jr., and Fank Munger. "Social Determinism and Electoral Decision: The Case of Indiana." In *American Electoral Behavior,* ed. Eugene Burdick and Arthur J. Brodbeck, 281–99. Glencoe, Ill.: Free Press, 1959.

Key, V. O., Jr., with the assistance of Milton C. Cummings, Jr. *The Responsible Electorate: Rationality and Presidential Voting, 1936–1960.* Cambridge, Mass.: Harvard University Press, 1966.

King, Anthony. "The American Polity in the Late 1970s: Building Coalitions in the Sand." In *The New American Political System,* ed. Anthony King, 371–96. Washington, D.C.: American Enterprise Institute, 1978.

King, Anthony, ed. *The New American Political System.* Washington, D.C.: American Enterprise Institute, 1978.

King, Michael E., and Lester G. Seligman. "Critical Elections, Congressional Recruitment and Public Policy." In *Elite Recruitment in Democratic Politics: Comparative Studies Across Nations,* ed. Heinz Eulau and Moshe M. Czudnowski, 263–99. New York: Halstead, 1976.

Kirkpatrick, Samuel A., ed. *American Electoral Behavior: Change and Stability.* Beverly Hills, Calif.: Sage, 1976.

Kirkpatrick, Samuel A., William Lyons, and Michael Fitzgerald. "Candidates, Parties, and Issues in the American Electorate." *American Politics Quarterly* 3 (July 1975): 247–83.

Kleppner, Paul. *Continuity and Change in Electoral Politics: 1893–1928.* Westport, Conn.: Greenwood Press, 1986.

Kleppner, Paul. "Critical Realignments and Electoral Systems." In *The Evolution of American Electoral Systems,* ed. Paul Kleppner et al., 3–32. Westport, Conn.: Greenwood Press, 1981.

Kleppner, Paul. *The Cross of Culture: A Social Analysis of Midwestern Politics, 1850–1900.* New York: Free Press, 1970.

Kleppner, Paul. "From Ethnoreligious Conflict to 'Social Harmony': Coalitional and Party Transformations in the 1890s." In *Emerging Coalitions in American Politics,* ed. Seymour M. Lipset, 41–59. San Francisco: Institute for Contemporary Studies, 1978.

Kleppner, Paul. "From Party to Factions: The Dissolution of Boston's Majority Party, 1876–1908." In *The Evolution of Urban Politics: Boston, 1700–1980*, ed. Ronald P. Formisano and Constance Burns, 111–32. Westport, Conn.: Greenwood Press, 1984.

Kleppner, Paul. "Partisanship and Ethnoreligious Conflict: The Third Electoral System, 1853–1892." In *The Evolution of American Electoral Systems*, ed. Paul Kleppner et al., 115–45. Westport, Conn.: Greenwood Press, 1981.

Kleppner, Paul. "The Political Realignment of the 1890s: A Behavioral Interpretation." In *Voters, Parties, and Elections*, ed. Joel H. Silbey and Samuel T. McSeveney, 184–95. Lexington, Mass.: Xerox, 1972.

Kleppner, Paul. *The Third Electoral System, 1853–1892: Parties, Voters, and Political Cultures*. Chapel Hill: University of North Carolina Press, 1979.

Kleppner, Paul. "Voters and Parties in the Western States, 1876–1900." *Western Historical Quarterly* 14 (January 1983): 49–68.

Kleppner, Paul. *Who Voted? The Dynamics of Electoral Turnout, 1870–1980*. New York: Praeger, 1982.

Kleppner, Paul, Walter Dean Burnham, Ronald P. Formisano, Samuel P. Hays, Richard Jensen, and William G. Shade. *The Evolution of American Electoral Systems*. Westport, Conn.: Greenwood Press, 1981.

Kousser, J. Morgan. "History QUASSHed: Quantitative Social Scientific History in Perspective." *American Behavioral Scientist* 23 (July–August 1980): 885–904.

Kousser, J. Morgan. "History – Theory = ?" *Reviews in American History* 7 (June 1979): 157–62.

Kousser, J. Morgan. "Key Changes." *Reviews in American History* 9 (March 1981): 23–28.

Kousser, J. Morgan. "Toward 'Total Political History': A Rational Choice Research Program." *Journal of Interdisciplinary History* 20 (Spring 1990): 521–60.

Knoke, David. *Change and Continuity in American Politics: The Social Bases of Political Parties*. Baltimore: Johns Hopkins University Press, 1976.

Knoke, David, and Richard B. Felson. "Ethnic Stratification and Political Cleavage in the United States, 1952–1968." *American Journal of Sociology* 80 (November 1974): 630–42.

Knoke, David, and Michael Hunt. "Social and Demographic Factors in American Political Party Affiliation: 1952–1972." *American Sociological Review* 39 (October 1974): 700–713.

Kramer, Gerald H. "Short-term Fluctuations in U.S. Voting Behavior, 1896–1964." *American Political Science Review* 65 (March 1971): 131–43.

Ladd, Everett Carll. "The 1988 Elections: Continuation of the Post–New Deal System." *Political Science Quarterly* 104 (Spring 1989): 1–18.

Ladd, Everett Carll. "The American Party System Today." In *The Third Century: America as a Postindustrial Society*, ed. Seymour M. Lipset, 153–82. Stanford: Hoover Institution Press, 1979.

Ladd, Everett Carll. *American Political Parties: Social Change and Political Response*. New York: W. W. Norton, 1970.

Ladd, Everett Carll. "As the Realignment Turns: A Drama in Many Acts." *Public Opinion* 7 (December 1984–January 1985): 2–7.

Ladd, Everett Carll. "The Brittle Mandate: Electoral Dealignment and the 1980 Election." *Political Science Quarterly* 96 (Spring 1981): 1–25.

Ladd, Everett Carll. "The Brittle Mandate Is Extended: An In-Depth Examination of the Voters' 1982 Verdict." *Public Affairs Review* 4 (1983): 23–37.

Ladd, Everett Carll. "Elections 1988: The National Election." *Public Opinion* 11 (November–December 1988): 2–3, 60.

Ladd, Everett Carll. "Liberalism Upside Down: The Inversion of the New Deal Order." *Political Science Quarterly* 91 (Winter 1976–77): 577–600.

Ladd, Everett Carll. "On Mandates, Realignments, and the 1984 Presidential Election." *Political Science Quarterly* 100 (Spring 1985): 1–25.

Ladd, Everett Carll. "Party Time, Realignment." In *Governing,* ed. Roger H. Davidson and Walter Oleszek, 114–18. Washington, D.C.: CQ Press, 1987.

Ladd, Everett Carll. "Politics in the 1980s: An Electorate at Odds with Itself." *Public Opinion* 5 (December 1982–January 1983): 2–6.

Ladd, Everett Carll. "The Reagan Phenomenon and Public Attitudes Toward Government." In *The Reagan Presidency and the Governing of America,* ed. Lester M. Salamon and Michael S. Lund, 221–49. Washington, D.C.: Urban Institute, 1984.

Ladd, Everett Carll. "A Rebuttal: Realignment? No. Dealignment? Yes." *Public Opinion* 3 (October–November 1980): 13–15, 54–55.

Ladd, Everett Carll. "The Shifting Party Coalitions from the 1930s to the 1970s." In *Party Coalitions in the 1980s,* ed. Seymour M. Lipset, 127–49. San Francisco: Institute for Contemporary Studies, 1981.

Ladd, Everett Carll. *Where Have All the Voters Gone? The Fracturing of America's Political Parties.* 2d ed. New York: W. W. Norton, 1982.

Ladd, Everett Carll, and Charles D. Hadley. "Party Definition and Party Differentiation." *Public Opinion Quarterly* 37 (Spring 1973): 21–34.

Ladd, Everett Carll, and Charles D. Hadley, *Political Parties and Political Issues: Patterns of Political Differentiation since the New Deal.* Beverly Hills, Calif.: Sage, 1973.

Ladd, Everett Carll, with Charles Hadley. *Transformations of the American Party System,* 2d ed. New York: W. W. Norton, 1978.

Ladd, Everett Carll, Charles Hadley, and Lauriston King. "A New Political Realignment?" *Public Interest* 23 (Spring 1971): 46–63.

Ladd, Everett Carll, and Seymour Martin Lipset. "Anatomy of a Decade." *Public Opinion* 3 (December 1979–January 1980): 2–9.

Lamb, Karl A. "Plotting the Electorate's Course in Dangerous Waters." *Political Science Reviewer* 2 (1972): 39–65.

Lamis, Alexander P. "The Realignment of Southern Politics, 1964–1988." Paper presented at the annual meeting of the American Political Science Association, Atlanta, 1989.

Lamis, Alexander P. *The Two-Party South.* Expanded ed. New York: Oxford University Press, 1988.

Lasser, William. *The Limits of Judicial Power: The Supreme Court in American Politics.* Chapel Hill: University of North Carolina Press, 1988.

Lasser, William. "The Supreme Court in Periods of Critical Realignment." *Journal of Politics* 47 (November 1985): 1174–87.

Lawrence, David, and Richard Fleisher. "Puzzles and Confusion: Political Realignment in the 1980s." *Political Science Quarterly* 102 (Spring 1987): 79–92.

LeDuc, Lawrence. "Canada: The Politics of Stable Dealignment." In *Electoral Change in Advanced Industrial Democracies,* ed. Russell J. Dalton, Scott C. Flanagan, and Paul Allen Beck, 402–24. Princeton: Princeton University Press, 1984.

LeDuc, Lawrence. "The Dynamic Properties of Party Identification: A Four-Nation Comparison." *European Journal of Political Research* 9 (September 1981): 257–68.

LeDuc, Lawrence. "Partisan Change and Dealignment in Canada, Great Britain, and the United States." *Comparative Politics* 17 (July 1985): 379–98.

LeDuc, Lawrence, Harold D. Clarke, Jane Jensen, and Jon H. Pammett. "Partisan Instability in Canada: Evidence from a New Panel Study." *American Political Science Review* 78 (June 1984): 470–84.

Lehnen, Robert H. "Realignment and Short-Term Crisis: A Case Study of Public Opinion During the Watergate Era." In *Realignment in American Politics: Toward a Theory,* ed. Bruce A. Campbell and Richard J. Trilling, 110–31. Austin: University of Texas Press, 1980.

Lenchner, Paul. "Partisan Realignments and Congressional Behavior: Some Preliminary Snapshots." *American Politics Quarterly* 4 (April 1976): 223–36.

Levine, Marc V. "Standing Political Decisions and Critical Realignment: The Pattern of Maryland Politics, 1872–1948." *Journal of Politics* 38 (May 1976): 292–325.

Levitin, Teresa, and Warren E. Miller. "Ideological Interpretations of Presidential Elections." *American Political Science Review* 73 (September 1979): 751–71.

Lewis-Beck, Michael S. "France: The Stalled Electorate." In *Electoral Change in Advanced Industrial Democracies,* ed. Russell J. Dalton, Scott C. Flanagan, and Paul Allen Beck, 425–48. Princeton: Princeton University Press, 1984.

Lichtman, Allan J. "Critical Election Theory and the Reality of American Presidential Politics, 1916–1940." *American Historical Review* 81 (April 1976): 317–50.

Lichtman, Allan J. "The End of Realignment Theory? Toward A New Research Program for American Political History." *Historical Methods* 15 (Fall 1982): 170–88.

Lichtman, Allan J. "Political Realignment and 'Ethnocultural' Voting in Late Nineteenth Century America." *Journal of Social History* 16 (Spring 1983): 55–82.

Lichtman, Allan J. *Prejudice and the Old Politics: The Presidential Election of 1928.* Chapel Hill: University of North Carolina Press, 1979.

Lipset, Seymour M. "Coalition Politics: Causes and Consequences." In *Emerging Coalitions in American Politics,* ed. Seymour M. Lipset, 437–63. San Francisco: Institute for Contemporary Studies, 1978.

Lipset, Seymour M. "Party Coalitions in the 1980 Election." In *Party Coalitions in the 1980s,* ed. Seymour M. Lipset, 15–46. San Francisco: Institute for Contemporary Studies, 1981.

Lipset, Seymour M. "The U.S. Elections: The Status Quo Re-affirmed." *International Journal of Public Opinion Research* 1 (Spring 1989): 25–44.

Lipset, Seymour M., ed. *Emerging Coalitions in American Politics.* San Francisco: Institute for Contemporary Studies, 1978.

Lipset, Seymour M., ed. *Party Coalitions in the 1980s.* San Francisco: Institute for Contemporary Studies, 1981.

Lipset, Seymour M., and Stein Rokkan, eds. *Party Systems and Voter Alignments.* New York: Free Press, 1967.

Lowe, Carl, ed. *New Alignments in American Politics.* New York: Wilson, 1980.

Lowi, Theodore J. "An Aligning Election, A Presidential Plebiscite." In *The Elections of 1984,* ed. Michael Nelson, 277–301. Washington, D.C.: CQ Press, 1985.

Lubell, Samuel. *The Future of American Politics.* 3d ed., rev. New York: Harper, 1965.

Lubell, Samuel. *The Hidden Crisis in American Politics.* New York: W. W. Norton, 1971.

Luebke, Frederick C. *Immigrants and Politics: The Germans of Nebraska, 1880–1900.* Lincoln: University of Nebraska Press, 1969.

Lyons, Michael S., Peter F. Galderisi, and Randy T. Simmons. "A Final Word: Realignment Present and Future." In *The Politics of Realignment: Party Change in the Mountain West,* ed. Peter F. Galderisi et al., 221–24. Boulder, Colo.: Westview Press, 1987.

McCormick, Richard L. "Ethno-cultural Interpretations of Nineteenth Century American Voting Behavior." *Political Science Quarterly* 89 (June 1974): 351–77.

McCormick, Richard L. *From Realignment to Reform: Political Change in New York State, 1893–1910.* Ithaca, N.Y.: Cornell University Press, 1981.

McCormick, Richard L. *The Party Period and Public Policy: American Politics from the Age of Jackson to the Progressive Era.* New York: Oxford University Press, 1986.

McCormick, Richard L. "The Party Period and Public Policy: An Exploratory Hypothesis." *Journal of American History* 66 (September 1979): 279–98.

McCormick, Richard L. "The Realignment Synthesis in American History." *Journal of Interdisciplinary History* 13 (Summer 1982): 85–105.

McCormick, Richard L. "Walter Dean Burnham and 'The System of 1896.'" *Social Science History* 10 (Fall 1986): 245–62.

McCormick, Richard P. "Political Development and the Second American Party System." In *The American Party Systems,* ed. William N. Chambers and Walter D. Burnham, 2d ed., 90–116. New York: Oxford University Press, 1975.

McCormick, Richard P. "Suffrage Classes and Party Alignments: A Study in Voter Behavior." *Mississippi Valley Historical Review* 46 (December 1959): 397–410.

McCrary, Peyton, Clark Miller, and Dale Baum. "Class and Party in the Secession Crisis: Voting Behavior in the Deep South, 1856–1861." *Journal of Interdisciplinary History* 8 (Winter 1978): 429–57.

MacDonald, Stuart Elaine, and George Rabinowitz. "The Dynamics of Structural Realignment." *American Political Science Review* 81 (September 1987): 775–96.

McDonough, Peter, and Antonio Lopez Pina. "Continuity and Change in Spanish Politics." In *Electoral Change in Advanced Industrial Democracies,* ed. Russell J. Dalton, Scott C. Flanagan, and Paul Allen Beck, 365–96. Princeton: Princeton University Press, 1984.

Mackelprang, A. J., Bernard Grofman, and N. Keith Thomas. "Electoral Change and Stability: Some New Perspectives." *American Politics Quarterly* 3 (July 1975): 314–39.

MacKuen, Michael B., Robert S. Erickson, and James A. Stimson. "Macropartisanship." *American Political Science Review* 83 (December 1989): 1125–42.

McMichael, Lawrence G., and Richard J. Trilling. "The Structure and Meaning of Critical Realignment: The Case of Pennsylvania, 1928-1932." In *Realignment in American Politics: Toward a Theory,* ed. Bruce A. Campbell and Richard J. Trilling, 21–51. Austin: University of Texas Press, 1980.

MacRae, Duncan, Jr., and James A. Meldrum. "Critical Elections in Illinois: 1888–1958." *American Political Science Review* 54 (September 1960): 669–83.

McSeveney, Samuel T. *The Politics of Depression: Voting Behavior in the Northeast, 1893-1896.* New York: Oxford University Press, 1972.

Maddox, William S. "Changing Electoral Coalitions from 1952 to 1976." *Social Science Quarterly* 60 (September 1979): 309–13.

Margolis, Michael. "From Confusion to Confusion: Issues and the American Voter, 1956-1972." *American Political Science Review* 71 (March 1977): 31–43.

Marquette, Jesse F. "Social Change and Political Mobilization in the United States: 1870-1960." *American Political Science Review* 68 (September 1974): 1058–74.

Masters, Nicholas, and Deil S. Wright. "Trends and Variations in the Two-Party Vote: The Case of Michigan." *American Political Science Review* 52 (December 1958): 1078–90.

Matthews, Donald R., and James W. Prothro. "The Concept of Party Image and Its Importance for the Southern Electorate." In *The Electoral Process,* ed. M. Kent Jennings and L. Harmon Ziegler, 139–74. Englewood Cliffs, N.J.: Prentice-Hall, 1966.

Matthews, Donald R. *Negroes and the New Southern Politics.* New York: Harcourt, Brace and World, 1966.

Mayhew, David. "Party Systems in American History." *Polity* 1 (Fall 1968): 134–43.

Meier, Kenneth J., and Kenneth W. Kramer. "The Impact of Realigning Elections on Public Bureaucracies." In *Realignment in American Politics: Toward a Theory,* ed. Bruce A. Campbell and Richard J. Trilling, 202–28. Austin: University of Texas Press, 1980.

Merelman, Richard M. "Electoral Instability and the American Party System." *Journal of Politics* 32 (February 1970): 115–39.

Miller, Arthur H. "Partisanship Reinstated: A Comparison of the 1972 and 1976 U.S. Presidential Elections." *British Journal of Political Science* 8 (April 1978): 129–52.

Miller, Arthur H. "Public Opinion and Regional Political Realignment." In *The Politics of Realignment: Party Change in the Mountain West,* ed. Peter F. Galderisi et al., 79–100. Boulder, Colo.: Westview Press, 1987.

Miller, Arthur H. "Realignment in the 1980 Election." *Economic Outlook* 8 (Autumn 1981): 88–90.

Miller, Arthur H., and Warren E. Miller. "Issues, Candidates, and Partisan Divisions in the 1972 American Presidential Election." *British Journal of Political Science* 5 (October 1975): 393–434.

Miller, Arthur H., Warren E. Miller, Alden S. Raine, and Thad A. Brown. "A Majority Party in Disarray: Policy Polarization in the 1972 Election." *American Political Science Review* 70 (September 1976): 753–78.

Miller, Warren E. "Challenges of Electoral Research." *American Politics Quarterly* 3 (July 1975): 340–45.

Miller, Warren E., and M. Kent Jennings. *Parties in Transition: A Longitudinal Study of Party Elites and Party Supporters.* New York: Russell Sage, 1986.

Miller, Warren E., and Teresa E. Levitin. *Leadership and Change.* Cambridge, Mass.: Winthrop, 1986.

Miller, William L. "Religious Alignment in England at the General Elections of 1974." *Parliamentary Affairs* 30 (Summer 1977): 256–68.

Miller, William L., and Gillian Raab. "Religious Alignment at English Elections between 1918 and 1970." *Political Studies* 25 (June 1977): 229–51.

Mishler, William, Marilyn Hoskin, and Roy Fitzgerald. "British Parties in the Balance: A Time-Series Analysis of Long-term Trends in Labour and Conservative Support." *British Journal of Political Science* 19 (April 1989): 211–36.

Moakley, Maureen. *Party Realignment in the American States.* Columbus: Ohio State University Press, forthcoming.

Nagel, Stuart S. "Court-Curbing Periods in American History." *Vanderbilt Law Review* 18 (June 1965): 925–44.

Namenwirth, J. Zvi. "Wheels of Time and the Interdependence of Value Change in America." *Journal of Interdisciplinary History* 3 (Spring 1973): 649–83.

Nechemias, Carol. "The End of Realignment?" *PS: Political Science and Politics* 22 (December 1989): 908–9.

Nelson, Michael, ed. *The Elections of 1984.* Washington, D.C.: CQ Press, 1985.

Nelson, Michael, ed. *The Elections of 1988.* Washington, D.C.: CQ Press, 1989.

Nesbit, Dorothy Davidson. "Changing Partisanship Among Southern Party Activists." *Journal of Politics* 50 (May 1988): 322–34.

Neuman, W. Lawrence, and Alexander Hicks. "Public Policy, Party Platforms, and Critical Elections: A Reexamination." *American Political Science Review* 71 (March 1977): 277–80.

Nexon, David H. "Methodological Issues in the Study of Realignment." In *Realignment in American Politics: Toward a Theory,* ed. Bruce A. Campbell and Richard J. Trilling, 52–65. Austin, University of Texas Press, 1980.

Nie, Norman H., with Kristi Anderson. "Mass Belief Systems Revisited: Political Change and Attitude Structure." *Journal of Politics* 36 (August 1974): 541–91.

Nie, Norman H., Sidney Verba, and John R. Petrocik. *The Changing American Voter.* Cambridge: Harvard University Press, 1976.

Niemi, Richard G., Richard S. Katz, and David Newman. "Reconstructing Past Partisanship: The Failure of the Party Identification Recall Questions." *American Journal of Political Science* 24 (November 1980): 633–51.

Niemi, Richard G., and Herbert Weisberg, eds. *Controversies in Voting Behavior.* 2d ed. Washington, D.C.: CQ Press, 1984.

Norpoth, Helmut. "Underway and Here to Stay: Party Realignment in the 1980s?" *Public Opinion Quarterly* 51 (Fall 1987): 376–91.

Norpoth, Helmut, and Michael R. Kagay. "Another Eight Years of Republican Rule and Still No Partisan Realignment?" Paper presented at the annual meeting of the American Political Science Association, Atlanta, 1989.

Norpoth, Helmut, and Jerrold Rusk. "Partisan Dealignment in the American Electorate: Itemizing the Deductions since 1964." *American Political Science Review* 76 (September 1982): 522–37.

Norris, Pippa. "The 1988 American Elections: Long, Medium, and Short-Term Explanations." *Political Quarterly* 60 (April–June 1989): 204–21.

Oestreicher, Richard. "Urban Working-Class Political Behavior and Theories of American Electoral Politics, 1870–1940." *Journal of American History* 74 (March 1988): 1257–86.

Orren, Gary R. "Candidate Style and Voter Alignment in 1976." In *Emerging Coalitions in American Politics,* ed. Seymour M. Lipset, 127–81. San Francisco: Institute for Contemporary Studies, 1978.

Orum, Anthony M., and Edward W. McCranie. "Class, Tradition, and Partisan Alignments in a Southern Urban Electorate. *Journal of Politics* 32 (February 1970): 156–76.

Page, Benjamain I. *Choices and Echoes in Presidential Elections: Rational Man and Electoral Democracy.* Chicago: Univeristy of Chicago Press, 1978.

Patterson, James T. "The Failure of Party Realignment in the South, 1937–1939." *Journal of Politics* 27 (August 1965): 602–17.

Pauly, Patricia R. "The Role of the Supreme Court in the Process of Partisan Realignments: A Preliminary Statement." Paper presented at the annual meeting of the Southern Political Science Association, Memphis, 1989.

Pelletier, Réjean, and Jean Crête. "Réalignements électoraux et transformation du personnel politique." *Canadian Journal of Poltical Science* 21 (March 1988): 3–33.

Perkins, Jerry. "Bases of Partisan Cleavage in a Southern Urban County." *Journal of Politics* 36 (February 1974): 208–14.

Petrocik, John R. "An Expected Party Vote: New Data for an Old Concept." *American Journal of Political Science* 33 (February 1989): 44–66.

Petrocik, John R. "Issues and Agendas: Electoral Coalitions in the 1988 Election." Paper presented at the annual meeting of the American Political Science Association, Atlanta, 1989.

Petrocik, John R. *Party Coalitions: Realignments and the Decline of the New Deal Party System.* Chicago: University of Chicago Press, 1981.

Petrocik, John R. "Realignment: New Party Coalitions and the Nationalization of the South." *Journal of Politics* 49 (May 1987): 347–75.

Petrocik, John R., and Frederick T. Steeper. "Realignment and 1984: New Coalitions and New Majorities?" *Election Politics* 2 (Winter 1984–85): 5–9.

Pfeiffer, David G. "The Measurement of Inter-Party Competition and Systemic Stability." *American Political Science Review* 61 (June 1967): 457–67.

Phillips, Kevin P. *The Emerging Republican Majority.* New Rochelle, N.Y.: Arlington House, 1969.

Piereson, James E. "Issue Alignment and the American Party System, 1956–1976." *American Politics Quarterly* 6 (July 1978): 275–308.

Pierce, Roy. "Changes that Time Hath Wrought: The French Electorate, 1967–1988." Paper presented at the annual meeting of the American Political Science Association, Atlanta, 1989.

Pierce, Roy, and Thomas R. Rochon. "The French Socialist Victories of 1981 and the

Theory of Elections." In *France at the Polls: 1981 and 1986,* ed. Howard Penniman, 179–95. Durham, N.C.: Duke University Press, 1988.

Pinkney, Robert. "Dealignment, Realignment, or Just Alignment: A Mid-term Report." *Parliamentary Affairs* 39 (January 1986): 47–62.

Polsby, Nelson W. "Coalition and Faction in American Politics: An Institutional View." In *Party Coalitions in the 1980s,* ed. Seymour M. Lipset, 153–78. San Francisco: Institute for Contemporary Studies, 1981.

Polsby, Nelson W. "The Democratic Nomination and the Evolution of the Party System." In *The American Elections of 1984,* ed. Austin Ranney, 36–65. Durham, N.C.: AEI/Duke University Press, 1985.

Polsby, Nelson W. "An Emerging Republican Majority? Review Essay." *Public Interest* 17 (Fall 1969): 119–26.

Polsby, Nelson W. "Party Realignment in the 1980 Election." *Yale Review* 72 (August 1982): 41–54.

Pomper, Gerald M. "Classification of Presidential Elections." *Journal of Politics* 29 (August 1967): 535–66.

Pomper, Gerald M. "Controls and Influence in American Elections (Even 1968)." *American Behavioral Scientist* 13 (November 1969): 215–30.

Pomper, Gerald M. "The Decline of Partisan Politics." In *The Impact of the Electoral Process,* ed. Louis Maisel and Joseph Cooper, 13–38. Beverly Hills, Calif.: Sage, 1977.

Pomper, Gerald M. "The Decline of the Party in American Elections." *Political Science Quarterly* 92 (Spring 1977): 21–41.

Pomper, Gerald M. "From Confusion to Clarity: Issues and the American Voter." *American Political Science Review* 66 (June 1972): 415–28.

Pomper, Gerald M. *Voters' Choice: Varieties of American Electoral Behavior.* Lanham, Md.: University Press of America, 1983.

Pomper, Gerald M. *Voters, Elections, and Parties: The Practice of Democratic Theory.* New Brunswick, N.J.: Transaction, 1988.

Pomper, Gerald M., with Susan S. Lederman. *Elections in America.* 2d ed. New York: Longman, 1980.

Pomper, Gerald M., ed. *The Election of 1976: Reports and Interpretations.* New York: David McKay, 1977.

Pomper, Gerald M., ed. *The Election of 1980: Reports and Interpretations.* Chatham, N.J.: Chatham House , 1981.

Pomper, Gerald M., ed. *The Election of 1984: Reports and Interpretations.* Chatham, N.J.: Chatham House, 1985.

Pomper, Gerald M., ed. *The Election of 1988: Reports and Interpretations.* Chatham, N.J.: Chatham House, 1989.

Poole, Keith T., and Howard Rosenthal. "The Regional Realignment of Congress, 1919–1984." In *The Politics of Realignment: Party Change in the Mountain West,* ed. Peter F. Galderisi et al., 101–27. Boulder, Colo.: Westview Press, 1987.

Price, H. David. "Critical Elections and Party History: A Critical View." *Polity* 4 (December 1976): 236–42.

Prindle, David F. "Voter Turnout, Critical Elections, and the New Deal Realignment." *Social Science History* 3 (Winter 1979): 144–70.

Prothro, James W., James Q. Campbell, and Charles Grigg. "Two-Party Voting in the South." *American Political Science Review* 52 (March 1958): 131–39.

Prysby, Charles L. "Electoral Behavior in the U.S. South: Recent and Emerging Trends." In *Party Politics in the South,* ed., Robert P. Steed, Lawrence W. Moreland, and Tod A. Baker, 101–26. New York: Praeger, 1980.

Przeworski, Adam. "Institutionalization of Voting Patterns, or Is Mobilization the Source of Decay?" *American Political Science Review* 69 (March 1975): 49–62.

Rabinowitz, George, Paul-Henri Gurian, and Stuart Elaine MacDonald. "The Structure of Presidential Elections and the Process of Realignment, 1944 to 1980." *American Journal of Political Science* 28 (November 1984): 611–35.

Rae, Douglas W., and Michael J. Taylor. *The Analysis of Political Cleavages.* New Haven: Yale University Press, 1970.

Ranney, Austin. "The Political Parties: Reform and Decline." In *The New American Political System,* ed. Anthony King, 213–48. Washington, D.C.: American Enterprise Institute, 1988.

Ranney, Austin, ed. *The American Elections of 1984.* Durham, N.C.: American Enterprise Institute/Duke University, 1985.

"Realignment Prospects: Are They Fading?" Opinion Roundup. *Public Opinion* 4 (December 1981–January 1982): 38–39.

Reiter, Howard L. "The Perils of Partisan Recall." *Public Opinion Quarterly* 44 (Fall 1980): 385–88.

RePass, David E. "Issue Salience and Party Choice." *American Political Science Review* 65 (June 1971): 389–400.

Reynolds, John F. *Testing Democracy: Electoral Behavior and Progressive Reform in New Jersey, 1880–1920.* Chapel Hill: University of North Carolina Press, 1988.

Riker, William. *The Theory of Political Coalitions.* New Haven: Yale University Press, 1962.

Rogin, Michael Paul, and John L. Shover. *Political Change in California: Critical Elections and Social Movements, 1890–1966.* Westport, Conn.: Greenwood Press, 1969.

Rose, Richard, ed. *Electoral Behavior: A Comparative Handbook.* New York: Free Press, 1974.

Rostow, Elspeth. "Realignment for Whom?" In *The Coattailless Landslide: El Paso Papers on the 1972 Presidential Campaign,* ed. Joseph M. Ray, 97–104. El Paso: Texas Western Press, 1974.

Rusk, Jerrold G. "The Effect of the Australian Ballot Reform on Split Ticket Voting, 1876–1908." *American Political Science Review* 64 (December 1970): 1220–38.

Rusk, Jerrold G. "The American Electoral Universe: Speculation and Evidence." *American Political Science Review* 68 (September 1974): 1028–49.

Rusk, Jerrold G., and Herbert F. Weisberg. "Perceptions of Presidential Candidates: Implications for Electoral Change." *Midwest Journal of Political Science* 16 (August 1972): 388–410.

Salisbury, Robert H., and Michael MacKuen. "On the Study of Party Realignment." *Journal of Politics* 43 (May 1981): 523-30.

Sandoz, Ellis, and Cecil V. Crabb, Jr., eds. *Election 84: Landslide Without a Mandate?* New York: New American Library, 1985.

Sandoz, Ellis, eds. *A Tide of Discontent: The 1980 Elections and Their Meaning.* Washington, D.C.: CQ Press, 1981.

Särlvik, Bo, and Ivor Crewe. *Decade of Dealignment: The Conservative Victory of 1979 and Electoral Trends in the 1970s.* Cambridge: Cambridge University Press, 1983.

Scammon, Richard M., and James A. Barnes. "Republican Prospects: Southern Discomfort." *Public Opinion* 8 (October-November 1985): 14-17.

Scammon, Richard M., and Ben J. Wattenberg. "Is It the End of an Era?" *Public Opinion* 3 (October-November 1980): 2-12.

Scammon, Richard M. *The Real Majority.* New York: Coward-McCann, 1970.

Schattschneider, E. E. *The Semi-Sovereign People: A Realist's View of Democracy in America.* New York: Holt, Rinehart, and Winston, 1960.

Schlesinger, Arthur M. "Tides of American Politics." *Yale Review* 29 (December 1939): 217-30.

Schlesinger, Arthur M., Jr., *The Cycles of American History.* Boston: Houghton Mifflin, 1986.

Schlesinger, Arthur M., Jr., ed. *The Coming to Power: Critical Presidential Elections in American History.* New York: Chelsea, 1971.

Schneider, William. "The November 4 Vote for President: What Does It Mean?" In *The American Elections of 1980,* ed. Austin Ranney, 212-62. Washington, D.C.: American Enterprise Institute, 1981.

Schneider, William. "The November 6 Vote for President: What Did It Mean?" In *The American Elections of 1984,* ed. Austin Ranney, 203-44. Durham, N.C.: AEI/Duke University Press, 1985.

Schneider, William. "Realignment: The Eternal Question." *PS* 13 (Summer 1982): 449-57.

Schreiber, E. M. "Where the Ducks Are: Southern Strategy vs. Fourth Party." *Public Opinion Quarterly* 35 (Summer 1971): 157-67.

Schulman, Mark A., and Gerald M. Pomper. "Variability in Electoral Behavior: Longitudinal Perspectives From Causal Modeling." *American Journal of Political Science* 19 (February 1975): 1-18.

Seagull, Louis M. "Secular Realignment: The Concept and Its Utility." In *Realignment in American Politics: Toward a Theory,* ed. Bruce A. Campbell and Richard J. Trilling, 69-81. Austin: University of Texas Press, 1980.

Seagull, Louis M. *Southern Republicanism.* New York: John Wiley and Sons, 1975.

Seagull, Louis M. *Youth and Change in American Politics.* New York: New Viewpoints, 1977.

Seagull, Louis M. "The Youth Vote and Change in American Politics." *Annals of the American Academy of Political and Social Science* 397 (September 1971): 88-96.

Segal, David R. "Partisan Realignment in the United States: The Lesson of the 1964 Election." *Public Opinion Quarterly* 32 (Fall 1968): 441-44.

Segal, David R., and David Knoke. "Social Mobility, Status Inconsistency, and Partisan Realignment in the United States." *Social Forces* 47 (December 1968): 154–57.

Seligman, Lester G., and Michael R. King. "Political Realignments and Recruitment to the U.S. Congress, 1870–1970." In *Realignment in American Politics: Toward a Theory,* ed. Bruce A. Campbell and Richard J. Trilling, 157–75. Austin: University of Texas Press, 1980.

Sellers, Charles. "The Equilibrium Cycle in Two-Party Politics." *Public Opinion Quarterly* 29 (Spring 1965): 16–37.

Shade, William G. "Political Pluralism and Party Development: The Creation of a Modern Party System, 1815–1852." In *The Evolution of American Electoral Systems,* ed. Paul Kleppner et al., 77–111. Westport, Conn.: Greenwood Press, 1981.

Shade, William L. *Social Change and the Electoral Process.* Gainesville: University of Florida Press, 1973.

Shafer, Byron E. "Dealignment Affirmed or Explosion Deferred? The American Midterm Elections of 1986." *Electoral Studies* 6 (April 1987): 47–51.

Shafer, Byron E. "The Election of 1988 and the Structure of American Politics: Thoughts on Interpreting an Electoral Order." *Electoral Studies* 8 (April 1989): 5–21.

Shaffer, William R., and David A. Caputo. "Political Continuity in Indiana Presidential Elections: An Analysis Based on the Key-Munger Paradigm." *Midwest Journal of Political Science* 16 (August 1972): 700–711.

Shamir, Michal. "Realignment in the Israeli Party System." In *The Elections in Israel—1984,* ed. Asher Arian and Michal Shamir, 267–96. Tel Aviv: Ramot, 1986.

Shaw, Malcolm. "Reinstatement: The American Presidential Election of 1976." *Parliamentary Affairs* 30 (Summer 1977): 241–57.

Shefter, Martin. "Party, Bureaucracy, and Political Change in the United States." In *Political Parties: Development and Decay,* ed. Louis Maisel and Joseph Cooper, 211–65. Beverly Hills, Calif.: Sage, 1978.

Shivley, W. Phillips. "Party Identification, Party Choice, and Voting Stability: The Weimar Case." *American Political Science Review* 66 (December 1972): 1203–25.

Shivley, W. Phillips. "A Reinterpretation of the New Deal Realignment." *Public Opinion Quarterly* 35 (Winter 1971): 621–24.

Shortridge, Ray M. "The Voter Realignment in the Midwest during the 1850s." *American Politics Quarterly* 4 (April 1976): 193–222.

Shover, John L. "The Emergence of a Two-Party System in Republican Philadelphia, 1924–1936." *Journal of American History* 60 (March 1974): 985–1002.

Shover, John L. "Was 1928 a Critical Election in California?" *Pacific Northwest Quarterly* 58 (October 1967): 196–204.

Silbey, Joel H. *The American Political Nation, 1838–1893.* Stanford: Stanford University Press, 1991.

Silbey, Joel H. *The Partisan Imperative: The Dynamics of American Politics Before the Civil War.* New York: Oxford University Press, 1985.

Silbey, Joel H. *The Transformation of American Politics, 1840–1860.* Englewood Cliffs, N.J.: Prentice-Hall, 1967.

Silbey, Joel H., Allen G. Bogue, and William H. Flanigan, eds. *The History of American Electoral Behavior.* Princeton: Princeton University Press, 1978.

Silbey, Joel H., and Samuel T. McSeveney, eds. *Voters, Parties, and Elections: Quantitative Essays in the History of American Popular Voting Behavior.* Lexington, Mass.: Xerox, 1972.

Silva, Ruth V. *Rum, Religion, and Votes: 1928 Reconsidered.* University Park: University of Pennsylvania Press, 1962.

Sinclair, Barbara D. "Agenda and Alignment Change: The House of Representatives, 1925–1978." In *Congress Reconsidered,* ed. Lawrence C. Dodd and Bruce I. Oppenheimer, 2d ed., 221–45. Washington, D.C.: CQ Press, 1981.

Sinclair, Barbara D. "Agenda, Policy, and Alignment Change from Coolidge to Reagan." In *Congress Reconsidered,* ed. Lawrence C. Dodd and Bruce I. Oppenheimer, 3d ed., 291–314. Washington, D.C.: CQ Press, 1985.

Sinclair, Barbara D. *Congressional Realignment: 1925–1978.* Austin: University of Texas Press, 1982.

Sinclair, Barbara D. "Party Realignment and the Transformation of the National Agenda: The House of Representatives, 1925–1938." *American Political Science Review* 71 (September 1977): 940–53.

Sinclair, Barbara D. "The Policy Consequences of Party Realignment: Social Welfare Legislation in the House of Representatives, 1933–1954." *American Journal of Political Science* 22 (February 1978): 83–105.

Smith, Eric R. A. N., and Peverill Squire. "State and National Politics in the Mountain West." In *The Politics of Realignment: Party Change in the Mountain West,* ed. Peter F. Galderisi et al., 33–54. Boulder, Colo.: Westview Press, 1987.

Stanley, Harold W. "The 1984 Presidential Election in the South: Race and Realignment." In *The 1984 Presidential Election in the South: Patterns of Southern Party Politics,* ed. Robert P. Steed, Lawrence W. Moreland, and Tod A. Baker, 303–35. New York: Praeger, 1986.

Stanley, Harold W. "Southern Partisan Changes: Dealignment, Realignment, or Both?" *Journal of Politics* 50 (February 1988): 64–88.

Stanley, Harold W., William T. Bianco, and Richard G. Niemi. "Partisanship and Group Support over Time: A Multivariate Analysis." A Research Note. *American Political Science Review* 80 (September 1986): 969–76.

Stanley, Jeanie R. "Party Realignment in Texas: The 1986 Elections." *Texas Journal of Political Studies* 9 (Spring–Summer 1987): 3–13.

Steed, Robert P., Lawrence W. Moreland, and Tod A. Baker, eds. *Party Politics in the South.* New York: Praeger, 1980.

Steed, Robert P., Lawrence W. Moreland, and Tod A. Baker, eds. *The 1984 Presidential Elections in the South: Patterns of Southern Party Politics.* New York: Praeger, 1986.

Sternsher, Bernard. "The Emergence of the New Deal Party System: A Problem in Historical Analysis of Voter Behavior." *Journal of Interdisciplinary History* 6 (Summer 1975): 127–49.

Sternsher, Bernard. "The New Deal Party System: A Reappraisal." *Journal of Interdisciplinary History* 15 (Summer 1984): 53–81.

Stewart, Charles V. "The Federal Income Tax and the Realignment of the 1980s." In
  Realignment in American Politics: Toward a Theory, ed. Bruce A. Campbell and
  Richard J. Trilling, 263–87. Austin: University of Texas Press, 1980.
Stokes, Donald E. "Parties and the Nationalization of Electoral Forces." In *The American
  Party Systems: Stages of Political Development,* ed. William Nisbet Chambers and
  Walter Dean Burnham, 2d ed., 182–202. New York: Oxford University Press, 1975.
Stokes, Donald E. "Party Loyalty and the Likelihood of Deviating Elections." *Journal
  of Politics* 24 (November 1962): 689–702.
Stokes, Donald E. "Some Dynamic Elements in Contests for the Presidency." *American Political Science Review* 60 (March 1966): 19–28.
Stokes, Donald E. "Spatial Models of Party Competition." In *Elections and the Political Order,* Angus Campbell, Philip E. Converse, Warren E. Miller, and Donald E.
  Stokes, 161–79. New York: John Wiley and Sons, 1966.
Stokes, Donald E., Angus Campbell, and Warren E. Miller. "Components of Electoral
  Decision." *American Political Science Review* 52 (June 1958): 367–87.
Stokes, Donald E., and Gudmund Iversen. "On the Existence of Forces Restoring Party
  Competition." *Public Opinion Quarterly* 26 (Summer 1962): 159–71.
Stone, Walter. "Regional Variations of Partisan Change." In *The Politics of Realignment: Party Change in the Mountain West,* ed. Peter F. Galderisi et al., 55–77. Boulder, Colo.: Westview Press, 1987.
Stonecash, Jeffrey M. "Political Cleavage in Gubernatorial and Legislative Elections:
  Party Competition in New York." *Western Political Quarterly* 42 (March 1989):
  69–81.
Strong, Donald S. "Durable Republicanism in the South." In *Change in the Contemporary South,* ed. Allan P. Sindler, 174–94. Durham, N.C.: Duke University Press,
  1963.
Strong, Donald S. "Further Reflections on Southern Politics." *Journal of Politics* 33
  (May 1971): 239–56.
Strong, Donald S. *Issue Voting and Party Realignment.* University: University of Alabama Press, 1977.
Sundquist, James L. "The 1984 Election: How Much Realignment?" *Brookings Review*
  3 (Winter 1985): 8–15.
Sundquist, James L. *Dynamics of the Party System: Alignment and Realignment of
  Political Parties in the United States.* rev. ed. Washington, D.C.: Brookings Institution, 1983.
Sundquist, James L. "Whither the American Party System?" *Political Science Quarterly* 98 (Winter 1983–84): 573–94.
Sundquist, James L., and Richard M. Scammon. "The 1980 Election: Profile and Historical Perspective." In *A Tide of Discontent: The 1980 Elections and Their Meaning,* ed. Ellis Sandoz and Cecil V. Crabb, Jr., 19–44. Washington, D.C.: CQ Press,
  1981.
Sweeny, Kevin. "Rum, Romanism, Representation, and Reform: Coalition Politics in
  Massachusetts, 1847–1853." *Civil War History* 22 (June 1976): 116–37.
Tate, C. Neal. "The Centrality of Party in Voting Choice." In *Western European Party
  Systems,* ed. Peter Merkl, 367–401. New York: Free Press, 1980.

Tedin, Kent. "The Transition of Electoral Politics in Texas: Voting for Governor in 1978–1986." In *Perspectives on American and Texas Politics,* ed. Donald Lutz and Kent Tedin, 233–51. Dubuque, Iowa: Kendall/Hunt, 1987.

Topping, John C., John R. Sazarek, and William H. Linder. *Southern Republicanism and the New South.* Cambridge, Mass.: privately printed, 1966.

Trilling, Richard J. "Party Image and Electoral Behavior." *American Politics Quarterly* 3 (July 1975): 284–314.

Trilling, Richard J. *Party Image and Electoral Behavior.* New York: John Wiley and Sons, 1976.

Trilling, Richard J. "Party Image and Partisan Change." In *The Future of Political Parties,* ed. Louis S. Maisel and Paul M. Sacks, 63–100. Beverly Hills, Calif.: Sage, 1975.

Trilling, Richard J., and Bruce A. Campbell. "Toward a Theory of Realignment: An Introduction." In *Realignment in American Politics: Toward a Theory,* ed. Bruce A. Campbell and Richard J. Trilling, 3–20. Austin: University of Texas Press, 1980.

Tubbesing, Carl D. "Predicting the Present: Realignment and Redistribution." *Polity* 7 (Summer 1975): 478–503.

Vanderbok, William G. "Cohorts, Aggregation Problems, and Cross Level Theorizing: The Case of Partisan Stability." *Western Political Quarterly* 30 (March 1977): 104–11.

Vertz, Laura L., John P. Frendreis, and James L. Gibson. "Nationalization of the Electorate in the United States." *American Political Science Review* 81 (September 1987): 961–66.

Wald, Kenneth D. "Realignment Theory and British Party Development: A Critique." *Political Studies* 30 (June 1982): 207–20.

Wald, Kenneth D. "Rise of Class-based Voting in London." *Comparative Politics* 9 (January 1977): 219–29.

Wanat, John. "The Application of a Non-Analytic Most Possible Estimation Technique: The Relative Impact of Mobilization and Conversion of Votes in the New Deal." *Political Methodology* 6 (1979): 357–74.

Wanat, John, and Karen Burke. "Estimating the Degree of Mobilization and Conversion in the 1890s: An Inquiry into the Nature of Electoral Change." *American Political Science Review* 76 (June 1982): 360–70.

Ward, James F. "Toward a Sixth Party System? Partisanship and Political Development." *Western Political Quarterly* 26 (1973): 385–413.

Ware, Alan. *The Breakdown of Democratic Party Organization: 1940–1980.* Oxford: Oxford University Press, 1985.

Wattenberg, Martin P. *The Decline of American Political Parties, 1952–1984.* Cambridge: Harvard University Press, 1986.

Wattenberg, Martin P. "The Decline of Political Partisanship in the United States: Negativity or Neutrality?" *American Political Science Review* 75 (December 1971): 941–50.

Wattenberg, Martin P. "The Hollow Realignment: Partisan Change in a Candidate-Centered Era." *Public Opinion Quarterly* 51 (Spring 1987): 58–74.

Wattenberg, Martin P. "The Hollow Realignment Continues: Partisan Change in

1988." Paper presented at the annual meeting of the American Political Science Association, Atlanta, 1989.

Wellhofer, E. Spencer. "Looking Backward: Stability and Volatility in the British Electorate, 1945–1974." *Western Political Quarterly* 39 (September 1986): 413–34.

Wildgen, John K. "The Detection of Critical Elections in the Absence of Two-Party Competition." *Journal of Politics* 36 (May 1974): 464–79.

Williams, Philip. "Review Article: Party Realignment in the United States and Britain." *British Journal of Political Science* 15 (January 1985): 97–115.

Wilson, James Q. "Realignment at the Top, Dealignment at the Bottom." In *The American Elections of 1984,* ed. Austin Ranney, 277–310. Durham, N.C.: AEI/Duke University Press, 1985.

Winters, Richard T. "Party Control and Policy Change." *American Journal of Political Science* 20 (November 1976): 597–636.

Wolfinger, Raymond E. "Dealignment, Realignment, and Mandates in the 1984 Election." In *The American Elections of 1984,* ed. Austin Ranney, 277–96. Durham, N.C.: AEI/Duke University Press, 1985.

Wolfinger, Raymond E., and Robert B. Arseneau. "Partisan Change in the South, 1952–1972." In *Political Parties: Development and Decay,* ed. Louis Maisel and Joseph Cooper, 179–210. Beverly Hills, Calif.: Sage, 1978.

Wolfinger, Raymond E., and Michael G. Hagen. "Republican Prospects: Southern Comfort." *Public Opinion* 8 (October–November 1985): 8–13.

Wright, James E. "The Ethnocultural Model of Voting: A Behavioral and Historical Critique." *American Behavioral Scientist* 16 (May 1973): 653–74.

Zanjani, Sally S. "A Theory of Critical Alignment: The Nevada Example, 1892–1908." *Pacific Historical Review* 49 (May 1979): 259–80.

Zingale, Nancy H. "Third Party Alignments in a Two-Party System: The Case of Minnesota." In *The History of American Electoral Politics,* ed. Joel Silbey, Allen G. Bogue, and William H. Flanigan, 106–36. Princeton: Princeton University Press, 1978.

Zuckerman, Allan, and Irving Lichbach. "Stability and Change in European Electorates." *World Politics* 29 (July 1977): 523–51.

Zukin, Cliff. "A Reconsideration of the Effects of Information on Partisan Stability." *Public Opinion Quarterly* 41 (Summer 1977): 244–54.

Index

Index

Abortion, 60, 70
Abramson, Paul, 111
Accommodationism, 30, 48, 55, 60, 61
Activists, 58, 59, 61, 70. *See also* Interest
   groups
Aldrich, John, 106, 108
Alignment-realignment cycle, 14-15, 17-18,
   121
American Labor party, 90
American Party System, The (Gosnell and
   Merriam), 27-28
American Political Science Review, 6
American Revolution, 45, 115-16, 117
Andersen, Kristi, 40
Anticommunism, 48, 70
Anti-Masons, 120, 121
Aristotle, 109, 112
Atomic war, 113

"Balance of power," 37
Ballot form, 11, 67, 71, 84n69
Banking, 89, 118, 120
Bass, Harold F., 40, 101
Beck, Paul Allen, 111
Beckett, Samuel, 24-25, 85
Bell, John, 97n9
Benson, Lee, 6, 16, 35n11, 111, 137n19
Benson, Richard H., 105
Biology, 109-10. *See also* Sciences, natural
Black Americans, 32-33, 45, 71, 89
Blue-collar Americans, 45
Blumenthal, Sidney, 106
Bogdanor, Vernon, 4
Breckinridge, John C., 88, 97n9
Britain, 72, 109, 111, 114, 117
Bryan, William Jennings, 9, 14, 93
Bureaucracy, 50, 90
Burnham, Walter Dean, 86, 101-39; Silbey

on, 4-7, 14, 16, 19n7, 20n9; Ladd on, 28,
   36n13; *Critical Elections and the Mainspring of American Politics,* 40, 41, 97n9,
   136n10; critique of critical criticism,
   103-9; *Presidential Ballots, 1836-92,* 106,
   136n8; on punctuational change, 109-12;
   on the United States and world politics,
   112-15; on "midlife crises," 113, 116-24;
   on postpartisan politics, 125-27
Bush, George, 35n9, 37, 53, 57, 84n69;
   Shafer on, 37, 53, 56-57, 103-4; speech at
   the Republican Convention (1988), 56; and
   the structure of politics, 71-73; Burnham
   on, 103-4, 125, 135
Butler, David, 40

California, 97n9
Campaigns, 29, 56; and mass media, 32;
   Shafer on, 39, 54-58; and subgroups,
   55-56, 65; themes of, 55, 56-57, 65; finan-
   cing of, 67, 71, 83n62
Campbell, Angus, 40
Capitalism, 33, 90
Caraley, Demetrios, 15
Carmines, Edward, 27, 104, 109
Carter, Jimmy, 33, 35n9, 69, 114; election of,
   51-52, 78n31
Catastrophe, 5-26, 91, 92, 109
Chambers, William N., 16
Civil rights, 33, 46, 47, 119
Civil War, 10, 13, 23n32, 31; as a realigning
   catastrophe, 26, 91, 92; political parties
   since, 43; and antecedent electoral orders,
   45-46; the secession of slave states during,
   89, 97n10; Burnham on, 104, 105, 108,
   117, 118-19, 122, 125
Class, social, 31, 33, 43, 45-46, 55
Clinton, George, 118

181

Clubb, Jerome M., 40, 87, 97*n10*
Cold War, 49, 70, 114, 115
Communism, 33, 48, 70, 112
Confederacy, 45, 89, 133
Congress, 49–51; and ticket splitting, 14, 30, 31, 32, 81*n54*, 94, 114–15, 133; Republicans in, 46, 67, 69, 88–89; and the realignment of the 1850s, 88–89; the Whigs and, 120; 1816 Congressional Caucus, 121
—Democratic control of, 30; Shafer on, 46, 51, 53–54, 62, 64, 69, 94; McSeveney on, 90–91, 100*n25*; and the New Deal, 90–91; Burnham on, 103, 119, 125, 126; and the budget deficit, 126. *See also* Congressional elections; House of Representatives; Senate
Congressional elections, 14, 133; and the "arrival of the party," 10, 11; campaign financing for, 67, 71, 83*n62*; in 1836 and 1840, Holt on, 86–87; incumbent-insulation effects in, 105
Congress of Industrial Organizations (CIO), 90–91
Connecticut, 100*n26*
Conservatives, 54, 55, 72, 94, 100*n26*, 112; and the general public, 57; cross-party coalition of, in the House, 69
Constitution, 5, 9, 10, 15, 18, 112, 116; national offices established in, 42; and the presidency, 49, 50, 127
Constitutional history, 106
Constitutional law, 114
Correlation coefficients, of party voting, 10–11, 22*n27*
Creation of a Democratic Majority, The (Andersen), 40
Crime issues, 57
Critical Elections and the Mainspring of American Politics (Burnham), 40, 41, 97*n9*, 136*n10*
Cultural values: conservative majority on, and the presidency, 39, 49–50, 54, 56, 72, 94; and traditionalists, 39, 51, 52, 55, 56, 60, 61, 62, 71; national consensus on, disintegration of, 46, 47–48, 52; and the Supreme Court, 47–48, 49–50, 70; concern about, within Congress, 49–50; progressivism and, 55, 60, 61; and the election of 1988, 57; and interest groups, 59, 60; and realignment/dealignment, 62; rising tensions on issues of, 70; and the 1976 election, 78*n31*

Dalton, Russell J., 41
Darwin, Charles, 105, 109
"Dealignment," 37, 41, 62–64, 85, 94
Decline of American Political Parties (Wattenberg), 41
Defense issues, 57, 70
Deficits, fiscal, 70, 89, 126
Delaware, 121
Democratic party, 10, 46, 61, 69, 71, 72, 86, 88, 97*n9*; loyalty to, 4, 12, 13; and gubernatorial elections, 11; and party norms, adoption of, 12; and ticket splitting, 14, 30, 31, 81*n54*, 94, 114–15, 133; and the Depression, 26, 93; and social change, during the 1960s, 28; control of Congress, 30; and organized labor, 32, 59, 90–91; in the South, 32, 45, 46; and the election of 1988, 55, 56, 57, 58; and "Reagan Democrats," 55; and economic well-being, 59, 61, 69, 70–71; and issue-based activists (interest groups), 59, 60, 62, 70, 94; and foreign affairs, 70; and voter registration, eased procedures for, 71; and the realignment of the 1890s, 94
—loss of presidential majority status: Ladd on, 32, 33, 35*n9*; and the realignment of the 1850s, 88–89; McSeveney on, 94–95; and national security issues, 114–15. *See also* Congress, Democratic control of; New Deal; Presidential elections
Democratic representation, 29–30, 36*n20*, 108
Depressions, 68; of the early 1890s, 13; and the Whigs, 87, 96*n7*. *See also* Great Depression; New Deal
Douglas, Stephen A., 88, 97*n9*
Doyle, A. Conan, 106
Dukakis, Michael, 57–58
Dynamics of the Party System (Sundquist), 40

Eagle Forum, 60
Earle, George H., 98*n15*
Eastern Europe, 114–15
Ecological regression procedures, 22*n27*
Economic welfare, 48, 49, 52, 57, 59, 61. *See also* Economy
Economy: market centered, 33; American domestic, 48, 57, 87, 89; international, 70. *See also* Depressions; Economic welfare; Great Depression; New Deal

Education, 32, 33, 55
Eisenhower, Dwight D., 25, 100*n25*, 119, 125
Eldredge, Niles, 110
Elections, listed by date; 1789, 5–8, 15, 16, 18; 1800, 8, 15, 101, 117, 118, 120, 122; 1810, 117; 1812, 122; 1820, 121; 1824, 10, 121, 122; 1828, 8, 9, 10, 15, 101, 121, 122, 124, 129; 1832, 122; 1836, 10, 86–87, 122; 1838, 8, 10–17 *passim*, 120, 122, 124, 133–34; 1840, 10, 12, 86–87, 120, 133; 1844, 10; 1852, 88, 134; 1856, 88, 133, 135; 1858, 133; 1860, 88, 97*n9*, 101, 133; 1872, 134; 1893, 10, 12; 1896, 10, 12, 92, 93, 94, 97*n9*, 101; 1900, 10, 104, 135; 1904, 133; 1910, 125; 1912, 134; 1914, 133; 1916, 90; 1918, 125; 1928, 92, 93, 99*n20*, 119; 1930, 125; 1932, 90, 101; 1934, 90, 134; 1936, 90; 1938, 91; 1940, 91, 92, 134; 1944, 91, 129; 1948, 16, 104, 129; 1952, 16, 25, 119, 122; 1956, 94–95, 134; 1960, 16, 119; 1964, 15, 47, 78*n31*, 95; 1966, 135; 1968, 47, 51, 52, 53, 62, 64, 69, 95, 106–7, 115, 135; 1972, 94–95, 106, 110, 115, 127, 135; 1974, 31; 1976, 51; 1980, 41, 69, 126, 127; 1988, 29, 38–39, 53–58, 62, 114, 115; 1990, 125; 1992, 51, 69, 125. *See also* Congressional elections; Gubernatorial elections; Presidential elections; Realignments, listed by date
Elections and the Political Order (Campbell), 40
Electoral Change in Advanced Industrial Democracies (Dalton, et al.), 41
Electoral college, 88
Electoral order, 37–84, 94, 95, 103; definition of, 38; and social divisions, patterns of, 38–39, 42; and cross-cutting issues, 39, 62, 70, 72; and political change, 39, 64–69; and political structures, 42–45, 67–68, 74*n11*; and "political culture," 43; and policy preferences, 44; antecedent, 45–46; and issue areas, 48–51; contemporary, 51–53; and the election of 1988, 53–58
Emancipation, 89
Emerging Republican Majority, The (Phillips), 28, 40
England. *See* Britain
Environmentalism, 59
Equilibrium, punctuated, 109–12, 115
Ethnicity, 43

Evolution, 109–10
Existentialism, 25

Farmer-Labor party, 90
Farmers, 46, 59, 90
Federalism, 7, 30, 114, 117–18
Feminism, 59
Field, Phyllis, 6, 16, 35*n11*
Fiorina, Morris P., 111
First Bank of the United States, 118
Flanigan, William H., 40, 87, 97*n10*
Ford, Gerald R., 52
Foreign policy, 39, 113, 114; conservative majority on, and the presidency, 39, 48–49, 50, 52–54, 56, 62, 72, 94, 114–15; and nationalism, 39, 51; national consensus on, disintegration of, 46, 47, 48, 52; after World War II, 48; and the election of 1988, 57; and interest groups, 59, 60–61; and realignment/dealignment, 62; and Congress, 69; and the changing international order, 70
Formisano, Ronald P., 6, 8, 9, 13, 117
Future of American Politics (Lubell), 93

Gallatin, Albert, 118
General Motors, 91
Generalizations, 29
Georgia, 22*n25*
Germany, 113
Gienapp, William E., 97*n9*
Gilbert, W. S., 105
God, 25
Goldwater, Barry, 100*n25*
Gorbachev, Mikhail, 115
Gosnell, Harold F., 27–28
Gould, Stephen Jay, 110, 137*nn 15, 16*
Gramsci, Antonio, 112
Great Britain. *See* Britain
Great Depression, 90; Ladd on, 26, 28, 31, 33, 35*n9*, 104, 105; as a realigning catastrophe, 26; Phillips on, 28; and antecedent electoral orders, 45–46. *See also* New Deal
Greeley, Horace, 134
Greenback/National party, 119
Gubernatorial elections, 35*n11*, 133; and the "arrival of the party," 10, 11; and the falling off in partisan voting, 14

Harrison, William Henry, 86, 87

Hartz, Louis, 29, 112
Hitler, Adolf, 33
Holt, Michael F., 86–87
Homosexuality, 59
Hoover, Herbert, 33, 119
House of Representatives: and concerns about
  social welfare and service provisions, 39,
  49, 50–51, 61, 62, 72, 94; and political
  structures, 43; and foreign policy, 49, 52.
  See also Congress
Huntington, Samuel, 112, 113

Ideology, 28, 29, 30, 59, 60, 87, 94, 105
Immigration, 26, 33, 91, 99*n19*
Illinois, 97*n9*
Independents, 4, 55, 79*n36*
Indiana, 22*n25*, 97*n9*
Industrialization, 26, 32, 91
Interest groups, 59–62, 89, 94; and cultural
  values, 59, 60; and the social base for pol-
  itics, 67
Iowa, 97*n9*
Iran Hostage Crisis, 69

Jackson, Andrew, 6, 8, 105, 124, 136*n8*. *See
  also* Jacksonian era
Jacksonian era, 6, 16, 117, 120, 121, 122
Japan, 70
Jefferson, Thomas, 8, 118. *See also*
  Jeffersonians
Jeffersonians, 16, 117–18, 121
Johnson, Lyndon B., 35*n9*
Johnson, Richard M., 124
Journal of Politics, 25, 39
Judiciary, federal, 89, 91. *See also* Supreme
  Court

Kentucky, 124
Key, V. O., Jr., 3, 5, 25–27; "The Future of
  the Democratic Party," 26, 91–92, 99*n20*;
  "A Theory of Critical Elections," 26,
  39–40, 92–93, 99*n21*; Shafer on, 63;
  McSeveney on, 91–94, 100*n24*; Burnham
  on, 101, 107, 129, 131
King, Clarence, 105
Kleppner, Paul, 7, 8, 93–94, 97*n10*, 98*n11*,
  100*n24*; Burnham on, 102, 111
Kuhn, Thomas R., 108

Labor, organized, 32, 90–91, 118–19. *See also*
  Unions

Ladd, Everett C., 15, 18, 24–36, 37; "Why
  Carter Will Probably Win," 30; on the
  preoccupation with realignment, 85;
  McSeveney on, 91–92, 95; Burnham
  on, 102, 103, 104–5, 108, 115, 127
Lakatos, Imre, 127
Liberalism, 31, 39, 54, 90, 120; classical, 29;
  position on economic well-being, 48, 51,
  53, 57; and social welfare, 55, 57, 72, 94;
  and the election of 1988, 56–58, 79*n42*;
  Burnham on, 110, 112, 114, 126
Lichtman, Allan, 104
Lincoln, Abraham, 35*n9*, 97*n9*
Locke, John, 29
Lubell, Samuel, 93
Lyell, Charles Stewart, 109

McCloskey, Robert G., 106
McCormick, Richard L., 6
McGovern, George, 95
McKinley, William, 9, 14
McSeveney, Samuel T., 40, 75*n15*, 85–100
Madison, James, 118, 121
Marshall, John, 114, 118, 124
Marx, Karl, 107
Mass media, 31, 32, 64
Massachusetts, 11, 99*n20*, 117
Mayhew, David, 16
Maysville Road Bill (1830), 120
Merriam, Charles E., 27–28
Michigan, 98*n14*, 111
Midlife crises, 113, 116–24
Minnesota, 134
Mississippi, 10, 22*n25*
Monroe, James, 121
Moral Majority, 60
Morality, private, 47
Murphy, Frank, 98*n15*

Namier, Lewis, 72
National identity, 70, 114. *See also*
  Nationalism
National Industrial Recovery Act, 90
Nationalism, 39, 48, 51, 52, 55, 56, 60, 61,
  62, 71; and declining international tensions,
  70; and the Supreme Court, 118. *See also*
  National identity
National Labor Relations Board, 91
National security, 114–15
New Deal, 4, 14, 15, 16; Ladd on, 25–34

passim, 35*n9*, 92; and "more government," 33–34; and the welfare state, 50, 57; political order, and the contemporary electoral order, 63, 64, 68; and dealignment, 85; McSeveney on, 90–93, 95; Burnham on, 105, 106, 117, 125, 129, 134; and postpartisan politics, 125, 134
New Hampshire, 129, 131
New Jersey, 22*n25*, 88, 97*n9*
New York, 10, 22*n25*, 88, 97*n9*, 121
Niemi, Richard G., 106, 108
Nixon, Richard M., 28, 40, 100*n25*, 125, 127; resignation of, 51–52
Nomination procedures, 29
Normalcy, 119, 134
North Carolina, 10
Nullification crisis, 120

Ohio, 22*n25*, 97*n9*

Parliament, 72
Partisan Realignment (Clubb, Flanigan, and Zingale), 40
Party Coalitions (Petrocik), 41
Party identification, 14, 111
Party loyalty, 4, 12–13, 15, 31
Party system(s), 4, 31, 64, 91; New Deal party system, 4, 14; five party systems, notion of, 6, 7, 15–16; in the post-1789 period, 7–8, 15; first party system, 7, 113–14; second party system, 7, 86; two-party system, 8, 30; and the "arrival of the party," 9–13; idea of, notion of political eras as a replacement of, 16; definition of, 21*n20*; and the "realignment focus," Ladd on, 25, 27, 29–34; and multipartyism, 30; and ticket splitting, 30, 31, 32; and postindustrialism, 32–33; and interest groups, 59, 60, 62; third party system, 86, 89; and lasting realignments, 87–88; fourth party system, 89; candidacies, 95, 119; sixth, 107. *See also* Partisanship; Party identification; Party loyalty
Patriotism, 48, 70
Peace movement, 59
Peace of Amiens (1803), 114
Pennsylvania, 97*n9*, 98*n14*
Periodicity, 6, 27, 28; Burnham on, 40, 82*n56*; Shafer on, 63, 66, 82*n56*, 85–86

Periodization, 37–38, 85–86; McSeveney on, 86; Burnham on, 101–2, 106
Petrocik, John, 41
Phillips, Kevin, 28, 35*n9*, 40
Pledge of Allegiance, 56–57, 79*n41*
Political Change in Britain (Butler and Stokes), 40
Politics of Depression (McSeveney), 40
Populism, 94
Postindustrialism, 32–33, 36*n17*, 91, 117
Potter, David, 112
Powers, separation of, 30
Presidency, 33, 134; and concerns about cultural values, 39, 49–50, 54, 56, 72, 94; and concerns about foreign policy, 39, 48–49, 50, 52–54, 56, 62, 72, 94, 114–15; and political structures, 43; and Congress, 49–50, 51; and the realignment of the 1850s, 88–89; repudiated, Burnham on, 127. *See also* Presidential elections
Presidential Ballots, 1836–92 (Burnham), 106, 136*n8*
Presidential elections, 113, 125, 129–35; and independent voters, 4; as significant markers of political currents, 7–8; turnout during, Burnham on, 7, 8, 121–23; and the "arrival of the party," 10, 11; and ticket splitting, 14, 30, 31, 32, 81*n54*, 94, 114–15, 133; and the nomination process, 67; and party control within states, 93; McSeveney on, 88–89, 90, 92, 100*n25*. *See also* Democratic party, loss of presidential majority status; Elections, listed by date; Republican party, success of, at the presidential level
Progressivism, 16, 55, 60, 61, 90, 119
Protectionism, 70
Punctuational change, 109–12, 115, 116, 117

Race, 32–33, 43, 46, 67
Random House Dictionary of the English Language, The, 25
Reagan, Ronald, 33, 100*n25*, 125, 127, 135; election of, 53, 66, 139*n35*
"Reagan Democrats," 55, 79*n36*
Realignment, 14, 16–17, 40; "party," 25–26; secular, 26, 92; "critical," 30–31, 63, 64, 65, 85, 92, 93, 97*n9*, 101–39; classical, 37, 41, 63–71 *passim*, 103, 107; minimalist definition of, 63

Realignment (*continued*)
—cycles: alignment-realignment, 14–15, 17–18, 121; realignment/dealignment, 17–18, 41–42, 62–64, 66
—listed by date: of the 1930s, 4, 5, 14, 25–27, 87, 88, 90–94; of the 1850s, 5, 13, 15, 26, 87–88, 90, 92, 119; of the 1890s, 4, 5, 6, 15–16, 87, 89, 90, 92–94, 119; of the 1960s, 3–4, 94, 95; of the 1980s, 95
Reconstruction era, 89, 118–19, 122
Reforms, 67–68; ballot form, 67, 71, 84*n69*
Regime orders, 116–24
Religion, 43, 47
Republican party, 4–5, 7, 56, 121; and ticket splitting, 14, 30, 31, 32, 81*n54*, 94, 114–15, 133; and Congress, 46, 67, 69, 88–89; and government's proper role, public opinion regarding, 34; and issue-based activists (interest groups), 59, 60, 61, 62; and the Moral Majority, 60; and foreign policy, 70, 71; during the 1920s, 90; and the Great Depression, response to, 93; and the election of 1894, 94; and the budget deficit, 125–26
—success of, at the presidential level, 4; Ladd on, 25, 30–33, 35*n9*; Shafer on, 39, 46, 51–52, 53–58, 62, 63, 66, 78*n31*, 94; and the realignment of the 1850s, 88–89, 96*n8*, 97*n9*; during the 1950s, 100*n25*; Burnham on, 103, 114–15, 135
Revolution, 109, 115–16, 124
Revolution of 1989, Eastern European, 114–15
Rhode Island, 88, 99*n20*
Riker, William, 111
Robinson, Eugene, 136*n8*
Roosevelt, Franklin D., 33, 35*n9*; election of, 90, 91, 99*n16*, 129; and the Supreme Court, 90–91

Savings-and-loan disaster, 126
Sciences, natural, 105, 109–10, 128
Second Bank of the United States, 120
Senate, 39, 50, 72; and political structures, 43; and foreign policy, 49, 52, 69; Republican majority in, in 1980, 69. *See also* Congress
Shafer, Byron E., 37–84, 94, 95, 100*nn 25, 26*; on dealignment, 37, 41, 62–64, 85, 94; Burnham on, 102, 103, 104, 127, 135
Silbey, Joel H., 3–23, 35*n11*, 37; McSeveney

on, 85, 86, 87, 89, 90, 91, 95; Burnham on, 102, 104, 108, 113, 117, 120, 136*n8*
Slavery, 89, 133
Smith, Alfred E., 35*n11*
Social class, 31, 33, 43, 45–46, 55
Socialism, 90, 112, 119
Socialization, 3, 8, 106
Social welfare: and Congress, 39, 49, 50–51, 61, 62, 72, 94; and the electoral order, Shafer on, 47, 48, 49–50, 52–53, 55, 59, 61, 62, 69, 70, 71; conservatives and, 55; liberal majority on, 72
Socioeconomic-status (SES) groups, 31
Sombart, Werner, 112
South Carolina, 23*n32*, 121
Soviet Union, 33, 70
Stacks, John F., 41
State elections, 5, 7, 10, 86–87, 133
Stimson, James, 27, 104, 109
Stokes, Donald, 40
Structure and Politics at the Accession of George III (Namier), 72
Sullivan, Arthur S., 105
Sundquist, James, 4, 20*n9*, 40
Supreme Court, 65, 90–91, 98*n16*; and cultural issues, 47–48, 49–50, 70; reforms regarding, 68; and abortion, 70; *McCulloch v. Maryland*, 118; "nationalist" decisions made by, 118; *Craig v. Missouri*, 124; *Worcester v. Georgia*, 124
Sutherland, Arthur B., 106
Swisher, Carl B., 106

Taney, Roger B., 121, 124
Taxes, 89
Tennessee, 11, 22*n25*
Texas, 88
Ticket splitting, 14, 30, 31, 32, 81*n54*, 94; Burnham on, 114–15, 133; and national security, 114–15
Tilden, Samuel, 35*n9*
Tocqueville, Alexis de, 112
Traditionalism, 39, 51, 52, 55, 56, 60–61, 62, 71
Twain, Mark, 129
Tyler, John, 9, 87, 120

Uniformitarian doctrine, 109
Unionists, Constitutional, 88
Unions, 45, 90–91; membership in, 32; and

the Democratic party, 46. *See also* Labor, organized
United States Steel, 91
Urbanization, 26, 91

Van Buren, Martin, 9, 86, 124
Vietnam War, 47, 49, 59, 114
Virginia, 121
Virginia Quarterly Review, The, 25
Voter: mobilization, 7, 71, 92, 104, 122; participation, 9, 11, 18
—turnout, 15, 71, 89, 122; in the post-1789 period, 7; in the 1890s, 14; and the inflation of voter numbers through corruption, 22*n24*; and the New Deal coalition, 90; depression, 113; statistics, 123

Wagner Labor Relations Act, 90, 91
Waiting for Godot (Beckett), 24–25
Wallace, George, 95
War of 1812, 114
War Powers Act of 1973, 49
Washington, Bushrod, 118

Washington, George, 5–6
Watergate scandal, 31, 51, 69
Watershed: The Campaign for the Presidency 1980 (Stacks), 41
Wattenberg, Martin P., 41
Weber, Max, 107
Wegener, Alfred, 128
Weicker, Lowell, Jr., 84*n69*, 100*n26*
Welfare state, 50–51, 61, 90. *See also* Social welfare
Whig party, 9, 11, 12, 13; McSeveney on, 87–88, 96*n7*, 97*n9*; and the upswing of 1836-40, 87; Burnham on, 120, 121
White Americans, 45, 112
White-collar Americans, 46
Willkie, Wendell, 97*n9*
Wilson, Woodrow, 90, 119
Wisconsin, 134
World War II, 32; American foreign policy after, 48, 49, 70, 113; preparation for, and growing prosperity, 91

Zingale, Nancy H., 40, 87, 97*n10*